British Cultural Identities

FOURTH EDITION

■ Edited by Mike Storry and Peter Childs

Routledge
Taylor & Francis Group

LONDON AND NEW YORK

First published 1997 by Routledge
Second edition published 2002 by Routledge
Third edition published 2007 by Routledge

Fourth edition published 2013
by Routledge
2 Park Square, Milton Park, Abingdon, Oxon OX14 4RN

Simultaneously published in the USA and Canada
by Routledge
711 Third Avenue, New York, NY 10017

Routledge is an imprint of the Taylor & Francis Group, an informa business

British Library Cataloguing in Publication Data
A catalogue record for this book is available from the British Library

Library of Congress Cataloging in Publication Data
A catalog record for this book has been requested

ISBN: 978–0–415–68075–2 (hbk)
ISBN: 978–0–415–68076–9 (pbk)
ISBN: 978–0–203–10504–7 (ebk)

Typeset in Sabon and Futura
by Keystroke, Station Road, Codsall, Wolverhampton

Contents

List of figures

List of tables

Contributors

Peter Childs is Professor of Modern English Literature at the University of Gloucestershire. He has edited, with Mike Storry, *The Routledge Encyclopedia of Contemporary British Culture*.

Jo Croft is Lecturer in Literary Studies at Liverpool John Moores University.

Edmund Cusick was Head of Department for Writing at Liverpool John Moores University until his untimely death aged 44.

Roberta Garrett is Lecturer in Literature and Cultural Studies at the University of East London.

Frank McDonough is Professor in Modern Political History at Liverpool John Moores University.

Gerry Smyth is Reader in Cultural History at Liverpool John Moores University.

Mike Storry was Senior Lecturer in English at Liverpool John Moores University. He has taught widely in Britain and abroad. He has published fiction and poetry and edited, with Peter Childs, *The Routledge Encyclopedia of Contemporary British Culture*.

Preface

A book about British cultural identities immediately raises a number of questions: Whose Britain? Whose culture? Whose identity? Do a majority of people in the UK think of themselves in terms of being British anyway?

British Cultural Identities is aimed at people interested in these questions. It approaches the idea of British identities through contemporary practices and activities: not through institutions or economics, but through culture. The book is written in a clear, accessible style, making it especially useful to the student, at home or overseas, who wishes to be introduced to the variety of British experiences in the twenty-first century. As in earlier editions, it has aimed to be a different kind of book about the contemporary UK: one that looks at Britain not in sociological or historical but in human terms. Each chapter is clearly structured around key themes, has a timeline of important dates, a list of recent cultural examples and a section of questions and exercises. The book is illustrated with photographs and tables throughout.

All the contributors to this collection outline the plurality of identities found across the UK. The essays begin from the belief that identities are the names we give to the different ways we all are placed by, and place ourselves within, our culture. The contributors have been asked to think of culture as the practices and beliefs that people encounter and share – events, ideas and images that shape their lives everywhere and everyday. The introductory chapter snaps a snapshot of Britishness, while the remaining seven chapters cover intersecting topics: gender and the family; religion and heritage; places and peoples; youth culture and age; class and politics; language and ethnicity; education, work, and leisure.

The chapters are organised in the following way. At the beginning of each one you will find a timeline, usually of the most significant dates for the area covered. There follows a structured discussion of ways in which that area can be understood from different perspectives and at different levels. The conclusions suggested by each chapter are usually open because all the contributors believe there are many Britains and many British cultural identities. You will find numerous opinions expressed, but all the writers aim to outline current debates, key moments and speculative questions rather than to supply definitive answers. Consequently, our collective aim is to explore the face of British culture today, while at the same time suggesting that it will have changed tomorrow.

At the end of each chapter, you will find some questions and exercises, preliminary clues to most of which will be contained in the text. However, some of the questions are designed to stimulate your thoughts and to encourage you to go online or to libraries, where necessary, to conduct research or to test our suggestions by looking at the numerous cultural products that supply a way into an understanding of cultural identity in contemporary Britain. The further reading shows you where to go next for more detailed study. Some of the books suggested will also have been chosen because they cover aspects which the chapter itself has not been able to treat at length. In an introductory text such as this we cannot cover the minutiae of all social, ethnic or even regional groupings; however, we intend to sensitise readers, particularly those outside the UK, to Britain's cultural diversity. Lastly, we have also listed at the end of each chapter some cultural examples which we feel will give you an insight into concerns, anxieties and tensions within contemporary British culture. These novels, films and TV programmes are of great importance because they provide specific British cultural representations relevant to the issues under discussion. We have chosen to select books, films and programmes that are either current or particularly illustrative and widely available in print, online or on video.

Introduction:
The ghost of Britain past

Mike Storry and Peter Childs

Timeline

43	Roman invasion
1066	Norman invasion
1215	Magna Carta (Great Charter)
1509	Accession of Henry VIII
1558	Accession of Elizabeth I
1616	Death of Shakespeare
1642–51	English Civil War
1815	Wellington at Waterloo
1901	Death of Victoria
1940	Churchill becomes PM
1952	Accession of Elizabeth II
1997	Death of Princess Diana
2002	Deaths of Princess Margaret and the Queen Mother Queen Elizabeth II's Golden Jubilee
2005	Third consecutive Labour victory under Tony Blair, 7/7 London bombings
2010	Conservative/Lib Dem Coalition comes to power
2011	Prince William marries Kate Middleton: public holiday *News of the World* closed Leveson Inquiry into phone hacking and press ethics

T HIS IS A BOOK ABOUT contemporary Britain and British people. On the one hand, Britain is a country with defined boundaries, a recognisable landscape, a long and contentious history, and a position in the various international economic, social and political league tables. On the other hand, British people are much harder to describe. To begin with, some British people do not live in Britain. Also, many people living in Britain do not think of themselves as British. Nationality is a matter of allegiance and cultural affiliation. Some people say that your nationality is indicated by where you choose to live or by the team you support at sports events; others say that it is a question of who you would fight for. It has also been argued that nationality is no longer a powerful force in Britain, that it is simply a matter of circumstance and that today it is far less significant than local or global identities: relatives, friends and communities are more important to us, and so is transnational culture, such that notions of national identity are both less persuasive and more contentious than they used to be. Above all, nationality is a question of identity and so is crossed by other kinds of identity, such as ethnicity, gender, sexuality, religion, age and occupation.

This book aims to outline some of the kinds of identity found at those intersections in Britain at the beginning of the twenty-first century. As such, it will implicitly question the difference between British cultural identities and cultural identities in Britain. Seventy years ago, T. S. Eliot famously said 'culture' was something that included 'all the characteristic activities and interests of a people'. He thought that this meant for England: 'Derby Day, Henley Regatta, Cowes, the twelfth of August, a cup final, the dog races, the pin table, the dart board, Wensleydale cheese, boiled cabbage cut into sections, beetroot in vinegar, nineteenth-century Gothic churches and the music of Elgar'. Seventy years on, conceptions of English and British identity have changed enormously and, for example, few people would attribute any significance to the twelfth of August, the opening day of the grouse-shooting season.

Contemporary British culture is a mixture of all the cultures of the past that people are influenced by – but certain figures, symbols and narratives exercise particularly strong control over the ways we imagine ourselves to be and to have been. In Dickens's *A Christmas Carol*, Scrooge is shown pleasant and unpleasant edited highlights of his life by 'The Ghost of Christmas Past'. Scrooge recognises the person he has been and understands how events have made him the way he now is, but, after seeing different glimpses of the present and the possible future, he rejoices in the fact that the life to come is only strongly influenced, not determined, by history. Dickens's ghost story, itself a potent narrative in British mythology, is a fable about self-knowledge; it concerns the importance of understanding the individual's responsibility within society and the significance of history in shaping identity. The figures and images that have shaped ideas of a British identity are the subject of this introductory chapter.

At sporting occasions like the Football Association Cup Final, annual events like the Last Night of the Proms concert, other events such as the funerals of soldiers brought home to (now Royal) Wootton Bassett, public celebrations like the 2011 royal wedding of Kate and William, there are signs of a traditional 'grass-roots' national culture, often accompanied by patriotic singing and flag-waving. But, in common with much of the world, Britain's major unifying influence today is the mass media (not all of which is British) and a connection between all of the events above is that they will be shown on television, broadcast on the radio and reported in the press. A popular magazine like *Hello*, a peak-time television show like *The X Factor* and a competition like the National Lottery lead to much discussion throughout the country. A recent book on Britain has said that 'Television is clearly the basic component of the national culture', but, at Eliot's time of writing, it was not even a part of any local culture. Table 0.1 shows the topics of conversation people say that they have, according to a 'TOM Attitudes to Advertising Survey'. This reveals that television, the cost of living, children and sport are arguably the most important subjects to most people.

Regional and local identities are extremely strong in Britain, and the diversity of beliefs, practices, loyalties and accents is immense. In George Bernard Shaw's 1913 play *Pygmalion*, the language specialist Professor Higgins believes he can, just by the sound of an accent, pinpoint any Londoner's place of birth to within two or three streets. Shaw's play was written at the start of the twentieth century when people were far less likely to move from area to area and yet distinct local identities are still easily discernible in the 2010s. The UK today is enhanced by diversity and difference, and for this reason, we must use the plural form and talk of 'identities'. Throughout the rest of this book you will find the multiplicity of British identities emphasised more than traditional single images.

But we need to say a little more about cultural identity. While culture may be seen as 'lived experience', shared by a community of people who relate to one another through common interests and influences, identity is concerned with how people see themselves, or are seen, in relation to others: as northerners or southerners, football or rugby enthusiasts, opera or blues

TABLE 0.1 Conversation subjects between friends and family

	Percentage of people who ever talk about subject
Advertising	2
Big business	2
Bringing up children	26
Clothes and fashion	19
Cost of living	43
Education	20
Gardening	16
Government	19
Health and welfare services	18
Law and order	16
Neighbours or workmates	21
Newspaper articles	19
Personal health	21
Politicians	8
Religion	6
Sport	25
Trade unions	1
TV programmes	48
Unemployment	16
None of above/don't know	3

Source: TOM Attitudes to Advertising Survey, 1991

fans and so on. In short, identity is perhaps two things: who people take themselves to be and who others take them to be. As the debate in Britain over whether or not to issue national identity cards has shown, questions of national and personal identity are highly complex and contentious.

At one end of the scale, identity is partly prescribed by what the state considers important about people: their physical characteristics, place of birth and area of employment. These details are usually included on passports, for example. At the other end of the scale, many people might consider the most important aspects of their identity to be their emotional life, their aspirations, their sporting or intellectual achievements and so on. So we are also inevitably left with *versions* of identity rather than a single definitive identity for each individual. *Guardian* columnist Armando Iannucci mocked the official view that 'identity' can be contained on a card when he suggested that children, who have developing personalities, will have to swap identity cards in the playground as they change week by week! This kind of identity, on an official form, similar to a gas bill or a birth certificate, is actually what is understood not as someone's identity but as their 'ID' – a kind of statistical identification far removed from any individual's notion of who they are. The lead character in a cult British television series, *The Prisoner*, famously used to say every week 'I am not a number, I am a free man'. The British response to 'identity cards' has been similar.

Then again, we have to consider individuals within their community and country. Collective identity and action can supply a focus for pride in a society and enable people to improve their material conditions, but, from another perspective, both patriotism and nationalism are uneasy notions in today's post-colonial world. As long ago as the eighteenth century, patriotism was described by Dr Johnson, compiler of the first authoritative English dictionary, as 'the last refuge of a scoundrel'. Similarly, nationalism, which has been linked so closely to imperialism and the resistance to it over the last two centuries, has unhealthy implications for those who define themselves as 'British'. Moreover we are looking for what emerges 'from below' rather than what can be imposed from above. People are nowadays more suspicious of authority and prefer to make up their own minds as to what they choose to share with their fellow citizens.

An interesting attempt to agree on shared values was made when *History Magazine* asked readers which significant anniversaries should be marked as a proposed British National Day. The ten most popular anniversaries were:

■   15 June 1215: Magna Carta signed
■   8 May 1945: VE day
■   6 June 1944: D Day
■   11 November 1918: Remembrance day
■   21 October 1805: Nelson and the Battle of Trafalgar
■   25 March 1807: abolition of the slave trade
■   18 June 1815: Napoleon and the Battle of Waterloo
■   30 November 1834: Winston Churchill born
■   19 May 1649: Cromwellian commonwealth established
■   7 June 1832: Reform Act passed

This list gives some idea of people's priorities. Issues of civil liberty, military prowess and political significance are most prominent. But overall there is still surprisingly little interest in a formal ceremonial celebration and very little consensus on what makes life worthwhile if you are living in Britain today rather than elsewhere. We must perhaps look for diversity rather than consensus if we are to offer an accurate snapshot of how people feel about the culture in which they are living.

Since the Second World War, most countries within the British Empire have, through revolt or reform, gained independence. Over the last few decades, perceptions of British expansion overseas have also undergone many changes as the traditional and dominant paternalist attitude Britain had towards its colonies has been reviewed as not benevolence but condescension overlaying economic greed. Comparisons between European fascism and imperialism, reflections on England's hold on Ireland, the only European country to have both an early and a late colonial experience and disapproval of the blustering patriotism associated with the Falklands War of 1981, have all added to a British reappraisal of its Empire.

A famous English novel, *The Go-Between* by L. P. Hartley, begins with the sentence, 'The past is a foreign country: they do things differently there'. No matter what view is held of the past, history provides many indications of how a country such as Britain has traditionally been perceived and the extent to which its people, often accused of living in the past, used to do things differently. There is still a fascination with this past. Stressful modern lives make people look back to calmer, more stable times through period costume TV dramas such as *Downton Abbey* or 'bonnet' series such as Mrs Gaskell's *Cranford*. Films like *Remains of the Day* are popular, as are historical novels, from *Birdsong* to *Possession*, *Atonement* to *Wolf Hall*. Patrick O'Brian's twenty-volume Aubrey–Maturin nautical novels, set in the early nineteenth century, still sell well. There seems to be no end to the pre-occupation British people have with their history, which is marketed back to them as heritage. We will look below then at how British history can serve as a starting point for the idea of a national cultural identity, partly framed by the perception of Britain as seen from overseas. In the next section we will consider past images of England and the UK, and in subsequent sections we will look at the icons and representatives who have portrayed or stood for this traditional Britain.

Traditional Britain

A simple overview of Britain might show the country as passing through a number of historical periods. It might identify them as 'rural', 'industrial', 'imperial', 'suburban', 'tourist', 'multicultural' and these would follow one another in time. In fact phases such as these are not just in sequence but overlap, though many people like to see Britain as still stuck in one of these stages.

Below we give you a little historical background information to contrast with the contemporary pictures drawn in the chapters that follow. We look at those formations of national identity that have held sway and attempted to define and delimit British culture. As we do so, we would like you to remember that Britishness never was a straightforward, uncomplicated term: it is and long has been a diverse, highly contested and varied label. For example, while the monarchy has provided the most famous icons of national identity, for the last millennium English monarchs have usually been foreign. England's figureheads have been Normans (Plantagenets),

Welsh (Tudors), Scots (Stuarts), Dutch (House of Orange) and German (Hanoverians).

The British Isles were invaded by the Romans in the first century AD and settled by Germanic tribes, the Jutes, Angles and Saxons in the fifth century. Some of the days of the week are still named after their gods: Tiw, god of War (Tuesday), Woden (Wednesday), Thor (Thursday), Frig, wife of Woden (Friday). These tribes drove the native Celts to the western parts of Scotland and to Cornwall, Ireland and Wales.

Life was precarious, and littered throughout the British countryside there are preserved places of refuge where early Britons could go when being attacked by neighbouring tribes and invaders. This accounts for the large number of Iron Age forts, medieval castles, Piel towers and fortified manor houses that still exist in Britain today. Britain's last invasion from overseas was in 1066, when it was conquered by Normans, Viking settlers from northern France. There followed after this many centuries of European rivalry and imperial expansion.

The most widely taught period of history in British schools is that of the Tudors (1485–1603). This is often taken to be the start of modern England because it included the revival of classical learning, the discovery of the Americas, the introduction of the printing press, the beginnings of the Church of England and notable military successes such as the defeat of the Spanish Armada. Its figureheads are Henry VIII, Elizabeth I, Walter Raleigh and Shakespeare: four figures who to this day would appear at the head of a schoolchild's list of important Britons. Thomas Carlyle, perhaps the greatest influence on British cultural thought in the nineteenth century, referred to the Elizabethan era as 'that strange outbudding of our whole English existence' in his influential book *On Heroes, Hero-Worship and the Heroic in History*. The continued prevalence of this view can be seen in the enormously successful comedy series *Blackadder*, which focused on one character's exploits in four stages of Britain's history: Medieval Britain, the reign of Elizabeth I, the period of revolutions and Romanticism at the threshold of the nineteenth century, and the First World War. Between the Middle Ages and the nineteenth century only the Tudor period was represented, omitting such key events as the English Civil War, the Glorious Revolution of 1688 and the American War of Independence. Literature courses at most levels taught across the country similarly devote little study to the period between Shakespeare and the Romantic poets. This ties in with popular notions of what it means to be 'British' and 'English', conceptions of a national identity that are often rooted in Tudor times but which are more recent in their articulation: products of the eighteenth and particularly the nineteenth centuries. Nationalism is a comparatively new invention, issuing from the formation of modern nation states since such eighteenth-century social upheavals as the French Revolution, and developing from, but often not superseding, identities based on such ideas as tribe, region, religion and class or 'blood'.

Broadly speaking, Britain has a historical heritage whose gross features everyone is aware of: colonised by the Romans; last invaded in 1066; a rural country up until the eighteenth century; unprecedented industrial growth in the nineteenth century; the largest empire the world has known; post-war decolonisation and economic decline. Its features have left a notion of Britishness, and more particularly Englishness, that remains today for many people and is prevalent in sections of the media: an island people 'unconquered' for centuries; a largely rural community, but the first industrial nation; an imperial leader; a land divided between north and south, or London and the rest of the country; and a class-ridden society, from the monarchy through the aristocracy and the middle classes to the working classes. Consequently, in the rest of this section we will look at three traditional ways of understanding Britishness and Englishness, beginning with an examination of the English countryside, followed by consideration of the national character and then of the British as an island race.

The English countryside

With the growth of London and the Industrial Revolution of the early nineteenth century, experience for many people in Britain became *urban* as the country entered its accelerated phase of trade and manufacturing. Factories and mills created areas of dense population such as Leeds, Manchester, Sheffield and Newcastle as people migrated there to work in the textiles, steel and shipbuilding industries. This was the time in which Britain saw itself as 'the workshop of the world' and the stamp 'Made in England' became famous across the globe. (Its supposed mark of authenticity and quality is still found, for example, in Elton John's recording of the same name in 1995.) However, throughout the industrial revolution the underlying idea of Britain did not change in many respects: it was still thought to be essentially a rural place even for those in the towns and cities, and the wealthiest people would choose to build houses away from the metropolitan centres. A 'countryside' outlook can still be found in the 1930s (when rambling and Sunday walks became national occupations). For example, J. B. Priestley in his famous *English Journey* dealt with three types of community: the metropolitan, the urban and the rural. He said England was at heart a rural country which had a countryside ethos. The implication of his model was that the cities, at a time of mass unemployment, financial crisis and widespread poverty, should become more like the rest of Britain. If cities were unsavoury places it was because they had lost touch with the innocence of their agricultural roots.

One can argue that Britain still has the self-image of the rural society (evident in magazines such as *Ideal Home* and *Country Life* for example). This belief lies behind immensely popular television series like *Inspector Morse* (set in Oxford) or *Midsomer Murders* (set in a fictional English village) in which the community must week by week be restored to a 'rightful' tranquillity. Many of the novels of Agatha Christie, Britain's most famous crime writer, are also principally about this restoration of a natural and lawful order of countryside innocence, and many of the most popular novels by writers such as Catherine Cookson indulge in a supposedly simpler past before the fast-paced and largely irreligious city living of present times.

A further example of the persisting non-metropolitan idea of Britain is the number of bookmaker's shops, principally for betting on horse races, of which there are many thousands in Britain – a retail industry unknown in Germany, for example. Here the country world comes to every British high street. Horse racing, a countryside pastime known as 'the Sport of Kings', enters into the urban environment and links the 'rural' aristocracy and the monarchy with the 'urban' working class. So, in many ways, contemporary Britain harks back to a localised and harmonious, but essentially feudal way of life.

In city pubs people drink the beer of the countryside. You can sit in London's Leicester Square and drink a bottle of 'Black Sheep Ale' or a pint of 'Shepherd Neame' bitter and eat a 'shepherd's pie' or a 'ploughman's lunch' (a recent invention containing bread, cheese, pickles and salad). Why not a coal miner's pie or a fireman's lunch? This is because these industrial or urban professions do not hold the appeal that the jobs of the rural past do and they cannot be romanticised in the same way. Such attitudes are by no means recent either. There is a long tradition in Britain of 'pastoral' poetry, where sophisticated court dwellers pretended to be simple country folk and wrote one another charming poems of seduction – such as Christopher Marlowe's *The Passionate Shepherd to his Love* ('Come live with me and be my love'). A similar Elizabethan nostalgia for a golden Arcadia is found in Shakespeare's *As You Like It* and *A Midsummer Night's Dream*.

A final indication of the appeal of the concept of rural England is that when builders sell houses that they have erected on agricultural land, the new roads are frequently named after what they have just destroyed (e.g. 'Four Acre Coppice', 'Oak Tree Farm Crescent'). Former habitats of birds are commemorated in 'Herons Way', or 'Tern Crescent'. As we will see in the next chapter, many people want the difficult combination of urban society and jobs with rural peace and beauty.

Character and accent

Perhaps the most enduring of all the tokens of a dominant traditional Britishness is the 'English character' itself, which is often easily encapsulated and parodied in terms of its accent(s).

Accent and dialect are both very important in British life and the public acceptability of regional accents has changed with a shift of focus from the capital to the regions. The English upper-class accent, as spoken by the Queen or announcers on the BBC World Service, was accepted until thirty years ago as the guide to correct pronunciation for Britain as a whole. Those with regional accents from the industrialised areas of the Midlands and north, let alone Northern Ireland, needed not apply for jobs as announcers on radio or TV. At one time it was thought that one of the effects of a national radio network would be to eradicate regional accents. This hasn't happened. Instead regional accents have persisted, and in areas of the media many more broadcasters and performers with northern or Scottish accents are employed. On television, Graham Norton has a Dublin accent, while the sixties pop singer turned presenter Cilla Black has steadily broadened her Liverpudlian accent in her appearances over the last 40 years. The following contemporary broadcasters all have strong regional accents: Cheryl Cole and Ant and Dec (north-east), Guto Harri (Welsh), Kirsty Young (Scottish) and Arthur Smith (south London).

There are wide variations in the use of dialect or slang across Britain. In terms of actual vocabulary, there are words throughout the UK whose use is purely local. For example the word 'bleb', meaning blemish, though found in the dictionary is only widely known in the north-east. There are regional variations in the words children use when playing games at school. In the playground chase of 'tick' or 'tag', when children are 'safe' (by standing on a stone for example) on Merseyside they will shout 'barley', while in London they will say 'home'. Because of greater mass communications and some increased mobility, regional variations are more commonly understood throughout Britain than they were in previously 'closed' communities.

Accents and expressions are diverse; but what about the myth of the British 'character'? British people are often themselves considered withdrawn and reserved. Stereotypically, they are supposed to undertake their tasks out of duty, without any thought of personal gain. Their aims are understated. They are meant to display characteristic (if often deceptive) British reserve, as in the stylised images of Hugh Grant or Princess Diana (or if not then an ostentatious class consciousness, as in the flamboyant manners of Noel Coward or the aggressive campaigning of trade union leaders such as Bob Crow). Such reserve is not considered to be confined to well-bred members of the upper classes. A typical story is that when the British soldiers, called 'Tommies' after a music-hall character, finally met the Russian counterparts they had been fighting with against the Germans in the First World War, they went up to them and shook hands. In a moment of national elation, this seems like a very understated action and is taken to indicate two things. First, at that time people practised British reserve; and second, it was displayed not just by those with 'stiff upper lips', the upper classes, but equally by working people.

Across all classes, few people shake hands. Handshaking on meeting is today a more widespread practice in much of the rest of the world than it is in the UK. British people do shake hands, but not routinely on meeting one another. It is usually when they are introduced to a stranger, whether at home or at work. While this is still often taken as a sign of reserve, such behaviour is equally part of a rejection and dislike of formality. Also, the image of reserve contrasts with that other enduring stereotype of British behaviour: eccentricity. This supposedly denotes a kind of outrageousness that has spanned upper-class eccentrics, the Masons, sixties fashions, punk rock and the contemporary artists Tracey Emin or Grayson Perry. Such images are most often reproduced in today's consumer culture as part of an idiosyncratic Britishness that can be successfully marketed and sold abroad. On the one hand, Rowan Atkinson's TV mime character 'Mr Bean' exemplifies this kind of awkward, inquisitive but repressed and easily embarrassed national stereotype. On the other hand, Richard O'Brien's camp reworking of the Gothic Frankenstein story in *The Rocky Horror Show* illustrates well the idea of British peculiarities and closeted sexual flamboyance.

An island race

The Germans live in Germany;
The Romans live in Rome;
The Turkeys live in Turkey;
But the English live at home.

(J. H. Goring, 'The Ballad of
Lake Laloo and other Rhymes', 1909)

Britain has been described as 'a tight little right little island'. In the early nineteenth century, the poet Byron wrote of 'the bitter effects of staying at home with all the narrow prejudices of an islander'. Later in the century, critics of Victorian overseas expansion were known as 'Little Englanders', but the term has since come to mean isolationists who believe in the concept 'my country right or wrong'. Winston Churchill, Britain's prime minister during the Second World War, used the title 'The Island Race' at the start of his history of the English-speaking people. He also tells in his memoirs of the time he was scheduled in his early career to meet Hitler, until the latter discovered Churchill had written articles condemning his Jewish policy. The Germans quietly cancelled the meeting and Churchill's conclusion was: 'Thus Hitler missed the only chance he ever had of meeting me.'

A story that further illustrates British insularity refers to a news announcement that said 'There has been a persistent fog at London airport during the weekend, and the Continent has been cut off for 24 hours'. That this parochialism is still common despite increased air travel and the Channel tunnel is illustrated by the politician Norman Lamont describing a united Europe as 'yesterday's idea' and by the fact that according to a recent MORI survey 48 per cent of Britons do not see themselves as Europeans but as having more in common with Americans. Meanwhile Europeans see the British as living on an island off the coast of the Continent.

The British have been considered an island race partly because of their imperialism, cultural isolation and international policies. Some of this attitude can be explained historically and it has been argued that, compared with most European countries, Britain's ethnic mix did not change greatly between the eleventh and the twentieth centuries, although there were, for example, some 20,000 Africans working in London in the mid-1700s and many Jewish settlers arrived at the end of the nineteenth century, while the oldest Chinese community in Europe was established in Liverpool as early as the eighteenth century. There have also been considerable influences from overseas, particularly from the exploitations of Empire, the architectural signs of which are still visible everywhere. For instance, Liverpool, one of England's largest ports and at one time Europe's major slaving port, has sheaves of corn moulded into cornices over the entrances to several of its buildings and the heads of African elephants and slaves carved in stone on its town hall, while London has a Great Pagoda at Kew Gardens and Moorish designs incorporated into many of its theatres and museums. Up to the early twentieth century there were Egyptian Halls in Piccadilly, while Bolton in Lancashire has Indian motifs cast into the stalls in its market and the oriental style of Brighton's Royal Pavilion makes it the town's most famous building. Additionally, Britain's language and food reflect its colonial history in India ('verandah' and 'bungalow', tea and pepper), while its Regency furniture adopted Egyptian designs and on its crockery, Chinese Willow Patterns have long been popular.

Today, Britain has sizable populations from, for instance, Australia, Bangladesh, Poland, Vietnam and West Africa. Particularly in the 1950s there was substantial immigration to Britain from the Caribbean. The other notable influx in the 1950s and 1960s was from both India and Pakistan (and later from Uganda, when Asians were expelled by Idi Amin). Both of these waves were encouraged by the British authorities and by employers such as London Transport, who set up recruitment offices in Jamaica and elsewhere.

Although quite small in relation to Britain's population as a whole (about 9 per cent, up from 6 per cent in 1991), these communities form the majority of certain areas of towns like Bradford and Leicester. The cultural tension for children in these communities is often greater than for their parents, who came to Britain with more positive expectations and often did not intend to settle. The second generation in these communities have had a profound effect on British culture but have also been sometimes faced with divided loyalties and opposite cultural pulls. Many have adopted (and modified) British pop music and clothes, and particularly in the case of Asian communities, many young people have developed much more casual attitudes than their parents towards the opposite sex.

Over the years, British social attitudes surveys have suggested that people in Britain are more optimistic than pessimistic about race relations. Facets of the island outlook of the majority population still remain, however. Statistics also show that black people are still discriminated against at immigration control, in the courts, by the police, at work and on the streets. Unlike the American 'melting pot' approach where minority ethnicities have been encouraged to blend into and become assimilated by the local culture, migrants to Britain have often not sought, nor been encouraged, to integrate into British society. Some academics bemoan the fact that immigrants to the US will call themselves 'Americans' quite soon, whereas migrants to UK develop local affinities but will not call themselves 'British'. In many respects this means that they have been excluded from the dominant culture. Moreover, if ethnic groups do not have a high profile on TV, the major national cultural arena, they are marginalised in social and political debates too. This awareness is behind Welsh-speakers' claims of the importance to their cultural survival of the TV channel S4C and also partly behind other communities' insistence on better and greater representation on television. The remit of Channel 4 was framed explicitly to address such issues and is perceived by some to show only 'minority' programmes, while others feel it does not have enough cultural variety and still caters for an ethnic mainstream.

The political left has tended to welcome the influx of other nationals. For the right, immigration remains a heated subject, hedged around by xenophobic myths and racist fears, based on the idea of 'our' beautiful island filling up with foreign nationals. For example, the Conservative MP Winston Churchill said in May 1993, in a speech at Bolton, that 'Immigration has to be halted to defend the British way of life'. Contrary to the belief of many, it is a fact that more individuals have left Britain each year since 1964 than have entered. (That situation has currently stabilised slightly because world recession has meant fewer overseas opportunities for British people.) Also, white immigration from countries such as Canada, New Zealand and Australia far outnumbers that from countries such as India, Bangladesh, Ceylon and Jamaica.

Recent debates have added extra significance to the versions of Britishness outlined in this section. On the one hand, some influential critics such as Stuart Hall have begun to explore seriously the possibility of 'New Ethnicities' that are black and British – thus redefining old notions of British identity. Tariq Ramadan objects to the very idea of 'integrating' minorities into a society into which many have been born and are already rightful citizens and contributors. Fathali Moghaddam posits the idea of an 'omnicultural' rather than 'multicultural' model of cultural identity. The latter emphasises difference where the former celebrates what people have in common: family values, regard for stability, respect for education, and so on. On the other hand, social commentators such as John Solomos have warned that a new right-wing conception of England as 'the island race', separate from Europe and distinct from minority ethnicities within the UK, is emerging once more.

National identities

Throughout this book we look at practices, artefacts, rituals, languages, customs and environments – shaping forces on *cultural* identity. However, national identity is often also embodied in public figures. Repeatedly the British image has been described in terms of certain strong individual people who stand for single aspects of Britain. This doesn't just apply to stock Shakespearean characters like Falstaff, or Henry Fielding's Parson Adams, or Dickens's Mr Pickwick or Sarah Gamp. It applies to single strong figures who somehow stand for or represent the nation as it has been seen at particular moments. British stereotypes have been created or reinforced by figures you may be familiar with from history, politics, sport or films. For example, the following is a list of symbolic individuals who have all been thought to be quintessentially British: Florence Nightingale and the Queen (sturdy, supportive English womanhood); Winston Churchill and Lord Kitchener ('boys of the bulldog breed', from a popular Victorian music-hall song called 'Sons of the Sea, All British Born'); W. G. Grace and Bobby Charlton (gentlemanly sportsmen); and David Niven, Joyce Grenfell, or Margot Fonteyn (the well-mannered, charming English performer). Particularly in fiction there are numerous strong characters in whom British readers are invited to invest their hopes and values. These are figures entrusted with fighting for the country (Biggles), or unravelling a mystery (Miss Marple or Sherlock Holmes), exploring the world (Allan Quatermaine in *King Solomon's Mines*), unmasking spies (Richard Hannay in *The 39 Steps*), redressing social and financial injustice (Robin Hood), or saving Britain, if not the world, from an evil mastermind (James Bond). These are idealised figures who express strong patriotic beliefs but, unlike the icons we will be looking at in this section, do not *personify* the country.

In the section that follows, we will look at a number of figures who offer alternative representative forms of British identity: Britannia, Albion, John Bull and the heroes of Arthurian mythology and other folk stories. These are foils against which we would like you to try your own views about Britain and the British: we hope you will register the obvious disparity between appearance and reality and that these images are not just part of history. They are powerful ideological images which are routinely used to exercise power in contemporary Britain.

Britannia or Albion

An important cultural and symbolic figure is Britannia, a personification of the country with the name the Romans put to the area of the islands they controlled – roughly equivalent to modern England and Wales (the islands were only named 'Britannia' because Claudius Caesar wrongly thought the Britanni, a Gaulish tribe from near Boulogne in northern France, had colonised them). Britannia was a mythical figure who came to represent Britain and she appears throughout the imperial period in engravings and paintings as the woman, often seated in a Roman chariot and accompanied by a lion, spear and shield, to whom colonised peoples make their offerings and show their subservience. A current use of Britannia herself as an offering to represent all-conquering achievement is given to winners of the annual

FIGURE 0.1 Britannia Building Society

Brit awards, or 'Brits'. These are the 'Oscars' of the British music industry, and the trophy is a small Britannia figure complete with helmet, trident and shield. There are numerous other cultural reminders of this heritage, such as the many 'Britannia' inns and the Britannia bridge that spans the Menai straits (between the island of Anglesey and the Welsh mainland). The royal yacht was called Britannia and so was Britain's foremost holiday airline, before being rebranded Thomsonfly by its new German owners in 2005. Meanwhile the oldest and largest English language encyclopedia, first produced in Scotland but now with a heavy American slant, is called the 'Encyclopedia Britannica', and is still widely advertised and sold at shopping complexes throughout the country. From the UK's Roman heritage, Britannia has therefore come to be associated to various degrees with learning, royalty, sea-faring and the figure of the woman warrior. The importance of the first three is perhaps easy to understand from British history, but what of the last?

This idea of the strong noble queen is easily invoked in Britain. Ancient familiar images are those of the warrior Boadicea who led the Iceni tribe against the Romans, the Celtic Fairy Queen Mab and Cathleen, the personification of Ireland. Queen Elizabeth I and Queen Victoria have both repeatedly been represented as such a defiant queen, leader of a war-like nation, for purposes of imperial rule as well as national pride. Margaret Thatcher's success and charisma were arguably associated with this symbolism, which is encapsulated in the song 'Rule Britannia':

> When Britain first, at heaven's command,
> Arose from out the azure main,
> This was the charter of the land,
> And guardian angels sung this strain:
> 'Rule, Britannia, rule the waves;
> Britons never will be slaves'.
>   ('Alfred: A Masque', 1740, James Thomson)

These words were put to music by Dr Thomas Arne and became a focus for patriotism when sung annually at the Last Night of the Proms summer concert at the Royal Albert Hall. Today, alongside 'Rule Britannia' will be sung William Blake's famous extract from his poem 'Milton', which envisages a new Jerusalem in 'England's green and pleasant land' (significantly, when Enoch Powell appealed to the British people in his argument against immigration he used this phrase). The other key song is Arthur Benson's imperial anthem 'Land of Hope and Glory':

> Land of Hope and Glory, Mother of the Free,
> How shall we extol thee, who are born of thee?

Wider still and wider shall thy bounds be set;
God who made thee mighty, make thee mightier yet.
('Song' from *Pomp and Circumstance*, Edward Elgar)

These songs are an expression of group identity and display an element just beneath the surface of some British attitudes. Rupert Brooke goes so far as to suggest that the death of a British soldier abroad should somehow hallow the place: 'there's some corner of a foreign field / That is for ever England'. The noble, sea-faring, essentially pastoral island is still the nostalgic image of Britain retained by some sections of the national press. It is also part of a traditional view that equates British identity with rural pastimes such as Morris dancing, clay pigeon shooting, beagling, fox hunting and other country sports. Additionally, it is tied up with the idea of Britain as a strong military and naval power: the conquering island race we considered earlier.

In his 1941 essay 'England Your England', George Orwell wrote that the diversity of British identity was illustrated 'by the fact that we call our islands by no less than six different names, England, Britain, Great Britain, the British Isles, the United Kingdom and, in very exalted moments, Albion'. Particularly since the French Revolution, Britain has been seen from abroad as *Albion perfide*, 'treacherous Albion'. The name Albion, or Albany, may have been the Celtic name for Britain, but the term itself probably comes from the imposing white (Latin: *albus*) cliffs of Dover, facing France.

In Britain, Albion is associated with English aspirations and high sentiment. So, in 1579, Sir Francis Drake intended that California would be called 'New Albion' when he annexed it. Two hundred years later, at the time of the French Revolution, William Blake, always critical of the English establishment, wrote 'Visions of the Daughters of Albion'. This poem of 1793 speaks out for the rights of women and against contemporary injus-

FIGURE 0.2 Morris dancers

tices such as slavery. It begins: 'Enslav'd the Daughters of Albion weep: a trembling lamentation'.

Together, the images of Britannia and Albion provide us with contrasting representations of Britain. Opposed to the image of the free imperial island and the strong female leader are Blake's less patriotic but more historically accurate references to Britain's involvement in the slave trade and its restriction of women's rights.

John Bull

A third image of cultural and symbolic significance is that of John Bull: a stubborn, kindly and affable but blustering farmer. In his 'Notes on the English Character' of 1920, the novelist E. M. Forster agreed with the Blakean view of Britain as Albion and thought that the principal British national characteristic was hypocrisy (followed by caution, integrity, solidity, efficiency and lack of imagination). But he also thought the English were 'essentially middle class' and afraid to have an emotional life:

> The national figure of England is Mr. Bull with his top hat, his comfortable clothes, his substantial stomach and his substantial balance at the bank. Saint George may caper on banners and in the speeches of Parliament, but it is John Bull who delivers the goods.

John Bull is the commercial, roast-beef-eating, imperialist Englishman. He is like a bulldog in appearance and temperament. He was established (though not invented) by Dr John Arbuthnot in 1712 and appears in numerous cartoons as the ebullient, well-fed, matter-of-fact, robust Englishman, dressed in a gaudy waistcoat and a jaunty hat. He is invoked at times of national crisis, especially war, and incorporates the England that attracts hostility abroad (British people are disparagingly known in France as *Les Rosbifs*). He is the narrowly patriotic Englishman who robustly defends his country's 'rights'. A figure from the mid-eighteenth century who resembles John Bull in many ways is the original Toby Jug decoration, the famous drinking-pot celebrating the traditional British male social space, the pub.

The Irish dramatist George Bernard Shaw wrote his play *John Bull's Other Island* in 1904 at the request of W. B. Yeats, for the Irish Literary Theatre. An historical allegory, it depicts the gradual takeover of an Irishman's life by an honest, but ambitious Englishman. Two years later, the name John Bull was adopted as the title for a staunch British weekly and so we can say that the enduring name is associated with Britain's belief in its world-purpose and its paternalistic attitude towards its empire. In the 1950s

FIGURE 0.3 Most pub drinkers are still men

FIGURE 0.4 A Toby Jug, whose origin has been attributed to Shakespeare's Sir Toby Belch

the word 'jumble' was a mocking contraction of 'John Bull' used by West Africans to describe a white English person. The figure is rarely seen today but the idea of a strong, free and independent country remains a dominant if outdated image of Britain and its role in the world; it surfaces in such assertions of national importance and identity as accompanied the Falklands War in 1981, when Prime Minister Thatcher insisted that Britain was still the country that had built an Empire and that its people still had the same 'sterling qualities'. Arguably, the idea of John Bull makes it easier for government to sell to its electorate British incursions into Iraq or Afghanistan.

Arthur and mythology

In this section, we will look at one further example of Britishness in modern popular mythology: Arthurian Britain. For many people, England is the land of St George and King Alfred, of Avalon, the Knights of the Round Table and King Arthur at Camelot. Historically, Arthur is a shadowy figure, a Dark Age chieftain possibly created in the Middle Ages by the Welsh historian Geoffrey of Monmouth but enshrined in literary history by Sir Thomas Malory in the fifteenth century in his *Morte D'Arthur*. The legend of Excalibur, the 'sword in the stone' that Walt Disney turned into a cartoon film, is famous here: 'Whoso pulleth out this sword of this stone and anvil is rightwise king born of all England' *(Morte D'Arthur*, Bk1, ch. 4). It is possible to think of such stories of the past as remote but, while they exert less direct influence than television programmes, for example, they in fact touch British lives every day. For example, the company running Britain's national lottery, which sells many millions of tickets every week, is called Camelot – to suggest a fundamental Britishness, a traditional identity and a sense of equality and fairness. Its three lottery machines are called Lancelot, Guinevere and Arthur.

In Victorian times the idea of Arthur's Britain was fostered by many romantic painters such as James Archer and by writers such as Lord Tennyson, whose sequence of Arthurian poems 'Idylls of the King' was a bestseller. During a period when Britain was heavily industrialising, this invented nostalgia enabled people to hark back to a mythical England of chivalry and romance. Even today, places like Glastonbury, where Arthur and Guinevere's bones were supposedly found in the twelfth century, are places of pilgrimage for those who seek an Arthurian version of Britain. Mythology and paganism still have a strong hold on the public imagination: the standing stones at Stonehenge on Salisbury Plain (where Thomas Hardy's *Tess of the D'Urbervilles* ends) have been roped off because they were a site of congregation for thousands of people on midsummer's night and other occasions.

FIGURE 0.5 Lord Nelson, hero of the Battle of Trafalgar, honoured in a pub name

National representatives

As we have seen from the examples above, cultural identity is in many ways about representation. This should be understood in two ways. On the one hand there is representation as portrayal and below we will look briefly at some figures, or 'heroes', who have come to represent Britishness (and who are honoured in pub names across the country, from the 'Duke of Wellington' to the 'The Nelson'. On the other hand, there is political and constitutional representation, where an individual or group 'stands in' or speaks for the whole country. So, before looking at some national heroes, we will begin this section by considering two groups of people who 'represent' Britain in both these ways – the monarchy and statespeople: those who act as figureheads, but also wield constitutional power in the name of the nation.

Royalty

Perhaps the most enduring stereotypical version of Britain is that which revolves around the idea of monarchy. As an institution, the British monarchy has been both popular and deeply unpopular at different times in its history. It has often survived because of its links outside the country, though most tourists would think of it as quintessentially British. The idea that the royal family should be an ideal British family, associated with morals rather than power, only really stems from Victoria and Albert, whose 'family values' of a close, loving relationship and a harmonious household have been held up by the press as a standard by which the current royals are found wanting. The family tree of the present royal family is shown in Figure 0.6.

Earlier, we mentioned the traditions of the countryside persisting in the present. The monarchy also stresses its rural and regional base. An example would be the ceremonial investiture in Caernarfon Castle of Prince Charles as Prince of Wales – a traditional and not a legal title of the sovereign's eldest son. This might be seen as a move to consolidate and symbolise the power of the monarchy in Wales, but a less obvious and more revealing indicator of the rural basis of monarchy is supplied by the widespread locations of the royal estates of Balmoral, Sandringham and Blenheim. Further, individual members of the royal family are officially known by their titles, such as the Duke of Edinburgh, Duchess of York and Duke of Gloucester, to indicate their regional responsibilities. At national sporting occasions, such as Wimbledon or the FA Cup Final, royalty are still invited to present the trophies in the way that barons and earls presided at jousts or tournaments in medieval times, where they would honour the knight-champion. Today,

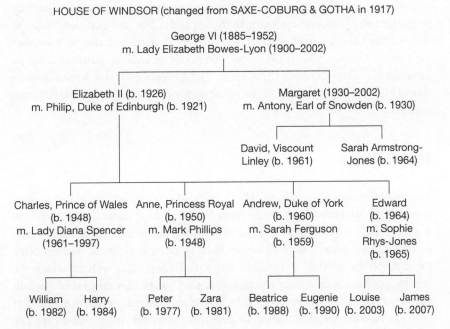

FIGURE 0.6 Family tree of the present royal family

in Britain as elsewhere, this function has been copied and localised, so while the Queen or other members of the royal family will still bless ships and officially inaugurate important public buildings, local TV and sports stars will 'open' supermarkets and fetes.

This awe and respect for monarchy sits alongside a disapproval of the royal family's social privilege and national income, particularly with regard to those members who are 'paid for' by the public but who are not in the Queen's immediate family. In the late 1960s, the American magazine *Time* described Captain Mark Philips, Princess Anne's future husband, as a 'semi-articulate dragoon' at a time when few English people, let alone the media, would use such insulting language about someone who was about to marry into the royal family. Nowadays, even quality newspapers in Britain are openly critical of the behaviour of younger members of the royal family and there is no doubt that in some quarters the popularity of the whole family has been eroded, despite the fact that the Queen herself is one of those monarchs, like Henry VIII, Elizabeth I and Victoria, who have enjoyed broad popular support. Hence, when Prince William and Kate Middleton were married in 2011 the palace were quick to point out that costs of the wedding would be borne not by the taxpayer but by the respective families.

However, as a focus for media fascination, the royal family remains unequalled: both the tabloids and the broadsheets regularly feature them in their main items and there are several royal documentaries made for television each year. Many of these are celebrations, or exposés, but others raise the perennial question of whether the monarchy brings in more money to the country, through tourism, than it spends. The ancient view that the state of the nation is embodied in the monarchy persists today in a weaker version that requires both propriety and profit as well as manners from its figureheads. The success of films like *The Queen* and *The King's Speech* shows how much the doings of the royal family are embedded in the national psyche.

Politicians

The second group of people who both wielded power and 'stood for' Britain are those politicians who have governed the nation at times of great success or crisis, such as William Pitt, Gladstone and Churchill. The traditional portrayal of these people in the UK has been as natural political leaders dedicated to public service. Because of Britain's strong class system, which we will be examining in a later chapter, it is easy to see this misplaced faith in 'noblesse oblige' as veneration for the aristocracy, based on the principle that only the rich can be relied upon to perform public service because they are beyond the reach of corruption. Partly for the same reason, the right-wing

Conservative party, traditionally the party of the aristocracy and commercial enterprise, has been portrayed as the 'natural' party of government. Elements of the idea that running the country was a part-time job, almost akin to running an estate, persisted up until the mid-nineteenth century, when Britain had its first 'professional' prime minister, Disraeli. Hitherto the office had been a part-time duty rather than a full-time occupation. It was not formally recognised as a government position until the twentieth century.

This respect for 'great statesmen' indicates a British distrust of professionalism and ambition. What people wanted was 'effortless superiority' (the attribute Prime Minister Asquith ascribed to men who attended Oxford University's Balliol College). The 'gifted amateur', someone who dispassionately worked for the public good, appealed more to the British public than a career politician. Britons traditionally favour the underdog at sporting events and in many situations believe that it is more important to 'play the game' than to win.

However, that tradition may have been mostly broken by the advent of Thatcherism. Margaret Thatcher's assertiveness and qualities of leadership gained her an international reputation such that she spent time after office on the lecture circuit, particularly in the United States, where, partly through her good relations with Ronald Reagan, she was able to champion market forces, commercial materialism and self-help. Though against the image of a reserved Britishness, Thatcherism has become synonymous with a revived kind of proud but narrow British 'island race' nationalism centred on the individual – Thatcher once said that there is 'no such thing as society'. By contrast, Tony Blair's 'New' Labour party promoted a 'stakeholder' society in which everyone was supposed to be involved. Their commitment would benefit them, so the argument went. And of course David Cameron's coalition government, elected in 2010, promotes The Big Society – a nebulous concept aimed at countering Denis Thatcher's reputed suggestion that compassion 'is not one of your words, is it, Margaret?' All politicians currently are labouring under the difficulties in public perception caused for them by the MP expenses scandals of 2010 and their proximity to powerful media interests. They have certainly lost the authority and respect that they may have held in former times.

Heroes

In addition to monarchy and certain politicians, a number of enduring cultural figures – or heroes – have been dominant in British society as role models and objects for national pride. Bertolt Brecht once said: 'Pity the land which has no heroes. No! Pity the land that has need of heroes.' It is perhaps to be regretted therefore that Britain's cultural commentators for at least the last two centuries seem to have felt a need to promote hero-worship. We will refer here to a number of representative heroes from Britain's past whose influence is still found in politicians' speeches, advertising, the media, class-rooms and the tourist trade.

William Shakespeare is Britain's most famous writer. However, in many ways, 'Shakespeare' is not so much an individual dramatist as a commercial enterprise that generates T-shirts, playing cards, tea cloths and pints of beers as well as plays and poetry. Also, despite the populism of the original Globe theatre in London his work has come to represent élite cultural values. The role of organisations such as the British Council is to bring this type of high art to the rest of the world, perpetuating the image of present-day Britain as in many ways a version of its past. The individual in the street in Britain may have no relation to the culture of this manufactured Shakespearean England, but the Shakespeare industry, as it now is, forms part of a cluster of 'heritage tours': to Anne Hathaway's cottage in Stratford-upon-Avon, to Wordsworth's Dove Cottage in Grasmere, to the Brontës' parsonage in Haworth.

Other figures who have long stood at the centre of groups or fan clubs but around whom there is now a newly minted heritage industry are Dickens in London, Grace Darling on the Farne Islands, Francis Drake in Plymouth and Jane Austen at Bath. The representation of many of these figures stresses the island or nautical aspect of Britain and such insularity has been credited with forming the war-like character of British Imperialists from Walter Raleigh to Winston Churchill. British political and military history provides many other cult figures. For example, the Duke of Wellington's defeat of Napoleon in Belgium in 1815 has been ingrained in the public consciousness (the equal presence of Belgian, Dutch and German forces is not widely known in Britain) and the expression 'met his Waterloo' has entered into the British vocabulary, along with the saying that 'the battle of Waterloo was won on the playing fields of Eton' – a reference to the importance of public-school sports in developing discipline, strategic thinking and a competitive spirit. The list of figures who are celebrated through stamps, banknotes, statues and speeches is too long for us to mention more than a few of the most prominent: Clive of India, Lord Kitchener, Lawrence of Arabia, Lord Mountbatten, Montgomery of Alamein and Admiral Nelson. In almost every case, these explorers and military men will be referred to as part of some appeal to national responsibility, destiny, or identity (against them, figures from an alter-native pantheon, such as the women's rights campaigners Mary Wollstonecraft and Emmeline Pankhurst, will be promoted by others).

Lacking a contemporary mythical personification as strong as Uncle Sam, old-fashioned British rhetoric is liable to turn to these historical figures when rallying people in the name of the nation. Most of them, of course, will alienate or offend many of today's British people, who do not feel they have a positive association with such people – consequently, more sensitive politicians will avoid celebrating such figures. Virginia Woolf said in 1938 that women were excluded from Britishness, and many others, from gay, youth or black communities, feel the same way today. It is ironic that the only English person whose name is given to a much-loved national annual event is a would-be regicide or king-killer: Guy Fawkes, who tried to blow up the Palace of Westminster in 1605.

Bonfire Night and other festivities and events we have discussed in this chapter form the popular mythology of Britishness, the ghost of Britain past that many would prefer to exorcise, or cast out, but which still haunts many people's notions of British identity. In 1995 there was a call, by government ministers and others, for British heroes to be systematically taught in history classes at school, precisely to instil a sense of national cultural identity. In the rest of this book, we will be concentrating not on these national representatives but on the ways in which a wide spectrum of different British people see themselves and on the importance they attach to the cultural influences by which *they* have been moulded.

Finally in this section, a look at the people regarded as contemporary popular heroes will tell us something about the British character. While younger people have their own music, fashion and TV heroes, from Kerry Katona and Lily Allen to Kate Moss and the late Amy Winehouse, Britain more generally has a pantheon of what are known as 'national treasures'. A 'list' of such heroes is always going to be debatable, but the following suggestions would chime with many people: David Attenborough, Pam Ayres, Alan Bennett, Richard Branson, Bruce Forsyth, Stephen Fry, Rolf Harris, Lenny Henry, Joanna Lumley, Patrick Moore, Jamie Oliver, J. K. Rowling and Terry Wogan.

Each one of them is known via the media. Most are in entertainment. None is a politician or a war hero. Several might be described as 'middlebrow', and yet they are deeply loved. Joanna Lumley's telling off of the Immigration Minister Richard Woolas on the issue of Gurkhas' settlement and Pam Ayres's 'They Should Have Asked My Husband' have scored huge numbers of hits on YouTube. Television appears to define the parameters of heroism, as once newspapers would have, and in many cases it is personality rather than public achievement that circumscribes our role models.

However, young people in particular admire Richard Branson for his derring-do. He is self-made, rich, zany, and takes part in dangerous sports such as ballooning and powerboat-racing. The young admire the megalomania of his ambition – he also owns an airline, a train company and now a bank. In the current age of austerity, the Conservative government is encouraging entrepreneurialism as Britain's best way out of recession, and so they are holding up as role models figures like Branson and the host of the hugely popular TV show *The Apprentice*, Alan Sugar.

Jamie Oliver, the TV chef, is also a 'local hero' partly because he was *not* born with a silver spoon in his mouth. His parents ran a pub in Essex and he left school without qualifications. And yet he built a career in which he helped other 'late starters' either through his Fifteen Foundation, which trains people for work in restaurants, or through reality TV programmes such as *Jamie's Dream School*. People feel he is genuinely putting something back into society.

David Attenborough is perhaps more respected than any other 'national treasure' and can be thought of as a role model as well as a hero. What appeals to many people about him is his typically British modesty and understatedness combined with his erudition and intellectual curiosity. He and the others certainly display values held in high esteem by people at large, though often they are just traditional values of good humour and common sense as well as charitable service beyond a media profile.

Conclusion

Obviously the above is not an exhaustive list of characters and characteristics in the formation of a dominant national cultural identity, but it gives an idea of the way in which Britain has traditionally been seen. Today, these aspects do not carry anywhere near as much weight as they did only fifty years ago and there is much current debate about the kind of Britain that is emerging in the twenty-first century and the problems attendant upon putting forward any coherent notion of 'Britishness' given the variety of people who now live in the UK. Even within organisations like the National Trust there is discussion about whether to preserve in aspic the many British stately homes and gardens, or whether it would be better to modernise and update 'our heritage' by preserving elements across the range of British culture, including mines, textile mills and wartime bunkers. Others see British culture (rather than heritage) as being in a constant process of evolution and being far more about the present than the past.

Many tourists, for example, are attracted to Britain for alternatives to its traditional culture of castles, cathedrals and village greens, described elsewhere as 'Theme Park Britain'. Those alternatives include events like the Notting Hill Carnival, Glastonbury Festival and the Edinburgh Festival Fringe – events that serve as magnets for tourists and also as a focus for local counter-culture.

Our aim is to encourage debate rather than to make fixed claims, but it seems safe to suggest that anxiety around British cultural identity is more prevalent among English people than Irish, Scottish or Welsh. It is suggested that the latter are more secure in their cultural status, particularly post devolution, while England lacks an exclusively English parliament and exercises less influence over the other three countries than hitherto. This leads to a lack of national pride, so one argument goes. Hence, just in relation to patron saints, while Ireland has made a worldwide phenomenon of St Patrick's Day on 17 March, Wales has free admission to its national monuments on St David's Day (1 March), and St Andrew's Day on 30 November has been a bank holiday in Scotland since 2006, in England there is still no strong lobby to mark St George's Day (23 April) as a special day of celebration.

In the rest of this book, we will be exploring some of the legacies of and the alternatives to traditional conceptions of Britain. It will be important to keep in focus the historical images of Britain outlined in this introduction, because they do continue to impinge upon the present, but they should be continually questioned by an awareness of contemporary people, alternative cultural practices and other versions of history. Whereas in the United States society is constituted by ethnic and cultural diversity, in the UK, many argue, there is still a desire for 'monoculturalism': an attempt to ignore difference in favour of a dominant idea of 'Britishness'. At bottom, the aim of this book is therefore to argue for broadening notions of British identity, to move from a narrow base to a spectrum of cultural plurality and multiple identities.

Exercises

1   How important do you think mythology and folklore are to a 'sense of identity'? From the descriptions in this chapter, and from your own knowledge, what common images of England and of Britain have you noticed, and what characteristics do you think they represent?

2   In relation to Hollywood movies, we'd like you to consider the following exercises.

■   Think of the American films you have seen. How many English actors can you remember? Have they usually played English characters? How have the English been stereotyped by Hollywood in the past?

■   In terms of recent Hollywood films, Harry Potter is perhaps the most famous English character. What other similar larger-than-life images of British people has Hollywood produced? How many of these originated in British novels?

■   Does Hollywood portray British women differently from British men (you might think of Keira Knightley, Julie Andrews, Emma Thompson, or even the Americans Katherine Hepburn in *The African Queen* and Bette Davis in *The Virgin Queen*)?

3 How important do you think wider geographical perspectives, such as those offered by Europe or the Commonwealth, are to understanding British identity? How is national culture altered by these larger communities? Can you name fifteen countries that are in the Commonwealth, and can you list them by (a) size of population and (b) year of independence?

4 British daily national newspapers are extremely varied, from the tabloid press to the broadsheets, and so are their readerships. A long-standing characterisation of newspapers categorises them in terms of the people who buy them. Listed below are the newspapers and the descriptions of their readers – can you match the one with the other?

   a) *The Times; The Daily Mail; The Sun; The Financial Times; The Guardian; The Daily Telegraph; The Daily Mirror; The Morning Star*

   b) ■ Read by the people who own the country.
   ■ Read by the people who think they run the country.
   ■ Read by the people who think they ought to run the country.
   ■ Read by the people who do run the country.
   ■ Read by the wives of the men who run the country.
   ■ Read by people who don't care who runs the country.
   ■ Read by those who think the country should be run by another country.
   ■ Read by those who think the country is being run by another country.

5 In this chapter we have looked at traditional British identities. What do you know of the following people and characters who have become important or comic cultural figures to the British: Lady Godiva, Henry VIII, Queen Guinevere, Dickens's Mr Podsnap, Shakespeare's Falstaff, Biggles, Bulldog Drummond, Robert the Bruce, Lord Nelson, Lawrence of Arabia, Clive of India and Bunyan's Christian? What are the problems with continuing to advance these characters as icons of Britishness?

6 How important do you think it is to consider language when describing other people? For example, the word 'immigrant' has not been used in this chapter, but you will come across it elsewhere in this book because it is the common term used by most of the British to describe other people who have come to settle in the UK. By contrast, the British abroad are almost never regarded (by the British) as 'immigrants' in other communities or even as 'emigrants' from Britain. Most often they are called 'expats' (short for expatriates). Why do you think this is?

Reading

Childs, Peter and Storry, Mike. *Encyclopedia of Contemporary British Culture*. Routledge, 1999. A wide ranging resource for those interested in the practices and people influencing British culture.

Porter, Roy. *Myths of the English*. Blackwell, 1993. Careful analysis of aspects of Britishness from cricket to the British 'bobby'.

Room, Adrian. *An A to Z of British Life*. OUP, 1992. Handbook containing a lot of information on background detail to British culture, history, idiosyncrasies and 'institutions' such as Ascot, Henley and Glyndebourne.

Samuel, Raphael. (ed.) *Patriotism*. 3 vols. Routledge, 1989. Detailed examination of kinds of British identity in terms of history, gender, race, politics, cultural icons and much more.

Thorne, Tony. *The 100 Words that Make the English*. Abacus, 2009. Language-based analysis of the evolution of such social phenomena as: Jobsworths, Barking and Innits.

Cultural examples

Films

Henry V (1989) dir. Kenneth Branagh. Tudor England. Latest film of Shakespeare's most pro-English play, with comic relief and small roles set aside for the Welsh, Scottish, Irish and French.

Tess (1979) dir. Roman Polanski. Nineteenth century. Loving evocation of the English rural way of life and countryside, filmed in France with a German playing Hardy's heroine. (It is worth comparing this with earlier versions of nineteenth-century classics, such as *Far From the Madding Crowd*, *Jane Eyre*, *Great Expectations*, *Oliver Twist* and *Wuthering Heights*.)

Chariots of Fire (1981) dir. Hugh Hudson. Early twentieth century. Famous Oscar-winning film about a Scottish missionary and a Jewish undergraduate at Cambridge running in the 1924 Olympics. Films of E. M. Forster's novels make other examples: *Maurice*, *Howards End*, *A Room With A View*, *Where Angels Fear to Tread* and *A Passage to India*.

Brief Encounter (1945) dir. David Lean. Mid-twentieth century. Noel Coward's play about repressed middle-class English passion.

Never Let Me Go (2010) dir. Mark Romanek. Based on Ishiguro's dystopian novel about schoolchildren in a classic English setting bred as organ donors.

Tinker, Tailor, Soldier, Spy (2011) dir. Tomas Alfredson. Latest film version of Le Carré novel about spying and the Cold War.

Books

Henry Fielding, *Tom Jones* (1749). One of the first highly praised English novels, this is a comic story of an orphan's adventures and travels across the English countryside and aristocracy.

Elizabeth Gaskell, *North and South* (1855). Class conflict and labour relations in industrial Manchester.

H. G. Wells, *Tono-Bungay* (1909). Analysis of the 'Condition of England' through country houses, patent medicines, romance, business enterprises, sea adventures and London's urban sprawl.

George Orwell, *The Road to Wigan Pier* (1937). An ex-Eton boy travels up north to report on the working classes for the Left Book Club.

Andrew Rawnsley, *The End of the Party* (2010). Though describing the rise and fall of New Labour, the book also gives an accurate account of the economic, political and social state of Britain.

TV programmes

The Jewel in the Crown. The British being terribly 'English' in India between 1942 and 1947. Drama of colonial relations under the Raj interspersed with clips from wartime newsreels.

Middlemarch. The BBC's version of George Eliot's text: the book most often cited as the greatest English novel.

Pride and Prejudice. Yet another extremely popular Jane Austen blockbuster adapted by Andrew Davies.

Little Dorrit. Davies's adaptation of Dickens's novel for the BBC.

Pobol y Cwm. This subtitled Welsh language soap has an audience of 100,000 on S4C.

Antiques Roadshow. Experts tour Britain's old cities and towns so that the middle classes can empty their attics of heirlooms and be amazed at the price they would fetch at auction.

Who Do You Think You Are? A BBC programme in which a variety of British people trace their roots.

The Apprentice. A reality series in which aspiring young businessmen and women aim to become apprenticed to Sir Alan Sugar.

Shameless. Charts the lives of a family on a housing estate in Manchester. Drug-dealing and the underclass are staples.

 Websites

www.royal.gov.uk

The official site of the British monarchy: royalists only!

www.ons.gov.uk

The Office for National Statistics. A reliable government source of information about the UK population.

www.npg.org.uk
> The National Portrait Gallery. A useful source of images of 'high culture'.

www.theworldinonecity.net
> A site depicting 202 people from countries taking part in the Olympics, based in London.

www.geograph.org.uk
> A project to photograph and comment on every Ordnance Survey grid square in UK.

Chapter 1

Places and peoples: region and nation

Peter Childs

Timeline

1536	England and Wales joined
1707	Act of Union for England and Scotland
1801	Ireland incorporated
1922	Independence of southern Ireland
1931	Commonwealth officially formed
1972	Direct rule imposed on Northern Ireland
1973	UK joins EEC
1974/5	Redrawing of county boundaries
1979	Devolution referenda
1994	Eurotunnel opened
1999	Scottish Parliament, Welsh Assembly
2000	Northern Irish Assembly
2014	Scottish Independence Referendum planned

Introduction

'BRITAIN' IS A SHORT FORM of the full name of the United Kingdom of Great Britain and Northern Ireland (the UK). Therefore, Great Britain strictly comprises the countries England, Wales and Scotland, whereas the UK also includes Northern Ireland. On the one hand, these four countries have become part of one nation over the last five hundred years: Wales was linked with England in 1536; an Act of Union joined the crowns of England and Scotland in 1707; Ireland was incorporated in a Union lasting from 1801 to 1921, when all but the counties of Northern Ireland gained independence (taking effect in 1922). On the other hand, as European history repeatedly demonstrates, political union is not cultural union and it has often been maintained that Scotland and Wales should have devolution, a transfer of power from the government in Westminster to home rule. The pressure of this view, following referenda of the populations, resulted in the creation of the Scottish Parliament and the Welsh Assembly in 1999, which give not independence but increased self-government. These elected bodies can be perceived as part of a transition to full national government in Wales and Scotland, though at present they are seen by some as an extra layer of government between the people and the UK government at Westminster, which retains overarching financial control and has generally centralised power rather than devolving it, especially in relation to local government below the regional level. By contrast, Northern Ireland had self-rule in most governmental areas except foreign affairs and defence prior to 1972, at which date direct rule from London was reintroduced following increased sectarian violence. However, following the Peace Agreement in 1998 and in line with Scottish and Welsh partial devolution the previous year, a Northern Irish Assembly and Executive was created in 2000 to end direct rule from Westminster, though continued violence and a lack of political commitment to the Agreement has threatened this, such that the reimposition of Westminster rule has been made at times and the Assembly suspended. Alongside this can be placed the fact that repeated polls report that more Britons believe Northern Ireland should join a united Ireland than believe that it should be a part of the UK.

FIGURE 1.1 Map of the British Isles

In terms of natural, as opposed to political geography, it can be argued that Britain is marked by great contrasts but few extremes. Its highest mountain is Ben Nevis (4,408 ft or 1,344 m) in Scotland; its longest river is the Severn (220 miles or 354 km), which rises in central Wales but also wanders as far east as Gloucester in England. Its largest lake is Lough Neagh (148 sq miles or 383 sq km) in Northern Ireland. Officially, the mainland stretches from Dunnet Head in the north of Scotland to Lizard Point in Cornwall, but most people will describe Britain as running from the famous names of Land's End, in the south, to John O'Groat's.

However, when situating British identity in terms of place in relation to culture, we should both turn to smaller geographical units, such as the ancient counties whose boundaries were contentiously redrawn in 1974/5, and look to the larger outside world, not least because many British people do not live in the UK. Britishness in recent years has often been defined in relation to the Continent as European political and economic links have become stronger: in 1973 the UK joined the European Community (now European Union) and in 1994 the Channel Tunnel was opened, providing a rail connection from England to France. From another perspective, their eventful history means that British people have ties throughout the world, particularly with the other 53 member states of the Commonwealth of Nations, a loose association of independent countries formerly of the British Empire. In between all these geographical and political groupings there has arisen not just a few but a multitude of British cultures and identities.

To give an initial outline of the UK in terms of place, we can begin by looking at three aspects: size, population and people. The United Kingdom has a land area of just over 94,000 square miles (243,610 square km), a little over half of which is in England. This is one reason why England is sometimes mistaken for Britain abroad, but a stronger factor is the relatively large size of England's population – an imbalance that allows it to dominate the union, beaming its television programmes to the rest of the nation for example. In 2009, the fairly stable UK population stood at nearly 61.8 million people (up from 58.4 million in 1994).

In terms of culture, the figures in Table 1.2 can be misleading. To begin with, we should not assume that strength of cultural identity increases with size of population – indeed, many people would argue that the opposite is more likely to be the case. It is therefore not surprising that to confuse

TABLE 1.1 Mid-2009 population estimates for UK (estimated resident population by age and sex) (in thousands)

Age	Persons	Males	Females
All ages	61792,0	30374,0	31417,9
15–24	8220,5	4210,9	4009,6
25–34	7993,3	4047,1	3946,2
35–44	9012,0	4465,7	4546,3
45–54	8349,7	4116,9	4232,7
55–64	7315,1	3585,3	3729,9
65–74	5278,7	2511,1	2767,6
75+	4827,1	1911,3	2915,8

TABLE 1.2 Mid-2009 population estimates for countries in UK

Area	Mid-2009 population (in thousands)
United Kingdom	61 792,0
Great Britain	60 003,1
England and Wales	54 809,1
England	51 809,7
Wales	2 999,3
Scotland	5 194,0
Northern Ireland	1 788,9

Sources: Office for National Statistics, General Register Office for Scotland, Northern Ireland Statistics and Research Agency

Britain with England can cause grave offence. History provides ancient reasons for this vehemence of feeling: England is named after the Angles, a tribe who invaded the country's south-east coast from northern Europe in the fifth century and, with other conquering tribes such as the Saxons, drove the older inhabitants, the Celts, to the west. Celtic influence is still notably present in Ireland, Scotland, Wales and Cornwall, and this ethnic difference remains one basis on which England, of the UK's four countries, is sometimes considered to have the least in common with the others. On the other hand, the breakdown into English, Welsh, Scottish and Irish histories can also be misleading when it comes to contemporary cultural identity. The domestic histories of these four countries do not adequately represent the people of the UK today because Britain now has a richer mix of ethnicities than those associated with the ancient Anglo-Saxon or Celt. Over the last century and before, the connections created by the Empire have led to the arrival in Britain of many people from the Caribbean, the Indian sub-continent and Africa, such that, for example, the number of British people of Asian descent is now greater than the population of Northern Ireland. Similarly, refugees from Bangladesh and Uganda, plus communities uprooted from Cyprus, Vietnam and China, have added to the different cultural identities found in Britain, which in recent years has been further enriched by migration from within the EU, especially from Eastern Europe. Also, while this book primarily discusses people within the UK, there are strong British identities to be found in, for example, Hong Kong (a British crown colony up to 1997), the Falkland Islands (over which Britain fought with Argentina in 1982) and the vast Commonwealth of Nations. So, while this chapter will focus on places within the UK, the cultural life of the British is both always in flux and much wider than geographical boundaries might suggest.

In among this discussion of British identities, it is also salutary to note that there are many rumours circulating about the end of Britishness as pressures for separation surface from time to time. Similarly, Britain's relationships with Europe, the Commonwealth and the United States fluctuate depending on numerous national debates and international changes. These speculations and proposals for major shifts usually settle down over time as governments and economies cycle through their changes, but occasionally they grow to pressure points that result in momentous action.

Most commonly they can be read, with hindsight, as at best premature, such as one from the turn of the millennium that I will quote. An article by expatriate Andrew Sullivan in the *New York Times* in 1999 (21 February 'There will always be an England') used the headline 'Farewell Britannia' on every page:

> The United Kingdom's cultural and social identity has been altered beyond any recent prediction. Its very geographical boundaries are being redrawn. Its basic Constitution is being gutted and reconceived. Its monarchy has been reinvented. Half its Parliament is under the axe. Its voting system is about to be altered. Its currency may well soon be abandoned. And its role in the world at large is in radical flux.

Sullivan anticipates a post-imperial attempt at dismantling:

> By quietly abolishing Britain, the islanders abolish the problem of Britain. For there is no problematic 'Great' hovering in front of Scotland, England or Wales. These older deeper entities come from a time before the loss of empire, before even the idea of empire. Britain . . . is a relatively recent construct, cobbled together in the seventeenth century in the Act of Union with Scotland . . .

And there are of course voices from Scotland and Wales that also look forward to the end of Britishness as the route to a fuller and better national future free from England. The Welsh poet R. S. Thomas once wrote: 'Britishness is a mask. Beneath it there is only one nation, England', while Gwynfor Evans, the former leader of Plaid Cymru, published a book entitled *The End of Britishness*, arguing that 'Britishness is Englishness'. Another poet, Robert Crawford, from north of the border, maintains that: 'It is hard to think today of what could be confidently called 'British' culture rather than English or Scottish culture . . . Scottish culture seems to have moved into a post-British phase.'

While we can therefore still talk about 'British cultural identities', the emphases need to remain on multiplicity and plurality, particularly given the resurgence of regionalism, suggesting that the weakness and strength of

Britain is the fact that many people see themselves as primarily some other nationality or ethnicity and 'British' only secondarily.

Nation

Separated from the European continent by the English Channel, the British mainland is the eighth largest island in the world. Its inhabitants are islanders and their attitude towards the rest of the world has sometimes been said to reflect this.

While the Commonwealth offers many indications of the cultural and ethnic influences on modern Britain, and is at the same time a sign of the UK's international links and imperial past, it is Europe's economic policies, legal dictates and bureaucracy that are increasingly forcing the British to reconsider their identity. For some people, 'Brussels' has become a major opponent, in the face of whose recommendations and legislation they are trying to assert a national culture that they feel is coming under attack. Alongside genuine fears, such as that of a loss of local languages, there has also arisen a mythology of European Union policies: rumours maintaining that traditional British foods, such as milk chocolate, crisps, fish and chips and Cornish ice-cream, are under serious threat because of EU standardisation. Through appeals to such recognisable staples of national heritage, a powerful resistance to the EU has built up, but other voices maintain that Britain's political, economic and legislative future has to lie within a united Europe, despite the crisis in the Eurozone in recent years. Consequently, the split over the EU within the Conservative Party has constituted its major policy stumbling block for many years. While the majority of British people are happy in principle to participate in a mutually beneficial union, they are also defensive of their distinctive traditions and their cultural separation from other European countries: in other words, of their identity.

Similarly, some people in the UK argue that while each of Britain's four different countries has a strong identity and inspires patriotic loyalties, there is no 'British' identity as such. Surveys of people 'north of the border' reveal that most would call themselves Scottish and not British. Arguably, the 'British' element to identity for many people is redundant and the United Kingdom is only England with other countries attached in the same way that the Soviet Union now appears to much of the outside world to have been just Russia with other communities uneasily tied to it. Such a view has made British Studies courses sometimes turn to a 'four nations' approach.

Country

To illustrate some traditional ways in which the countries of the British Isles have developed separate cultural identities, we can begin with examples of their various images and emblems. England's patron saint (and also Portugal's) is the probably fictional St George, a knight who slew a fire-breathing dragon in medieval mythology. St George's cross is the name of the English flag, which depicts a red cross on a white background – and English national teams still play rugby and football predominantly in white. The English emblem has been the rose since the War of the Roses in the fifteenth century, when the House of Lancaster, whose symbol is a red rose, fought for the English crown against the House of York, whose symbol is a white rose. More recently, as a symbol of both tradition and socialism, the red rose has been adopted as its emblem by the Labour Party. Red is also the colour of Wales, whose mascot (interestingly, given England's patron saint is St George) has since 1801 been the red Welsh dragon, which is the central figure on the country's flag. The patron saint of Wales is a sixth-century monk called St David and his day, 1 March, is regarded as the country's unofficial public holiday. Wales's twin emblems are the leek and the daffodil. English and Welsh hostility is rooted in history, the relative size of populations arguably giving rise to English condescension and Welsh resentment. Welsh identities are distinctive in terms of language, literature and culture, but it is also divided by language (most people speak English), politics (between those who want a republic and those who would wish for a self-governing nation within a federal UK) and geography (as in England, there is a perceived split between south and north). The Welsh emphasise their sense of community more than the English (except those in the north of England who are often as hostile to southern Englanders as are the Scots or Welsh) and according to surveys see themselves as more caring, genuine and responsible than their English neighbours. Economic regeneration, the new Welsh Assembly, the resurgence of the Welsh language and the characteristic landscape of the valleys has added to a recent growth in Welsh national feeling.

Intranational rivalry is suggested by two other adopted animals: the warring lion (England) and unicorn (Scotland). Since James VI of Scotland became James I of England in 1603, these animals have featured on the Royal Arms holding the monarch's shield. The lion has become a symbol of the strength of the crown and Britain in general, while the Scottish unicorn represents purity. In politics, the Scottish National Party is the strongest voice for the country's distinctive identity and its most famous campaigning supporter, Sean Connery, has vowed to move back to Scotland if the country wins independence. The Scots have a stronger sense of national identity and allegiance than the English or the Welsh, perceiving themselves as tough, friendly, outdoor people who are proud of their traditions and history. Consequently, and partly because of the distinctive Scottish accent(s), they have a higher profile abroad than the Welsh and in some ways a more positive profile than the English. Scotland's patron saint is one of the twelve apostles, St Andrew, and its emblem is the thistle, a symbol of defence. St Andrew's cross forms a part of the British flag, known to most British people as the Union Jack, together with the crosses of St George and St Patrick, the patron saint of Ireland.

A fifth-century ex-slave, St Patrick made the base for his gospel preaching in Armagh, and from there led the successful resurgence of Christianity against chieftains on the British mainland. His feast day, 17 March, is an official holiday in Northern Ireland and his cross is the country's flag (it is not that of the Republic of Ireland). Northern Irish identities contain strong English, Scottish and Irish connections, although there are people in the six counties who identify neither with traditional Irishness nor with Britons from the mainland, seeing themselves instead overwhelmingly in terms of their own local culture, with its emphasis on both hard work and an easy-going character. Ireland's emblem is the shamrock, whose three-in-one leaf was supposedly used by St Patrick to demonstrate the Holy Trinity, but on the British coat of arms Ireland is represented by a harp, now most widely recognised as the logo for Guinness, the famous Irish stout. The majority of these symbols have become signs of a collective heritage and the degree to which people align themselves with such images today is negligible, but there is still strong national pride and people do sing their national anthems, display their flags on major sporting occasions and even wear badges with their country's emblem in their lapels on the saints' days. Since the Second World War and the decline of Empire, the national flag has faded from being a major emblem of national solidarity to most often figuring as a design on a style accessory. In terms of popular culture, the Union Jack had already become primarily a minor fashion image in the 1970s, appearing on watch faces and T-shirts. It was also taken up in the 1980s by football fans, who since then have visited Europe with the flag daubed on their faces (reminiscent of the Ancient Britons who would paint their faces blue with a substance called woad to frighten their enemies). In those decades, the flag represented a legacy left over from Britain's old place in the world, but since the 1990s it has also come to be again a sign of contemporary identity, losing some of the irony or resentment it might have attracted before.

Ireland is the second largest of the British Isles. However, unlike smaller islands, which are wholly British, such as the Isle of Wight and the Shetlands, Ireland is officially partitioned. In 1921, when an agreement was signed giving the rest of the country independence, six of the nine Irish counties that constituted the ancient province of Ulster remained part of the United Kingdom – these were the north-eastern counties that were predominantly

FIGURE 1.2 Mini with Union Jack design

Protestant. Northern Ireland therefore has national and official links with the rest of Britain, but its people share deep roots with histories and traditions south of the border, and since the Anglo-Irish agreement of 1985 the Republic of Ireland has participated in its political and legal matters. Ireland is politically divided but in several respects it is culturally united for many people, not least because the Irish have retained a national distinctiveness despite the globalising influences that are so evident in England. In the 1960s, traditional Irish music saw a resurgence, which has continued; government policy has been to revive the Irish language; indigenous sports such as hurling and Gaelic football have remained popular; and Irish literature is flourishing. For example, in Seamus Heaney, the Irish have arguably produced the finest poet writing in the English language since W. B. Yeats – who was also Irish. Ireland retains a vibrant literary culture and in 2007 Anne Enright won the most well-known literary award in Britain and the Commonwealth, the Booker Prize, with her comic novel *The Gathering*, a bleak but distinctively Irish story about a family reunion drawing together relations who had grown apart geographically and emotionally.

The last Scottish winner of the Booker was James Kelman, in 1994, with his novel *How Late it Was, How Late*. This is a story written in Glaswegian slang, and its part-abusive, part-aggressive patter is peculiar to that city, such that its idioms are not always readily intelligible in much of Scotland outside Glasgow, let alone in the rest of Britain. In addition to a unique vocabulary, the Scots have their own legal and educational systems, a stronger Calvinist tradition than the English and a history that has forged closer links with the French and Irish than the English. When the Scots move abroad, it is said that their national identity emigrates with them, which is significant when approximately four times as many Scots live outside of Scotland as within. It is important to remember that such feelings of belonging do not cease at the border and, in England for example, there is a strong sense of Scottish identity – as any 25 January spent at thousands of English pubs will demonstrate. This is Burns Night, when the birth of Scotland's national poet, Robert Burns, is celebrated with drink, song and dance in a way that Shakespeare's very seldom is.

Officially, the most closely tied countries in the UK are England and Wales, which includes the large island of Anglesey across the narrow Menai Strait. Often mentioned as one unit for purposes of surveys, censuses and polls, England and Wales are joined administratively as well as politically and economically. However, many of the arguments for devolution have rested upon the view that Wales, as well as Scotland, is readily distinguishable from England in terms of language, culture and history. For example, a traditional cultural event which identifies Wales separately from the rest of Britain but which is held in many forms is the Eisteddfod, a bardic competition from pre-Christian times. The name, meaning 'chairing' or 'session', derives from the ceremonial seating of the bard or poet whose work has been awarded the first prize. The Royal National Eisteddfod, conducted entirely in Welsh, is held annually in different locations throughout the country. It involves music, drama and other arts, as well as poetry. The Eisteddfod is announced over a year in advance at a harp ceremony conducted by the Gorsedd, or Court, encircled by specially laid stones. The festival is associated with a nationalistic Welsh identity, and Plaid Cymru, 'the party for

Wales', was founded in a hotel room in Pwllheli during the Eisteddfod in 1925. As a cultural event the Eisteddfod remains identifiably Welsh, even though there are English language spin-offs, just as Highland reels and sword dancing are Scottish. In terms of place, it is country rather than nation that remains the major cultural (though not necessarily political) grouping with which people identify.

Representations of the British are not only generated from within Britain, however. In terms of culture, Hollywood remains a dominant influence. In the 1940s and 1950s, English actors commonly played the roles of well-mannered, upper-class socialites. At the end of the last century, there was an identifiable trend in which male English actors took the roles of 'bad guys': killers, psychopaths or terrorists. There was a run of such films in which the villain, though not English, was played by an Englishman: *Schindler's List* (Ralph Fiennes), *Air Force One* (Gary Oldman), *Die Hard* (Alan Rickman) and *Reversal of Fortune* (Jeremy Irons). An actor such as Anthony Hopkins, who played the part of Hannibal Lecter in *Hannibal* and *The Silence of the Lambs,* is likely to be lumped in with this group because the Welsh, unlike the Scottish and Irish, who have large populations in the US, seem not yet to have a strong cultural identity in Hollywood. By contrast, the *Star Wars* film *The Phantom Menace* had a Scottish actor, Ewan MacGregor, and a Northern Irish actor, Liam Neeson, as its heroes. Arguably, Celtic sympathy in the USA, combined with an increased awareness of colonialism, has meant that, post-Cold War, the English have been frequently cast in the guise of oppressors and their role in, for example, the Second World War, has been ignored or downplayed by Hollywood in films like *Saving Private Ryan.*

Region

It is important to remember that culture varies for Irish, Welsh, Scottish or English people depending on which region of their country they come from. In Wales, three-quarters of the population live in the valleys and coal regions of the south, which instil a different sense of Welsh identity from the mountains and seaside towns of the more militantly anti-English north; while in England it is the heavily populated metropolitan areas that have created several of its strongest regional identities. People from these different areas are associated with specific names and local characteristics, though it is their dialect that most obviously distinguishes them. For example, those from Newcastle and Tyneside, in the north-east of England, are called 'Geordies' after a mining lamp designed by George Stephenson, while people from Liverpool are known as Scousers, after a sailor's stew of meat and potatoes called lobscouse, and anyone brought up in the vicinity of London's

Cheapside is known as a Cockney, originally the name for a spoilt city child. Each of these has a strong regional identity, which is reflected in television series devoted to personalities from the major cities: *Auf Wiedersehen Pet* and *The Likely Lads* about canny, tough-minded Geordies, *Brookside* and *Boys from the Blackstuff* about long-suffering but brave-faced Scousers, *EastEnders* and *Only Fools and Horses* about wily, enterprising east Londoners 'on the make'. The importance of regional identity can also be understood from any phone-in radio programme where presenters will almost invariably cite the area that callers are from, as though this in some significant way influenced their viewpoint, determined their record request, or mattered greatly to the show's listeners.

England is often talked about in terms of a north/south divide, which is cultural, economic and political (the Labour Party has far more support in the north and the Conservative Party in the south). This can be particularly accentuated by differences in unemployment levels, crime rates, house prices and standards of living, all of which in recent decades have been worse in the north – for example, compare these 2009 figures for Middlesbrough in the north-east with the average for England: life expectancy (55 versus 86 years), average wage (£17,000 versus £23,500), unemployment (10.7 per cent versus 5 per cent). The perceived divide does not occur in the middle of the country, however, and southerners sometimes refer to a cold, industrial region that is everywhere 'north of Watford', a town not particularly far north of London. In turn, some northerners caricature many southerners as both 'soft' and unsociable. This is because people from the south-east, and particularly London, are sometimes seen as fast-living, career-minded and unfriendly, while they are also more comfortably off and enjoy better weather than those further north. Differences between north and south have evolved over the last two centuries and are more cultural than simply industrial or economic (during parts of the nineteenth century the north was more prosperous than the south).

However, the largest number of 'enterprise zones' and development areas, assisted by government funding and incentives for industry, are in regions such as the Midlands, the north-east, east central Scotland and south Wales – but this economic difference from the south of England is frequently exaggerated. That a southern English region such as south-west Cornwall is also a development area is often ignored because it is distant from London and the financially dominant south-east. The greatest financial distinction between London and the rest of the country is the cost of housing. In 2001, the average house price in Britain was £90,000, but it would have been almost impossible to buy a home in London for anything like this price. At the time of writing, it is feared that most younger people cannot afford to buy houses, the cost of which has escalated far in excess of wages, such that over ten years the average price has risen to over £160,000.

Other regional differences are evident in sport, food and housing: the north has rugby league, the south rugby union; the north has butties, barmcakes and baps (all breadcakes) while the south has sandwiches and rolls; terraced housing is more common in the north, detached houses and bungalows in the south. Between these two regions lies the Midlands, a band of counties such as Staffordshire and Nottinghamshire across central England, which, caught between two cultures, often seems to be regarded as the north by people in the south, and vice versa. However, a strong regional identity associated with the dales, hills and moors is felt by people in the Midlands, and the countryside of a county such as Derbyshire is often considered the most beautiful in England (by Jane Austen in *Pride and Prejudice,* for example). Also, an individual personality attaches to Birmingham, the UK's second-largest city, and the distinctive 'Brummie' downward intonation is as recognisable as a Scottish or Welsh accent.

Language, accent, vocabulary and idioms of speech form important regional differences. For example, Welsh, a version of which was spoken in Britain when the Romans invaded in 55 BC, is one of the oldest languages in the British Isles. Tens of thousands of people still speak Welsh, adult educational institutions run language courses, and since the 1970s bilingual education in Wales, or *Cymru*, has become firmly established. About a quarter of the Welsh population speak both languages, and because Welsh and English are both officially supported it is usual to see signs written in the two languages. Also, Gaelic, another variant of the ancient Celtic languages, is still spoken by some people in Ireland, Scotland and, to a lesser extent, the Isle of Man. Accent and idiom vary enormously throughout Britain, although there has been concern expressed over the spread of 'estuary English': an outer London accent and dialect characterised by features of pronunciation such as lisped 'r's and by words such as 'basically' (it is thought by some to be reducing speech variations). In England there are still great differences in regional accent, but the clearest boundary is that between north and south. No English person is likely to mistake the long, soft vowels of a west Londoner who could rhyme 'garage' with 'large', for the short, hard ones of a Lancastrian, who could rhyme 'garage' with 'ridge'. As for local vocabulary and idioms, if we take Scotland as an example, some words have become national expressions and most British people will understand 'ken' (know) or 'wee bairn' (small baby). However, an English person would be unlikely to know the meaning of such words as 'wabbit' (tired and weak), 'toom' (empty), or 'reidh' (smooth).

Scottish words come from different languages that lie either side of an ancient regional divide. The majority of Scots are Lowlanders and have an ancestry that is part Teutonic and part Celtic. In the past, they were considered different from the traditionally more aggressive, independent, Gaelic-speaking Highlanders, who were a minority but supplied the national symbols of the tartan, bagpipes, kilt and sporran (like the Highland games, these are largely produced for tourists nowadays). However, except in the crofting (loosely, farming) communities of the west, this division is historical more than contemporary, and religious denomination, football team allegiance and city of birth are more likely to form points of cultural identity, especially for Lowlanders. Today, Gaelic is the principal language only in the Outer Hebrides and a few other, mainly island communities.

While it is a comparatively small country, Britain still has regional television companies, which, as well as making and carrying the nationally transmitted programmes, provide localised information to areas such as Granada in the north-west of England and Central in the Midlands. Since the 1980s, regional accents have been increasingly welcomed onto the BBC airwaves, which were previously saturated by announcers with the clipped tones of Received Pronunciation, an upper-class accent used to standardise speech by public schools in the nineteenth century. Today, there are also local radio broadcasts in Welsh and since 1982 there has been a Welsh-language television channel called Sianel Pedwar Cymru, which means Channel 4 Wales and is abbreviated to S4C. However, national stations are more culturally influential for most people and satellite stations for some. While there are regional weekly and even daily papers, a similar picture is true of newspapers: even locally, national media are frequently more popular than regional.

TABLE 1.3 Mid-2009 population estimates for regions in UK

Area	Mid-2009 population (in thousands)
North East	2 584,3
North West	6 897,9
Yorkshire and the Humber	5 258,1
East Midlands	4 451,2
West Midlands	5 431,1
East	5 766,6
London	7 753,6
South East	8 435,7
South West	5 231,2
Wales	2 999,3
Scotland	5 194,0
Northern Ireland	1 788,9

Sources: Office for National Statistics, General Register Office for Scotland, Northern Ireland Statistics and Research Agency

County

After region, the largest area with which the British identify themselves is their county, a geographical fusion of landscape, culture and administration most likely to affect people in terms of its natural scenery and its historic landmarks. County boundaries partitioned ancient Britain, and three counties in the south (Sussex, Kent and Essex) were Anglo-Saxon kingdoms. Modified in 1975, counties may be ceremonial or administrative and still form the basis of local government in some areas of the UK, though reorganisation in 1997 again changed the map (for example, Gwent used to be a county in south-east Wales but, since the 1997 local government reorganisation, it officially no longer exists). In terms of county types, the most famous grouping in England is the 'home counties', a nineteenth-century phrase referring to the counties around London, such as Kent, Surrey, Berkshire, Middlesex and Essex. Some counties are known for their countryside: Cumbria's Lake District (made famous in Wordsworth's poetry) and Hampshire's New Forest (a royal hunting ground for William the Conqueror). Others are known for their industry: Lancashire's factories and mills (described in novels by Charles Dickens and Elizabeth Gaskell) and Nottinghamshire's mines (as in D. H. Lawrence's *Sons and Lovers*). Historic county affiliations remain very strong, in some parts of England particularly, but not everyone by any means has a sense of a county identity, identifying much more strongly with a modern city, for example.

Northern Ireland is sometimes known simply as 'the six counties'. Local government there operates now on the basis of small district and borough councils, but ancient county identities are stronger. To take one example, Antrim, which derives its name from the fifth-century monastery of Aentrebh, occupies the north-east corner of Ireland. A county of moorlands and wooded glens, it is bordered by the sea on three sides. On the north coast is the famous Giant's Causeway. This is a promontory of vertical basalt columns formed by a volcanic rift which stretches under the sea to the Hebrides, islands off the west coast of Scotland. However, Irish legend holds that a giant built this as a walkway from Ireland to a cave on the Hebridean island of Staffa, so that he could attack the legendary Scottish hero Fingal. The roof of Fingal's Cave is also formed of straight six-sided rock columns which the two giants supposedly threw at each other. Celtic mythology adds a magical dimension to local identities and has been used in Ireland in attempts to forge a national consciousness, but even English Romantic poets such as Keats, Wordsworth and Tennyson have written about Fingal's cave.

Most of England's forty-eight ceremonial counties have a recognisable identity and will be said to have their own particular characteristics and distinctive inhabitants. Counties have given their names to famous stretches of countryside (e.g. Surrey hills or Devon moors), to types of people (unsophisticated socialites are 'Essex girls' and those with determination have 'Yorkshire grit'), to food (Cumberland sausages and Cornish pasties), and even to breeds of animal (Staffordshire bull terrier and Berkshire pig). However, one of the strongest ways in which county loyalties are continued is through sport. For example, one of the seventeen county cricket clubs, Yorkshire, refused up until 1992 to allow anyone not born in the county to play for the team. Despite this, Yorkshire had up to that date won the County Championship more often than any other team.

Of course, geographical features are also significant. Yorkshire is separated from its historic rival Lancashire by the Pennines, a range of limestone hills popular with walkers and sometimes described as the backbone of England. Yorkshire is famous abroad for the moors on which the Brontë sisters used to live, but the county is also well known in Britain for a section of the Pennines, the Yorkshire Dales, which was designated a National Park in 1954. These parks are areas of significant natural beauty in England and Wales protected under an Act of 1949. The act prohibits building or development in such areas as Dartmoor and the New Forest in England, Snowdonia and the Pembrokeshire coast in Wales. Similar protection applies to 'listed buildings', usually those dating back before 1840. Such measures preserve the past for the heritage and tourism industries and, partly in consequence, listed buildings and National Parks are sometimes put forward as representative of an authentic Britishness that is at threat from the architecture, pollution and city-oriented life of the present.

Yorkshire is particularly famous for having a strong identity, but this is actually true of most counties. For example, in 1995 inhabitants of Britain's smallest ex-county, Rutland, which was merged with Leicestershire in 1974, were trying to have the county officially recognised again, by raising funds through a 'Rutland' credit card – this campaign succeeded in 2007 when the county was once again recognised as a postal county, though officially it had become a unitary authority (the smallest in the country apart from the City of London). In the 1970s, this sense of local county identity was satirised in a TV series called *Rutland Weekend Television*, a spin-off from *Monty Python's Flying Circus* that had nothing to do with the county – it just pretended to be run on a low budget by a small community of amateur enthusiasts.

In 1975, the Welsh counties were rearranged with others to reduce their number from thirteen to eight. Powys, in mid-Wales, covers the old counties of Montgomeryshire, Radnorshire, and most of Breconshire, but the name itself is that of an ancient province dating from about the fifth century. Like all British counties, it is steeped in history. The county contains Powis and Montgomery Castles, the Dan-y-Ogof Caves, Brecon Cathedral and Gregynog Hall, but its most famous landmark is the Brecon Beacons, or *Bannau Brycheiniog* in Welsh. These are a collection of mainly red sandstone mountains, designated a National Park in 1957, that run for forty miles away from the English border. Along and between the mountains are standing stones from 5,000 to 6,000 years ago, ancient castles and cairns (hill markers made from piles of stones). The forests, mountains and reservoirs of the Beacons provide excellent grounds for outdoor activities such as angling, gliding, riding, boating, trekking and cycling. The 1974 counties were themselves abolished in 1996 and officially since then Wales has been entirely divided into a system of unitary authorities, also known as principal areas.

Since the local government reorganisations of 1974/5, Scotland has been divided into nine large administrative regions, districts and three island areas, instead of thirty-three counties. Fife was the only county not to be renamed as a region and it covered roughly the same area as it did before. The administrators of the Local Government Act had intended that the county be split in two but the people of Fife protested so vehemently that the plans were dropped. It is also nationally and politically significant that off the coast of Fife are the drilling ships and rigs that have been exploring for oil and gas in the North Sea since the 1970s. Some of the arguments put forward for devolution by the Scottish National Party, which has seats at Westminster and campaigns for an independent Scottish Parliament, turned on the standpoint that North Sea gas and oil are Scottish and would enable the country, free from England, to run a prosperous economy. England, for its part, makes occasional gestures at Scottish inclusion, as when the economist Adam Smith became the first Scot to feature on a English banknote when he replaced the composer Edward Elgar on the Bank of England's £20 note in 2007 – a fact that left the leader of the Scottish National Party, Alex Salmond, distinctly unimpressed given that Smith already featured north of the border on the Scottish £50 note. The regions and districts were themselves abolished in 1996, in favour of unitary Scottish council areas.

City

As of 2010, the United Kingdom has sixty-six cities, a title many British people wrongly think is given to a town with a cathedral. City is actually a title of dignity conferred on towns of religious, commercial or industrial importance by statute, royal charter or tradition (for example, Coventry, Exeter and Norwich are mentioned as cities in William the Conqueror's eleventh-century *Domesday Book* of landholdings). Occasionally, new cities are created, sometimes bidding for the status, as happened in 2012 when, after a competition, Chelmsford, Perth and St Asaph were made cities to mark the Queen's Diamond Jubilee. Britain's cities vary enormously, from the industrial giants Manchester, Glasgow and Newcastle in the north and

Scotland to the southern ports such as Southampton and Bristol. There are also the cities noted chiefly for their cathedrals, such as Hereford and Ely, and the heritage cities such as the Roman town of Chester, whose entire medieval surrounding wall has survived, or Winchester, a small city of only 41,000 people which in Anglo-Saxon times was the capital of England.

According to an EU publication, the first five things that spring to mind when someone thinks of the UK are Shakespeare, the BBC, the Beatles, royalty and London, the capital. Within London there is a 'square mile' of offices and banks that encompasses the original walled area that is also sometimes referred to simply as 'the City' and is the financial hub of Britain's business activities. At nearly 8 million in 2011, London has the largest population of any city in Europe, although people have been steadily moving away to the outer suburbs and commuter zones since the Second World War. Britain's capital is one of the best-known cities in the world, but in many ways it is different from the rest of the UK. London fashions are likely to sample different clothes and styles of the past, specialist shops sell anything from military armour to body jewellery, and musical styles are eclectic, forming such hybrids as Bungle, a mixture of Bhangra and Jungle music, or Gujarati Rock, a fusion of Western guitars with Indian sitars and tablas. Such meetings illustrate the blended histories that London now represents because its 'conglomerate nature', as Salman Rushdie records in his controversial 1988 novel *The Satanic Verses*, now echoes the cultural diversity of the old Empire. To reflect London's particular interests and identity, the position of Mayor was revived in May 2000, and its first elected incumbent was Ken Livingstone, the ex-leader of the former Greater London Council, which was itself reborn in the form of a Greater London Assembly created to run affairs in the capital. Livingstone, a Labour socialist, was replaced in 2008 by the Eton-educated Conservative Boris Johnson (full name Alexander Boris de Pfeffel Johnson), and the battle between the two to become London Mayor at the time of the Olympics was set to be the major political tussle of 2012.

Britain's high culture is famously represented everywhere in London from the National Gallery in Trafalgar Square and the Royal Academy of Arts in Piccadilly to the Royal Opera House in Covent Garden and the National Theatre on the South Bank. Museums in central London are around every corner, from the Museum of the Moving Image (MOMI), which celebrates film and television, to the vast British Museum, which was the world's first public museum and is currently Britain's second most visited tourist attraction. As much as anything in London, the British Museum serves as a reminder of Britain's imperial history, and yet it is only one of around a hundred major museums in the capital. These, from the Museum of the Jewish East End and the Museum of Eton Life to the Sherlock Holmes Museum and the Florence Nightingale Museum, represent the variety of Britain's lucrative cultural heritage industry.

Tradition is still celebrated all year round, from the Lord Mayor of Westminster's New Year's Parade through to November's Lord Mayor's Show (the Lord Mayor is an office of the City 'Square Mile' only). However, in a modern consumer culture such as Britain's, the past is often used for commercial profit or for charity: 'punks' are quite likely to be arts students looking to supplement their grants by simulating a Britishness for photographers; Pearly Kings and Queens, who were originally arbitrators in arguments between traders, are now usually on show, with their coats covered in mother of pearl buttons, to raise money for local causes.

To many people outside the capital, 'London' conjures up a collection of buildings, landmarks, and monuments such as Buckingham Palace, St Paul's Cathedral, the Tower of London, Westminster Abbey, Big Ben and Piccadilly Circus. However, London is best seen as not one city but a patchwork of distinct districts stitched together: the cockney East End, the Docklands development, the Parliament at Westminster, the administration at Whitehall, the parks and the Thameside areas, the museums, theatres, shops and galleries of the West End, the residential areas such as Hampstead and Belgravia, the City, the exhibition area around Earls Court and the famous suburbs from Richmond in the west to Greenwich on the east. Despite this diversity, it is the tourist attractions that survive in the popular imagination as representative of London: a fascination with Britain's past

FIGURE 1.3 Tower Bridge

that was illustrated in the 1960s when London Bridge was bought by wealthy Americans who had it taken apart and rebuilt in Arizona.

A further, less well-publicised characteristic of London and other British cities is the rise in the number of homeless people sleeping on the streets, or in makeshift back garden temporary accommodation more often associated with Mumbai or Rio. Though housing in the capital is very expensive, in London and elsewhere, 'inner-city' areas are generally less well off than the suburbs, to which the more affluent sections of society have moved (a counter-trend has brought the middle classes into the renovated dockland areas of London and other cities). Lifestyles are different too: in the inner cities the neighbourhood and street in which people live impinge more on their sense of identity than they do in the suburbs where people's home and garden are major preoccupations and sources of pleasure. Inner-city regeneration has become a central policy for successive governments since the war, and more especially since the 'riots' that broke out in the early 1980s in the inner cities of London, Liverpool, Bristol and Birmingham, and led to violent clashes between police and protesters against the government's race, housing and employment policies. The riots of the summer of 2011, by contrast, appeared not to be about rights and discrimination so much as a consumer society's frustrated response to the recession as opportunistic stealing became a leisure activity and many cities saw a temporary flare-up of lawlessness fuelled by social networking that could direct groups to underpoliced areas, almost in the manner of crowdsourcing.

Until recently, the capital city of Northern Ireland was most famous throughout the world for its violence. Between 1968 and the end of the millennium, Belfast had chiefly made the front pages of British newspapers for its sectarian killings, although statistically it had been a safer place to live than many American cities. Separated as they are by the fortified wall of the 'Peace Line', the Falls Road (Catholic) and the Shankhill Road (Protestant) became notorious throughout Britain, and 'the Troubles', as they were locally known, contributed to Belfast's population of around 300,000 having one of the highest unemployment levels in Britain. Following the peace negotiations begun in 1995 and the Celtic Tiger economic boom of the early years of the new century, the Northern Ireland Tourist Board has been active in bringing visitors back to the country through a publicity campaign including newspaper and television advertisements. A largely rural country without the crowded motorways or the fast-paced life of England, Northern Ireland's difference from the rest of Britain is illustrated by the fact that Belfast is the country's only industrial city.

The capital of Scotland is Edinburgh, cut across by the famous Royal Mile – central streets that run through the old town marking the area walked or ridden by numerous kings and queens. Though it is Scotland's first city, Edinburgh is smaller than Glasgow, whose population of 600,000 is about a third greater. Culturally, while Glasgow is currently deemed to be one of the 'coolest' cities in Britain, Edinburgh is probably more famous because of its annual summer Festival and Fringe, which has grown since 1947 to be a series of different summer festivals devoted to drama, film, literature, music and dance (Edinburgh is sometimes called 'The Athens of the North'). The Festival, and its famous Fringe, sells tickets to hundreds of thousands of visitors each year and claims to be the largest arts festival in the world. On New Year's Eve, which is known as Hogmanay in Scotland, people gather round Tron Church in Edinburgh, just as they do in Trafalgar Square in London, to celebrate the coming year and sing 'Auld Lang Syne'.

Cardiff, or *Caerdydd* in Welsh, in the county of South Glamorgan, is the capital of Wales and its largest city, with a population of just over 340,000. Built on a site originally developed by the Romans in the first century, the city stands alongside the river Taff (though the common nickname for the Welsh, 'Taffy', does not come from this but derives from the pronunciation of the Welsh equivalent of David, 'Dafydd'). In the nineteenth century, Cardiff became a major port when it provided an outlet for the coal mined in local valleys such as the Rhondda. In the late decades of the twentieth century, as the coal industry declined so did the Cardiff docks, which used to export more coal than any other port in the world. However, now, Cardiff's docklands, like those of London, Liverpool, Bristol and many other cities, have been greatly renovated and the extensive redevelopment has meant the entire waterfront has been restructured. Cardiff is also home to two strong Welsh passions: rugby union and singing. Since 1946, Cardiff has also been the base for the Welsh National Opera, which started from amateur roots and is the oldest of Britain's regional opera companies (the others are Scottish Opera and Opera North). A new opera house was being commissioned for the inner harbour of Cardiff Bay as the centrepiece for the docklands area development but, after difficulties, a Wales Millennium Centre to house an international arts and cultural complex opened instead, along the bay from the Richard Rogers designed Welsh Assembly Senedd building. These add to the Millennium Stadium in west Cardiff, built on the site of the old Cardiff Arms Park rugby ground in 2000. The impressive new sport stadium even staged the English FA Cup Final for several years while Wembley Stadium in London was being rebuilt.

Town

On the one hand, many people regret a creeping sameness in British cities and towns – for example, in most high streets you will see more or less the same shops, such as Boots, Marks and Spencer, Next, Mothercare, Debenhams, Primark, Burton and WH Smith, plus the common charity and 'pound' shops that flourish in times of recession. On the other hand, British towns are still enormously varied, from the seaside towns, market towns, country towns, tourist towns and industrial towns, to the post-war 'new' towns. Some coastal towns such as Blackpool and Bournemouth are chiefly known as seaside resorts, and these are extremely popular with British holidaymakers, although overseas tourists are more likely to visit historic towns such as Roman Colchester or Shakespeare's Stratford. Other popular spots, famous since the seventeenth century for their 'healing waters', are spa towns such as Harrogate, Cheltenham and Buxton. Many northern towns like Wigan and Huddersfield retain for southerners the unfair image of industrial decline they gained between the wars, while market towns in the Midlands such as Melton Mowbray in Leicestershire still suggest the traditions of the English country-side. Towns do not have the large cultural life of cities or the close-knit community feel of small villages, but they combine aspects of each, providing a balance that many people feel is preferable to the bustle of the urban areas or the relative isolation of the countryside. Each county also has a 'county town' which traditionally, but in many cases no longer, was the seat of county government. County towns can often be inferred from their names, such as Lancaster (today a city) in Lancashire and Shrewsbury (still a town) in Shropshire.

Traditional English towns retain many of the architectural signs of the nineteenth century. Victorian, iron-framed, glass-roofed, covered markets remain in the centres of Bolton and Halifax, for example. Many towns still have magnificent municipal buildings from their heyday over a hundred years ago and grand public houses from the turn of the century. Impressive corn exchanges, where samples were auctioned or sold, still stand in many country towns like Bury St Edmunds and Bishop's Stortford, while imposing workplaces like the Bliss Valley Tweed Mill at Chipping Norton in the Cotswolds and the Clocktower Mill in Burnley stand out as reminders of the Industrial Revolution in mill towns. Every sizable British town has a central park such as Jephson Park in Leamington Spa or Stratford Park in Stroud, and while each town is different its development of terraced housing, shops, factories and schools around church, railway station, market, town hall and square will be familiar.

Many modern towns arose because of the New Towns Act of 1946. These include Harlow and Stevenage near London, East Kilbride near Glasgow and Cwmbran in south Wales. However, of the total of thirty new towns the most well-known example is Milton Keynes in north Buckinghamshire. The new towns were designed to enable a redistribution of the metropolitan populations and they had to cope with the preferences indicated by commuter life: a traditional British liking for the countryside wedded to a practical need to be able to reach the city. The intention was always to plan towns for modern living in every aspect by blending industrial

FIGURE 1.4 A typical small-town street scene

and residential areas with full leisure facilities and by separating traffic from pedestrians through a network of underpasses and walkways. However, Milton Keynes was not built up from nothing: it was designed to unite thirteen existing villages, which are now enclosed by sweeping 'bypass' roads. Britain's largest new town in terms of area and population, Milton Keynes covers 34 square miles and has about 195,000 inhabitants. Despite its image of cleanliness and hi-tech living, much of the large town remained underdeveloped such that in 2004 the government announced plans to double the population of Milton Keynes by 2026, continuing its trajectory as the most ambitious town project in the last fifty years, with a diverse range of amenities and accommodation, from solar-powered to timber-framed houses.

Most British towns have their own distinctive characteristics or annual events that promote a local cultural identity. For example, two Welsh towns in the county of Powys are Hay and Brecon. Hay-on-Wye is a small town which has become the book trade capital of Britain. Almost every shop in the town is an antiquarian or second-hand booksellers and people drive great distances to spend a whole day searching the shelves; club, university and school trips are sometimes especially arranged to come and browse at what has become the largest collection of second-hand books in the world. While Hay has developed a prestigious annual literature festival, the nearby town of Brecon is the site of a distinctly Welsh community-based jazz festival each August which attracts some 30,000 people and takes place throughout the town in the cathedral, halls and pubs, as well as the streets themselves. Partly because jazz is enjoyed by its fans for its musical anarchism, flair and improvisation, its celebration at such festivals has been seen as one of the less obvious assertions of Welsh independence from English culture.

However, against this individuality, we must also note that the look of larger modern British towns has been greatly influenced by the United States. British planners, in the light of a general cultural imitation of American trends, are adopting stateside practices such as the 'doughnut effect' where town centres become abandoned by shoppers for malls on the outer ring. A largely consumer culture has been imported from across the Atlantic and modern buildings reflect this: shopping complexes, multiplex cinemas, theme parks, out-of-town supermarkets, Disney stores and fast-food restaurants, some of them drive-ins. The result is a sameness that is convenient and reassuring but also, on a national scale, numbing. Most cities and towns in Britain can be expected to have a number of fast-food outlets such as Burger King, a range of clothes shops like Gap, a Tesco or similar supermarket away from the town, a Super Bowl, Laserquest or ten-screen cinema complex, leisure centres with computerised workout gyms and hoardings that advertise the American Dream. Milton Keynes is a prime example of this cultural saturation. It has imitation sheep and cows, acres of Astroturf, a grid road network, huge parking lots, a Milton Keynes National Bowl for rock concerts and 'California Collection' houses. The planners' aim has been to emulate the values and facilities of the ideal American town: efficiency, convenience, easy access, cleanliness and even air-conditioning, plus such un-British aspects as indoor gardens, straight roads and parking for thousands of cars. In this, the designers have probably succeeded, but Milton Keynes more than any other town remains the butt of numerous jokes for the many

British who still unfairly caricature it as a place lacking culture, history or interest.

Village

By stark contrast, little international influence will be found in Britain's villages, some of which can to this day be described as rows of thatched cottages nestling in country fields between hedgerows and small streams. In the last sixty years, many people have moved back to rural areas, resisting the trend started by the industrial revolution, but the dominant migration is towards cities. In 1950, the population living in UK cities was already 79 per cent, but it is now about 90 per cent, and urban living is set to rise to a figure of 92 per cent by 2030. Less than 1 per cent of the overall workforce is employed in farming, with a total labour force of 534,000 in 2006, down 80,000 on a decade earlier. Agriculture accounts now for only about a half of one per cent of the gross domestic product, but there are around 300,000 farms in Britain. Over half of these are devoted to dairy farming or to beef cattle and sheep, while the farms primarily involved in arable crops are chiefly found in eastern and central southern England or eastern Scotland – the main crops by area are wheat and barley, though the production of potatoes and sugar beet in tonnes exceeds that of barley.

Villages in Britain are traditionally associated with a close-knit society centred on a hall, which serves as a kind of community centre, a market, parish church, pub and a 'green', which is a grass area for fairs, shows, cricket matches and other sporting events, or public gatherings. Most villages therefore promote a strong blend of social identity, because people usually have a number of roles within the community, traditionally associated with land ownership and family history. A village's focus is likely to be on continuity and familiarity, and it is often said that everyone will know everyone else's business. Village life, it is said, is synonymous with community, which is symbolised by church-going, jumble sales, charity collecting, fetes and flower shows: those who join in are welcomed and those who do not are treated with suspicion.

However, village life is changing. A modern phenomenon is the commuter village. These are hamlets or villages which have sufficiently good transport links for office workers to travel by road or rail to the major cities, such as London and Birmingham, sometimes on journeys that take several hours. Many city workers live in villages for the peace and quiet, the clean air, scenery and wildlife – but they probably have little involvement in the life of the village unless they also have children they want to bring up locally in the comparatively friendly, unpolluted and safe environment of the countryside. Similarly, second homes in villages throughout, for example,

FIGURE 1.5 Summertime British musical village concert

the Yorkshire Dales, are not unusual. City workers come out to them at weekends or just in the summer for holidays. Such city people are sometimes resented by the local villagers because they may force up property prices and they also pose a threat to the continuity of village life. In the past, 'holiday homes' in Wales were occasionally targets for arsonists resentful of this intrusion by outsiders, particularly from southern England. Village populations have also changed because more and more people, who are also living longer, are retiring to the countryside from the city. Historically, village work has been based around a farming community, but the size of the agricultural workforce decreases year by year. Britain now has nine counties that are classed as rural and, to give an indication of how they are still in some ways isolated from city life, about a quarter of the villages in these areas still have no food shop, post office or doctor's surgery. An article in *The Times* in 2001 claimed that there was still a 'village pecking-order', with landowners and farmers at the top, long-established residents (of 30 or more years) in the middle and 'newcomers' (of less than 15 years) at the bottom. The article argued that low down even within this echelon came 'new incomers', and way down at the bottom, Londoners.

Oddly, Britain's most talked about village is fictional. Ambridge is the setting for *The Archers*, the world's longest running radio serial. Begun by the BBC in 1950, the programme is broadcast during the week for fifteen minutes, twice a day, and by radio's standards it has a large, devoted following. In the serial, Ambridge is close to the market town of Borset in the fictional county of Borsetshire (shire is a term for the central English counties whose names have that suffix – *The Archers* was initially broadcast just in the Midlands). The on-going saga revolves around the Archer family at Brookfield farm and portrays a close-knit village community in which everyone interacts with everyone else. Episodes are full of domestic incident and minor moral dilemmas, but there are fewer exaggerated, intense emotional scenes and revelations than in the television soaps. The programme has always aimed to reflect realistically and unsensationally the concerns and interests of a village community, and it has a farming correspondent who ensures the serial's treatment of agricultural issues is factual and accurate. Ambridge's counterpart in reality is Hanbury in Worcestershire, where some outside location scenes have been recorded, and the programme also has a tradition of including real people, the most noted of whom have been several members of the royal family. In 1989, the Post Office issued a set of commemorative stamps to mark the 10,000th episode. A similar stalwart of BBC Radio 4 has been *Gardeners' Question Time*, which has taken a panel of experts around the country from village hall to village hall since 1947. Like much of Radio 4's broadcasting, the programme thrives on consistency and from 1951 to 1980, the trio of gardening authorities remained the same, but in 1994 an entirely new panel was introduced. Such changes, seemingly trivial, are extremely contentious for the station's loyal and conservative following, not least because Britain is a country in which gardening is often cited as the most common outside hobby.

Unsurprisingly for a people who are statistically more likely to give to animal charities than to the homeless, the British have long fashioned themselves as a nation of animal lovers, and Britain has a great variety of wildlife, with an estimated 30,000 animal species. Television reflects this with many sentimental shows about pets supplementing the broad appetite for nature and wildlife programmes. One issue in 2001 centred on animals tested this affection and also pointed up many differences between town and country: the foot and mouth crisis, which by September 2001 had resulted in the killing of three million sheep and over half a million cattle. The crisis arose in February 2001 and soon pointed up several areas of disagreement: some people resented the compensation farmers received for culled animals because they refused to use vaccines and also because they have long been subsidised, to the tune of a third of annual turnover (this is because when Britain joined the EC in 1973, land prices more than doubled after the Common Agricultural Policy raised the prices paid for arables, milk, beef and sheep); farmers felt that walkers and others, as much as the movement of livestock, spread the disease; tourist agencies resented the closing of country paths in spring, while farmers disagreed with their reopening months later; farmers were dismayed that compensation (£926 million by August 2001) was paid in euros, which, because of the strength of the pound, was less than it otherwise appeared; towards the end of the initial crisis, in the summer of 2001, an outrage was sparked by accusations that some farmers had deliberately contaminated their livestock to get compensation. The priorities in the to-ing and fro-ing were foregrounded by the spring general election, which farmers wanted postponing until after the crisis so that the disease was not spread by the large movement of people, while others argued that postponing the election would give out the wrong signals internationally, suggesting that Britain had been 'closed down' by the disease. The crisis added to growing concerns over food scares and the general safety of meat products.

More recently has arisen a furore over the traditional English pursuit of fox hunting, which will be discussed later. City-dwellers under the last Labour government successfully advocated a ban, which was opposed by the Countryside Alliance, whose influential and moneyed land-owning classes now expect the Conservative-led government to overturn the ban. Such issues highlight one of the many divisions within a complex culture, where a traditional image of national identity has to sit alongside the reality of different lives and changed priorities in the present. Though nine out of ten people live in cities, Britain likes to see it itself as rooted in the countryside, and most people have strong views about perceived class-based issues such as the red-coated upper-classes hunting animals in the countryside even if city-dwellers primarily only go there on holiday and most foxes now live in cities, where there are easier pickings.

Conclusion

In this concluding section, as well as summing up we will look at four thematic aspects to British culture that are linked to place but are shared by everyone throughout the UK: the country–city divide, travel, the weather and the environment. As a preface to this, however, it is worth noting that there is increasing pressure for decentralisation, if not devolution in some regions, with Scottish First Minister Alex Salmond arguing that this is a time for regionalism, and other parts of the country are increasingly angry at the disparity between London's wealth, especially among bankers and financiers, and much of the rest of the country's comparative poverty. A vocal pressure group, The Campaign for the English Regions, pointed out that London has had a public spending budget almost a quarter higher than that of Yorkshire and a fifth higher than the whole of the north-east. The appetite for further devolution among the public is less strong, however, as adversity leads to a general conservatism in which Britain appears a safer bet as a whole for most people.

Apart from political borders, one of the strongest kinds of geo-graphical division in Britain is that between those who look for the natural life of the countryside and those who prefer the amenities at hand in the city. As suggested above, this is a long-standing difference of experience and in the eighteenth-century, the poet William Cowper, in his poem 'The Task', wrote the famous line 'God made the country and man made the town'. Today, culture in cities tends to be diverse, reflecting the highly concentrated rich mix of different peoples with varied lifestyles: existence is mostly anonymous, formal and based around groups with specialised interests. Country life by contrast is generally associated with tradition, custom, community, cultural unity and 'the outdoor life'. The antipathy between the two is pointed up by the common expressions of pity each makes towards the other: those in the towns are stereotyped as believing country people are deprived of life's 'basics', ranging from adequate heating to convenience stores, while those in the country are caricatured as feeling that their lives are morally superior and that urban people only live in cities because they have to (according to *The Observer's* 2001 survey 66 per cent of people would rather live in the country).

An article in *The Times* this century observed that 'although there is a part of every Anglo-Saxon soul that is pastoral . . . there is a tradition of antipathy between yokel and townie which runs through English history'. It is often maintained that rural and urban people have different attitudes to the traditions of British life and, as already touched on, one cultural pursuit that many feel marks a division between people in cities and villages is fox-hunting (interestingly, at first attempt in 2001, the bill to ban hunting was passed by the House of Commons but overwhelmingly rejected by the House of Lords). It is a frequent generalisation that city people want what they call 'blood sports' banned; and it is just as common to hear from those in favour of what they call 'field sports' that anti-hunting campaigners do not under-stand, as villagers do, the need for control of the population of predatory animals in the wild. For reasons such as this, the kind of cultural division in England between north and south is also sometimes found throughout the country between 'townies' and 'yokels'. As farmers are considered by those in the towns to provide the country's food, they are blamed whenever prices are thought to be too high, as they usually are, but farmers are also resentful because they claim it is the supermarket chains who are hiking up prices while forcing producers to accept low payments or be dropped. Similarly, feeling that again they have been penalised, farmers led fuel-duty protests that brought Britain almost to a halt in the summer of 2000. The feeling that the priorities of the countryside are being sacrificed was concentrated in the formation of the above-mentioned Countryside Alliance, whose use of the slogan 'Listen to Us' expressed a belief that in the face of London's policies it is powerless. Under a Conservative government its stance has shifted to the more optimistic words 'Love the Countryside'. The Alliance fashions itself as the rural community fighting for its liberty, and it defends hunting, fishing, shooting and the interests of farming communitites as well as campaigning on conservation and the environment.

Before moving on to consider travel and the weather, we must note that in addition to the country and the city, there is a third place of escape for people from either of these communities: the coast. Because all Britons within the UK live on an 'island' there is a strong coastal culture incorporating trawler fishing, watersports, ports and docks, shipping, yachting and, for visitors, the British tradition of seaside holidays, with its staple ingredients of piers, buckets and spades, postcards, amusement arcades, deckchairs, donkey rides and promenading. Again, there are also dozens of smaller islands off the British mainland and the largest of these, the Isle of Wight below the south coast of England, is a county in its own right.

These areas are of course linked by travel on road, rail, air, river or sea. Three in four British households today own at least one car. In the 1930s, more miles of road in Britain were covered by bicycle than by car, but now it is mainly those conscious of their health and the environment who choose two wheels over four. Commuting by train, on the main network or the London Underground, is a daily activity for millions of Britons – many of whom will complain that the rail services are far worse than on the Continent. In response to this constant criticism, a charter was introduced to compensate people for delays, cancellations and poor reliability. London's main airport, Heathrow, is one of the busiest in the world, although only a fraction of its 66 million annual customers take domestic flights. Additionally, though they were superseded as a mode of transport in the nineteenth century by the railways, Britain is carved across by hundreds of streams and rivers, some with houseboats, and over 4,000 miles of canals and waterways. Also, recently trams have been reintroduced in cities such as Manchester and a light railway links the city area in London with the docklands.

An influence that on another level links city, country and coast is a shared climate. In the eighteenth century, Samuel Johnson said that 'When two Englishmen meet, their first talk is of the weather'. Throughout Britain today the weather is still the most frequent topic of conversation, and not usually for agricultural reasons but simply because it is so changeable. Many British people will be only too willing to offer a forecast of likely shifts in the weather. On top of experience and barometers, several other, often proverbial methods of prediction are sworn by. For example, a herd of cows sitting in a field is thought to indicate rain, as do twitching bunions and rheumatic attacks. Similarly, the old saying, 'Red sky at night, shepherds' delight; red sky in the morning, shepherds' warning' is passed down from generation to generation as a sure method of anticipating fair or foul weather throughout the country. The national hobby of predicting rain, sunshine, hail, thunder, snow or sleet is nicely summed up by the annual bets on whether there will be a white Christmas. Perhaps because of their obsessive interest in weather, the British are generally sceptical of official forecasts. While this scepticism is distinctly unfair, it was famously bolstered in October 1987 by a freak hurricane, which a BBC television weather forecaster famously asserted would pass Britain by. The storm blew over fences and light buildings, brought down telegraph wires and poles, put television stations out of action, resulted in eighteen deaths and left many cars crushed by fallen trees. Memories of 1987 were frequently invoked in the winter of 2000, when 'freak' floods left many villages under water and thousands of people homeless, and again in the devastating floods of 2007, then the severe winter of 2010–11, all of which seemed to catch the authorities by surprise.

Britain in fact has a moderate climate in terms of its temperature, which has never been recorded as high as 100 degrees Fahrenheit or as low as −18°F. Generally, it is between 35 and 65°F, and the climate is milder in England, Northern Ireland and Wales than in Scotland. The weather remains a constant talking point in Britain because of its local variations and its seasonal oddities: for example, though winter runs from December to February, a cricket match has been 'snowed off' in Buxton, Derbyshire, in June. August, in high summer, is one of the wettest months of the year and many Britons will swear that May and September are usually sunnier months. Rainfall differs greatly between regions and average annual levels vary from 500 mm in East Anglia in southern England to 5,000 mm in the Scottish Highlands.

Lastly, a country is frequently discussed in terms of its environment. For different reasons, the human maintenance and manipulation of the environment is of particular interest to two groups of people: environmentalists and the disabled. While they lagged behind other Europeans, the British became increasingly sensitive to ecological concerns, as the following examples indicate. The Green Party, founded in 1973 as the Ecology Party, won 130 seats on 43 Principal Authorities (county, city, borough and district) in the local elections of 2011, more than three times that of a decade ago. Most large cities are now circled by a 'green belt' on which little building is allowed. The Forestry Commission, which has its headquarters in Edinburgh, was set up in 1919 because of the timber shortage that became apparent in the First World War and as a non-ministerial government department manages almost one million hectares of land. Recycling centres have also been stationed at shopping centres and other public places, for people to bring along their old newspapers, glass, clothes and aluminium, but these are now supplemented by regular home collections of glass, paper, plastic and food, requiring people to sort and leave out their waste in different containers. The campaigning environmental group Friends of the Earth has been prominent in Britain since 1970, lobbying on world issues such as rain forests and global warming, as well as on local British concerns including beach pollution and alternative energy sources. Greenpeace, the Campaign for Nuclear Disarmament, Earth First! and various 'New Protest' groups, have all also been active in Britain over the last thirty years. A major issue here is that of pollution and congestion. There are now over thirty million cars on the road in Britain, twice the number of forty years ago, and congestion is such that the average journey speed is 25 mph even though the lowest speed limit is 30. Congestion is expected to increase by half again on motorways by 2015, adding hugely to concerns about gas emissions, compounded by the British love of short breaks abroad and cheap flights. A 'congestion charge' now applies to everyone who takes a vehicle into central London and there is an emission charge for much large transport, yet most British people also think the privatised train services are poor, with overcrowding on London commuter trains doubling between 1996 and 2006, while fewer and fewer people use bus services outside the capital.

A further issue of the (particularly built) environment is disability. Though many people in Britain have been slow to recognise the special needs of the disabled, supermarkets nearly always now have designated parking spaces close to the entrance, theatres often have signed performances, public buildings may be denied planning permission if they do not include wheelchair access and most employers now claim that their equal opportunity policies mean that jobs are open to all people regardless of age, ethnicity, gender, or disability. Despite this, legislation has been difficult to pass, and disabled people are not well represented in films or on television, although there are attempts made to cater for this audience on television (signed reruns of programmes at night) and radio (e.g. *In Touch* on Radio 4), while the BBC website *Ouch*! seeks to provide a platform for issues of disability and the representation of the 'differently abled'. However, with respect to people's misconceptions, a high-profile figure like the scientist Stephen Hawking (who has motor neurone disease) or the staging of the Paralympics in 2012 can do more than minority programming to raise general awareness. A major controversy was sparked by the decision in 2005 to place Marc Quinn's white marble statue 'Alison Lapper pregnant' on the vacant fourth plinth in Trafalgar Square alongside long-standing statues of military leaders, including Havelock and Napier, on the other plinths. The chosen subject of a naked pregnant woman with no arms was a brave one for London's busiest square, with the landmark of Nelson's column in the middle, but its statement about gender, inclusivity and human beauty was itself a landmark for the disabled. Overall, the campaign for responsible and fair adaptation of the natural and built environment has been seen as one of slow progress as organised groups lobby and protest on specific issues of personal or social importance against businesses whose interests are, by contrast, short-sightedly commercial.

FIGURE 1.6 Alison Lapper statue on the plinth in Trafalgar Square

As a final word, it can be said that while the Union Jack will be seen flying at international conferences and decorating lapel badges, it is as often used today as a design for underpants, a pattern for dyed hair or face-painting and a favourite symbol of the far-right British National Party. In other words, it is still going through a process of recuperation after being chiefly an emblem of Britain's past that will be used nostalgically and ironically – or even callously as a sign of solidarity against others. Britons have always defined themselves as an island people, whose singularity and separateness is illustrated by the channel of water dividing them from the Continent. However, the British now have an undersea tunnel that connects them with France; they are hostile to federalism but broadly committed to Europe; they are soaked in influences from the USA and are succumbing to a global culture that may leave them disunited, but curiously alike. This chapter has illustrated how, in terms of place, 'Britishness' is a varied and sometimes problematic tag for people living in the UK, and that it perhaps best serves as an emblem of traditional values on the one hand and on the other hand a geographic label for national issues that lie between the local or global concerns with which individuals are increasingly more likely to identify themselves. The label also stands for a certain history, increasingly positioned as heritage. This will be apparent when considering the role that tourism now plays in the UK. Tourism constitutes the fifth biggest industry in Britain, employing 2.7 million people overall and generating over £86bn for the economy each year (tourism has been assessed as worth about 8 per cent of GDP). The industry will have a boost this decade because of a series of international sports tournaments: the Ryder Cup in Newport, Wales in 2010 and in St Andrews, Scotland in 2014; the 2012 Olympic Games; the 2013 Rugby League World Cup, the 2014 Glasgow Commonwealth Games, the 2015 Rugby Union World Cup; and the 2017 World Athletics Championships. For the 2012 Olympics and Paralympics alone, £3.5bn of contracts have been released to business and the games are expected to bring 32 million extra visitor nights across the country. This income will supplement the tourist pounds brought into the country by the appeal of the major destinations that in their own way define the British nation and its people: Windsor Castle, Stonehenge, Snowdonia, Hadrian's Wall, St Ives on the Cornish coast, York Minster, the Roman Pump Rooms in Bath, the Giant's Causeway, Stratford-on-Avon and Edinburgh Castle. In many ways these icons, to choose ten prominent examples, constitute the jigsaw pieces of Britain that make up the country for the visitor, if not for the native inhabitant.

 ## Exercises

1   What different kinds of regional identity do you think there could be said to be in Britain? How many regional variations in accent can you think of?

2   Can you name any personalities or politicians who seem to you representative of a distinctive kind of Britishness? Can you say which country or region they grew up in?

3   Do you think there is any correlation between climate and culture or character, and do you think there are any dangers in promoting such beliefs?

4   Try to locate six other British cities on the map in Figure 1.1. What do you know of each city and how do you think cultural identities might be different in each?

5   At the end of this chapter, ten iconic British places were listed. What do you know of each? Could you locate them on a map of the UK?

 ## Reading

Bryson, Bill (ed.) *Icons of England*. Black Swan, 2010. A range of well-known English people select their definitive essences and images of Englishness.

Champion, A. G. and Townsend, A. R. *Contemporary Britain: A Geographical Perspective*. Edward Arnold, 1990. Still illuminating look at Britain and at the relationship of policies and practices with the land (considers the north/south divide and the rural/urban debate).

Fox, Kate. *Watching the English*. Translated by Isabelle Daudy. Hodder & Stoughton, 2004. An entertaining and wide-ranging view of English people and behaviour.

Kearney, Hugh. *The British Isles: A History of Four Nations*. Cambridge University Press, 1989. Suggests that while English, Irish, Scottish and Welsh identities are strong, a British identity is lacking.

Simpson, J. (ed). *Dictionary of English Folklore*. Oxford University Press, 2000. Comprehensive guide to the arcane aspects of English heritage.

Cultural examples

Films

Tamara Drewe (2010) dir. Stephen Frears. Typically British rural gentle sex comedy focused on prurience and repression. Can be contrasted with the village in buddy cop comedy *Hot Fuzz (2007)*.

Solomon a Gaenor (2000) dir. Paul Morrisson. Best Foreign Language Oscar-nominated movie, set in the Welsh valleys in 1911. A local girl falls in love with a Jewish boy, but the traditional community threaten their happiness.

Filth (2012) dir. Jon S. Baird. Film based on the Irvine Welsh novel of the same name about a corrupt Scottish policeman.

The Full Monty (1998) dir. Peter Cattaneo. Social comedy about unemployed workers in Sheffield who become male strippers. The biggest box office attraction of the year in the UK.

Into the West (1992) dir. Mike Newell. Irish mythology, travellers and inner city life.

Jubilee (1978) dir. Derek Jarman. Anatomy, and dissection, of modern urban life set around the Queen's jubilee in 1987.

Local Hero (1983) dir. Bill Forsyth. Poignant film about a Scottish coastal community threatened by a multinational oil corporation.

Riff-Raff (1990) dir. Ken Loach. Social comment, set on a building site: strong regional characters.

24-Hour Party People (2002) dir. Michael Winterbottom. Film about the 'Madchester' years, concentrating on the rise of Factory records and the Hacienda club, putting Manchester at the heart of the British music scene.

Books

Sue Townsend, *The Queen and I* (1992). Fantasy about the queen living on a Midlands housing estate.

R. S. Thomas, *Neb* (1985). Autobiography, written in Welsh, of Wales's most celebrated late twentieth-century poet.

James Kelman, *How Late it Was, How Late* (1994). Novel of Glaswegian street life.

Seamus Heaney, *North* (1975). An attempt by the Nobel-winning poet to place contemporary Northern Irish history in the context of European history and pre-history.

Gautam Malkani, *Londonstani* (2007). Novel of Desi life in London focused on a gang of middle-class but masculinist Hindustani youths in Hounslow, near Heathrow.

Laurie Lee, *Cider with Rosie* (1959) Most famous and still much-loved celebration of English village life.

TV programmes

The Only Way is Essex. Half soap, half reality show: called a 'dramality'. This is a soap based in one of the home counties and shot only a few days before broadcast. A typically wittily named similar show set in Liverpool was titled *Desperate Scousewives*.

Monarch of the Glen. Spoof drama series about life on a Highlands country estate.

Hollyoaks, EastEnders, Coronation Street. Urban living in Chester, London and Manchester, respectively.

Emmerdale. Set in Yorkshire, this is a serial about a semi-rural village community in England.

The League of Gentlemen. A satire of rural life set in the fictional village of 'Royston Vasey', where outsiders are treated with deep suspicion and the standard question asked of any unfamiliar person is 'are you local?'

Gavin and Stacey. Popular comedy about the family and friends surrounding a young man from London and a young woman from Barry in the Vale of Glamorgan, Wales.

 # Websites

www.statistics.gov.uk
   The latest official UK statistics, grouped in 13 themes.
www.ukvillages.co.uk
   Over 27,000 websites and online community centres for villages across Britain.
www.thisislondon.co.uk
   News and information site for the capital.
www.edinburghfestivals.co.uk
   Guide to the annual Edinburgh festival.
bbc.co.uk
   Excellent online BBC news coverage.
www.whatthepaperssay.co.uk
   Digest of regional and national British press.
www.londonnet.co.uk
   Claims to be the best guide to London on the Web.
www.countryside-alliance.org
   Website of the Countryside Alliance Foundation.
www.24hourmuseum.org.uk
   Vast access point to Britain's musuem collections.
www.ordnancesurvey.co.uk
   Free map service with historical mapping of Britain.

Education, work and leisure

Mike Storry

Timeline

597	Foundation of King's School, Canterbury
1249	Foundation of Oxford University
1284	Foundation of Cambridge
1440	Eton College founded
1803	Introduction of Income Tax
1902	Education Act establishes state secondary education
1936	Scheduled TV starts in England
1944	Education Act establishes free secondary education for all
1954	Independent Television Act licenses alternative broadcasters to BBC
1963	Labour Exchanges become JobCentres
1967	National Health Service (Family Planning) Act
1967	Plowden Committee recommends child-centred learning
1969	Foundation of Open University
1970	Equal Pay Act
1971	Industrial Relations Act (judiciary to arbitrate industrial disputes)
1975	Sex Discrimination Act
1975	Employment Protection Act
1976	Foundation of (private) University of Buckingham
1976	Education Act school-leaving age raised to 16
1982	Channel 4 started
1990	Education (Student Loans) Act
1993	Trade Union Reform and Employment Rights Act
1994	Criminal Justice Act opposed by Ramblers' Association
1994	Sunday Trading Act allows shopping on Sunday
1995	Rugby Union allows professionals
1999	Bluewater shopping centre, Europe's largest, opens in Kent
2005	2012 Olympics awarded to London
2006	Age Discrimination Act allows people to work longer
2011	First 24 'Free Schools' started
2012	£9,000 university fees introduced

Introduction

Introduction

W E HAVE LINKED WORK, education and leisure in this chapter in the belief that very often people's work is determined by the education they receive and that their leisure activities often complement their work.

The timeline at the start of this chapter picks out a number of significant historical points. From it you will see that schooling for the most exclusive echelon of British people started in 600 AD, through royal patronage. Schooling for the rest came only in the eighteenth and nineteenth centuries. Children had to work to contribute to their families' income. That remained so until the Factory Acts of the nineteenth century aimed to prevent child labour and to restrict work to 10 hours a day. Today, the 'working week' generally covers 9 am to 5 pm, Monday to Friday, although few people still work those exact hours and many are now employed on 'flexi time', with unfixed times for arriving at and leaving work. Britons work the longest hours in western Europe and attempt to express their real selves through leisure activities, both in the private space of the home and outside it. This chapter will look at the part played by education, work and leisure in forming British people's identities, and will deal with those topics in sequence.

Schools

There are about 27,000 schools in Britain, with 8,600,000 pupils and 610,000 teachers. The state offers 'primary' (for ages 5–11) and 'secondary' (for ages 11–18) schooling. There are a very few 'middle' schools for children aged 10–13 and some 'special' schools for children with learning difficulties. These are the main state schools, although there are others in, for example, hospitals and youth custody centres. England, Scotland and Wales have respectively 3,446, 372 and 222 state secondary schools. Of the English schools, 1,300 are academies (a Labour invention which morphed into 'free schools' under the Coalition government) and 6,955 are faith schools. Most are Christian, with 36 Jewish, 6 Muslim, 2 Sikh, 1 Hindu, 1 Greek Orthodox and 1 Seventh

Day Adventist. There are a few hundred faith schools in Scotland and Wales. Additionally and separately there are 790 independent schools (educating about 7 per cent of the school-age population) and 164 grammar schools.

The school year runs from September to July and children normally start school in the September following their fifth birthday. The school day is usually from 9 am to 3.30 or 4.00 pm and children are allocated places by the Local Education Authority (LEA) in the schools nearest to them. The government has encouraged the exercise of parental choice by promoting competition among schools and adopting a policy of incentives for 'good' schools and a laissez-faire attitude to the closure of those that are becoming less popular. League tables of school exam results have been published since the early 1990s. Ofsted (Office for Standards in Education) reports are available online. Pupils are permitted to leave school at 16, but a majority (73 per cent in 2010) stay on or move to local authority controlled further education (FE) or sixth-form colleges.

The present state system evolved from a gradual move towards universal educational provision, which started in the nineteenth century. Poorly funded 'board' and 'hedge' schools (the former managed by a local school board, the latter outdoors) taught pupils up to the standard leaving age of fourteen. This became fifteen in the 1930s, and sixteen in 1972.

In 1944, R. A. Butler's Education Act introduced the '11 plus' examination. All children took this test at the end of primary school, and those who passed had their fees paid at the local grammar school. This change had significant social and cultural effects in Britain. It enabled a degree of social mobility hitherto unknown and eroded notions of those with ability coming only from higher social strata. It introduced to post-war Britain a 'meritocracy', and made a significant contribution to the affluence of the 1950s and 1960s.

On the negative side, the system also distanced children from their less well-educated parents. Moreover, opportunity was still very limited. Speaking in 2011 the veteran film-maker Ken Loach said:

> In Nuneaton, with a population of 70,000 there were sixty boys who got into grammar school. The rest were written off at the 11-plus. And then there were only twelve of us in the sixth form, and six of those went to university. You forget how narrow those chances were.

While student fees (which are in the form of loans) make higher education less attractive, it remains true that access to university has improved with participation rates in the 2010s now over 40 per cent. As to school fees, Manchester Grammar School for boys (whose alumni include the actor Sir Ben Kingsley and the former England cricket captain Mike Atherton) charges £10,000 a year, while the Prime Minister's *alma mater* Eton charges fees of over £30,000 to Oppidans (common entrance pupils as opposed to scholarship winners).

Perhaps the worst effect of the 1944 Education Act was that some people saw it as 'discarding' the 80 per cent of children who were assigned by the test to secondary-modern schools. Children were labelled as 'failures' at the age of eleven, and this led to a cumulative loss of ambition, achievement and self-esteem. Many became alienated and reluctant to integrate into society. In due course, this offered fertile ground for the growth of such subcultural youth groups as mods, rockers and punks. Secondary-modern school pupils and teachers were demoralised by the knowledge that the most favoured students had been 'creamed off' to the grammar schools and by the fact that despite the rhetoric of 'appropriate provision', they were part of second-class educational establishments in a system of 'separate development', a sort of cultural 'apartheid'.

Partly because of the above malaise, the Labour government, in the 1960s, endorsed a system of 'comprehensive' schools. These were co-educational (most grammar schools were single-sex) and for all abilities. Some 'comps' exchanged grammar-school type streaming (grouping pupils according to performance) for mixed-ability teaching. Here pupils of differing capabilities shared the same classrooms in the belief that the bright would help the weak, and that improved social development would compensate for any lack of intellectual achievement. It was hoped that this would eventually lead to cohesiveness rather than competitiveness in society at large. Other comprehensive schools adopted what they saw as the best of existing educational practices, including intellectual rigour, while reducing emphasis in their curriculum on classics and sport.

In the private system, 'preparatory' schools educate children from the age of 5, prior to their entering the 'public schools' at 13. Confusingly, famous private schools like Eton and Harrow, Winchester or Stonyhurst are known as 'public schools'. (The expression 'public school' originally referred to a grammar school endowed for the public.) That system of education is now, as *Chambers* dictionary puts it, 'for such as can afford it'. The independent school sector is disproportionately important in British life for a variety of reasons: although only 7 per cent of British children attend independent schools, their alumni figure much more significantly as entrants to the universities, particularly Oxbridge (Oxford and Cambridge), and figure prominently in the higher echelons of British society (both the Prime Minster David Cameron and the Mayor of London Boris Johnson went to Eton and Oxford, where they were members of the elite Bullingdon dining club).

To monitor pupils' performance, in the 1990s the government introduced a series of 'Standardised Assessment Tests' (SATs) – taken at age 7, 11 and 14. However, the major public exams pupils face are those taken in individual subjects at 16 and 18 respectively: the General Certificate in Secondary Education (GCSE) and Advanced ('A') levels. In Scotland students gain Lower and Higher Certificates. University entrance is typically based on good grades in approximately 6 GCSEs and 3 A levels. Other qualifications open to those school leavers who want to attend college are AVCEs, BTECs, HNCs, City & Guilds, RSA and GNVQs.

The school system has a reputation for quality. However, a number of factors – continual reforms, the over-prescriptive National Curriculum, inspections without feedback – have produced low morale among teachers, many of whom leave the profession. The government is trying to address these problems through various initiatives to improve educational opportunities for children, including setting up fifteen City Technology Colleges in disadvantaged areas, plus Beacon Schools and the Leading Edge Partnership programme to share the best practice of successful schools. In 2006, amid public scepticism, the government was promising to raise the average spend per state secondary school pupil to that of the independent sector (i.e. from £5,000 to £8,000). Five years later the figure had only risen to £5,200.

In 2011, twenty-four so-called 'free schools' were allowed to open. The idea of them is based on US Charter Schools and on Swedish models. They may be run by special interest groups, faith groups, or parents. They are free in that they do not charge fees to parents but are funded by the taxpayer. They are also freed from the intervention of the local authorities. They do not need to teach the full National Curriculum and teachers do not need teacher-training qualifications. Nine of the twenty-four are faith schools and because they are a bold experiment, they have not been introduced without controversy. The fact that Maharishi free school in Lancashire will teach transcendental meditation, Phoenix school in Manchester will employ only former members of the armed forces, and that money may be siphoned off from the existing schools provision has aroused qualms.

In these circumstances, unsurprisingly, the independent schools sector has continued to flourish – partly because of their comparative stability and their high academic standards. In 2010 a claimed 93 per cent of all GCSE candidates at independent schools achieved A* or A grades (national average: 74 per cent). At A level 69 per cent of independent entrants achieved A or B grades (national average: 44.5 per cent). Several top public schools (Dulwich College, Harrow and Shrewsbury) have 'exported' their successful ethos by setting up in the Far East, and Brighton College plans to open in Moscow.

Colleges and universities

At the official school-leaving age of 16, 73 per cent (2005/06) of pupils continue in education either in schools, sixth form colleges or FE colleges. Higher education has a 40 per cent participation rate, but there is a gender imbalance with more young women entering university than young men.

There are 116 universities in the UK: 89 in England, 14 in Scotland, 11 in Wales and 2 in Northern Ireland. They have 1.96 million students and 138,805 lecturers (2008). The standard length of undergraduate study in Britain is three years for a Bachelor of Arts or Science degree (BA/BSc) and up to seven years for 'vocational' degrees (ones linked to a specific job), like medicine, dentistry, veterinary science or architecture. Students of subjects such as civil engineering spend an intermediate year in industry (a 'sandwich' course). Many universities offer the Bachelor of Education (BEd) degree, which is a four-year course geared towards classroom experience. The majority of primary school teachers qualify by this route. The standard way to train to be a secondary school teacher is to do a three-year university course in a specialist subject such as biology, history or mathematics followed by a one year Post Graduate Certificate in Education (PGCE), which includes teaching practice.

Students on Master's courses (MA/MSc) study for at least one year and those doing Doctorates (PhDs) for upwards of three years. Students finance their studies with great difficulty. Grants were pegged at 1982 levels and abolished altogether in 1994. A system of loans was introduced in 1990/91 and in 1997 students had to pay £1,000 towards fees for the first time. Annual tuition fees of £3,000 became payable in 2006 and fees of £9,000 per annum are proposed for 2012. Hence, today, students experience real financial hardship. Only those whose parents can afford to subsidise them are without money worries. The percentage of working-class children attending university is declining as tuition fees have risen over the course of fifteen years from nothing to in most cases £9,000 (the most expensive in the world after the United States and Korea, according to the Organisation for Economic Co-operation and Development).

Oxford and Cambridge (known collectively as 'Oxbridge') are the oldest universities in Britain. Though much expanded, their student numbers are still small, compared with (say) London's 102,000. In 2010/11 Oxford had 11,225 students, Cambridge, 11,515. Other old universities are Durham and St Andrews, and they are distinguished from the so-called 'Redbrick' universities founded around the beginning of the twentieth century (for example Birmingham, Liverpool, Manchester) through their emphasis on traditional subjects. 'New' universities created in the 1960s include Lancaster, York, Keele and Sussex. In 1992 all the former polytechnics changed their names and joined the existing 44 universities.

Apart from the European campuses of several American universities, Britain has two other main universities. The Open University (250,000 part-time students in 2010) offers a wide range of degree programmes delivered formerly by TV and radio, now also by DVDs and podcasts, especially for people already engaged in full-time work. The University for Industry (UfI) is a public–private partnership that offers basic and technological skills, 80 per cent online, through 2000 Learndirect centres. In 2011 The College of the Humanities was set up by Professor Anthony Grayling and others to charge fees of £18,000 p.a. Professor Terry Eagleton expressed his opposition trenchantly in the *Guardian*: 'British universities, plundered of resources by the bankers and financiers they educated, are not best served by a bunch of prima donnas jumping ship and creaming off the bright and loaded.' A precedent exists in the University of Buckingham, an independent university established in the 1960s, partly by renegade Oxford academics distressed by the turn of higher education. The founders wished to follow the model of private foundations in the US and as of September 2012, undergraduate fees will be £11,250.

Participation in higher education is still largely determined by the class one happens to be born into. There are deep divisions in education as in society. For example five schools, four independent and one state sixth form college, accounted for more Oxbridge places over three years than 2,000 comprehensives, according to analysis published by the Sutton Trust in 2011. The schools were Eton, Westminster, St Paul's Boys and St Paul's Girls and a Cambridge state community college. Moreover in Britain as a whole, currently 80 per cent of children from professional middle-class families study at university, compared with 17 per cent from the poorest homes. Finally at the extremes of opportunity, in 1999 in the Solihull suburb of Knowle, a population of 11,700 had 150 pupils starting degree courses, while Clifton East in Nottingham, with a population of 8,400 failed to send a single pupil to university.

The educational sector which has been most influential in raising Britain's profile abroad, the public (that is private) schools' one, has benefited from the difficulties experienced by the state sector. The proportion of pupils attending public/independent secondary schools has risen, as the public sector has atrophied. Independent school pupil numbers have remained fairly constant at around 615,000 despite hard economic times. Parents are eager to benefit from the fact that the private sector has always had a disproportionately high influence on British culture and society, dominating very many aspects of British public life, from Whitehall to Shire Hall, from Parliament to local constituency parties, from the Institute of Directors to local Chambers of Commerce.

Educational changes and trends

Major educational changes have been: the imposition of a national curriculum, as opposed to one agreed with local authorities and Her Majesty's Inspectors (HMIs); the introduction of pre-GCSE examinations; and the publication of league tables of schools' performances (since abandoned in Wales and Northern Ireland). Opponents of a national curriculum felt it was closing down room for individual initiative and saw it as sinister in its regimenting of pupils. They referred to a French Minister of Education who boasted that he knew at any hour of the day which page of which book pupils would be turning. Supporters of a national curriculum promoted it as a necessary educational reform which would ensure uniform standards in schools.

In 2007 the head of Ofsted said that the educational system wasn't working and needed fundamental reform. It currently had a 'one size fits all' approach and had to become more child centred. Children should be allowed to proceed at their own pace in response to teaching tailored towards them individually. This aim was very worthy but had huge resource implications and contributed further to the destabilising process of constant change within education.

Some would argue that reform is always necessary if only because of the underachievement and disaffection of many children in school. People

FIGURE 2.1 League tables mean schools 'advertise' their achievements to both pupils and prospective parents

can still relate to George Orwell's statement in the 1930s: 'There is not one working-class boy in a thousand who does not pine for the day when he will leave school. He wants to be doing real work not wasting his time on ridiculous rubbish like history and geography' (*Road To Wigan Pier*, 1937).

Seventy years later, journalist Neil Doyle, writing about the school he attended, made a direct link between poor schooling and disaffection leading to terrorism: 'With over 1,000 pupils on the roll in soul-destroying conditions, teaching methods that relied heavily on dictation . . . it made for perfect conditions for gangs to coalesce . . . There's now a British Mujahideen in our midst and it's been State-nurtured and funded' (*Terror Base UK,* 2006).

Because many children in school are bored by the GCSEs they are doing, the government is proposing to enable them to embark on apprenticeships two days a week at 14 years of age, once 40,000 industrial placements have been found. Previous such initiatives have failed amid complaints that firms have exploited students on work-experience as unpaid labour. Ken Spours, of London University's Institute of Education, said: 'In the era of league tables, it could mean schools just getting rid of their disruptive pupils – and I don't see industry falling over themselves to take them.' Some see this leading to a divisive two-tier education system where some children are denied quality education and others, with a privileged background, are enabled to flourish.

Schools matter to people because education is not just about the delivery of syllabuses. Primary schools in particular are the sites for the transmission from one generation to the next of shared culture. The culture is of the classroom, but also of the playground. Children socialise there. The playground is a concrete jungle where children practise their games and learn, where society's folk memories and myths are recycled through chants. The song 'A ring a ring a roses / A pocketful of posies / Ashoo! Ashoo! / We all fall down' contains memories of the Black Death, which swept Europe in the Middle Ages. Children in Yorkshire sing 'Wind the bobbin back', an echo of work in the woollen mills.

In choosing a school for their children, parents worry about potential academic progress, but also about the prevalence of bullying, the development of life skills and the kind of social, cultural and spiritual experience offered by the school. Furthermore, because schools are so important in the formation of shared cultural identity, people are interested in the way in which prominent public figures choose to educate their children. For example, Prince Charles was the first member of the royal family not to be educated by palace tutors. He was sent to Gordonstoun in Scotland. His own sons William and Harry were sent to Eton (where Tory leader David Cameron was also educated). For ordinary parents this humanised the royal family, who became subject to the same anxieties and uncertainties of sending children to school as they were. Conversely, people sensed hypocrisy when those members of the Labour Party who advocated state schooling sent their own children to public schools. For example, the then prime minister Tony Blair bypassed the state system and sent his sons to the exclusive Catholic public school Brompton Oratory.

Many parents send their children to public schools because of the availability of an 'Old School Tie' network, which may help their child to get a job and develop socially useful life-long friendships. In Britain as elsewhere, those who have shared experiences during their formative years forge a common cultural bond which enables them to operate along co-operative and self-help lines. The most famous of such networks may be the grouping of old Etonians, Harrovians and other public schoolboys, known as 'the Establishment'. Girls' schools offering access to this network would be Roedean, Benenden or Cheltenham Ladies College. Britain traditionally works on a system of contacts among people whose business, professional, sporting and social lives produce a shared cultural *milieu*. This is evident in the number and social status of clubs nominally representing various interests but in practice enabling members to socialise. Such organisations include golf and sailing clubs or Rotary, Round Table and Lions. Youth organisations like Cubs and Brownies and Scouts and Guides induct British children into this club mentality.

FIGURE 2.2 Roedean School, adjacent to Brighton Marina, enjoys a favoured location, like many independent schools

It has always been the case that pupils from single-sex schools have performed better than those at mixed ones – without the distractions of the opposite sex, so the argument goes. In the 2011 GCSE tables the ten top schools nationally were single-sex. Recently, moreover, the trend in school and university education is that girls seem to be performing much better than boys. Various factors have contributed to their increased pre-eminence. Today more women in prominent jobs offer role models. Feminism has changed girls' expectations and encouraged their ambition. A profound shift appears to be taking place where boys are 'the weaker sex', the ones who need encouragement and the raising of their self-esteem. This is one of the problems being addressed by educators who argue that boys perform better at exams while the education system has moved more towards continuous assessment.

There is constant anxiety about the state of education in society at large. For example a 2000 report by the National Skills Task Force found that seven million adults in Britain were 'functionally illiterate'. That is, they would not pass an English GCSE and have literacy levels at or below those expected of an 11-year-old. This was described by Estelle Morris, the then Education and Skills Minister, as 'quite frightening'. This perhaps explained Labour's claim to tackle 'education, education, education'. Ten years later the situation had improved only slightly with Britain's functional illiteracy rate estimated at 21.8 per cent and the Conservative–Lib Dem coalition seeing itself as equally committed to improving education.

Recent governments have encouraged a shift from education to training. The word 'education' comes from the Latin *educo*, meaning to lead out or develop qualities which are within. Education thus produces the fully rounded individual with a healthy mind in a healthy body (*mens sana in corpore sano*). Critics suggest that because the majority of students are still in a formative phase of their lives it is a mistake to concentrate solely on *instruction*, which implies pouring knowledge into them and ignores the stage of personal development that they have reached. Training is more to do with the supply of workers than with the personal fulfillment of the individual. Education, on the other hand, develops qualities like creativity, encourages curiosity and allows personal development. Opponents, meanwhile, say that publicly funded education should be pragmatic and does have a duty to supply society's need for skills and employers' requirements in the knowledge economy.

Some educational trends remain disturbing. For example studying modern languages has always been a minority pursuit in Britain. Britons are less likely than any other Europeans to speak a second language. Since 2004 they have become even less likely. The government made it no longer compulsory for pupils aged 14 to 16 to study a foreign language. Consequently, numbers of pupils studying German and French have declined by 45 per cent since that time to 73,000 and 188,000 respectively. University language departments are concerned at the shortage of prospective students if this trend continues. And of course the UK was already massively under-represented in the European public service – before the decline in language learning started. By contrast, in the independent sector, Brighton College has made the study of Mandarin Chinese compulsory for all its pupils, in the belief that this will ultimately advantage them.

In 2002 apprehensions about the political apathy of the young and a 'moral crisis' in society saw the teaching of citizenship made compulsory in schools. Four years later, an Ofsted report found that the subject was being taught inadequately in most schools. Teachers felt ill prepared and were not adhering to the curriculum laid down. They were expected to inform and enthuse pupils about, for example: legal and human rights and responsibilities; central and local government; the electoral system and voting; Britain's relations with the EU, Commonwealth and UN. Unsurprisingly, Ofsted found that often such classes were 'dull, irrelevant and even counterproductive'. In 2011 the Education Minister Michael Gove was thought to favour making the teaching of citizenship optional, despite the fact that currently 100,000 pupils take it annually at GCSE.

Universities

University education is generally less contentious for the general public and in recent years Britain has had in Europe the highest percentage (over a third) of 21-year-olds graduating from university. Moreover, in 2001 a report on graduate employment commissioned by the Higher Education funding council found that more new UK graduates expressed satisfaction with their college courses than did their counterparts in Europe. Government figures in 2010 showed that only 17 per cent of students in the UK leave universities without a qualification, the second lowest drop-out rate in the world (after Japan).

Universities are still central to the development of future leaders of Britain. Even when the lines of political division are being redrawn, university graduates (especially from Oxbridge) still dominate the political leadership. For example, Margaret Thatcher and Tony Blair both went to Oxford and almost two-thirds of the people appointed by Tony Blair to his Labour Cabinets were educated at Oxford or Cambridge. Seventy per cent of the Coalition government of David Cameron and Nick Clegg are Oxbridge graduates.

Despite sometimes rancorous debate, individuals still feel positive about their own education. A wide range of them, having had the experience of being in the school play, practising team sports like hockey or soccer, or such extra-curricular activities as chess or judo, develop and retain a shared sense of pride in their schools. Rivalry between schools is felt by children who are publicly labelled by the uniforms that most British schools make them wear. When they leave school, reports of their achievements will often indicate their schools – so, for example, members of the Oxford and Cambridge Rugby Teams have their colleges *and* schools listed thus: Carr, Kenneth: Merton; St Anthony's Comprehensive, Luton. Smith, John: Churchill; Shrewsbury School. Students will often visit their old schools and join Old Girls or Boys Associations, which meet to arrange social functions. This perhaps explains the phenomenal success of the website Friends Reunited.

Throughout their lives people who went to Eton, Harrow, or Winchester schools are referred to by others as Old Etonians, Old Harrovians, or Wykehamists (Winchester School was founded in the fourteenth century by Bishop William Wykeham). And they see themselves in this way also. Well into middle age someone will pride himself on being a *public* school boy. Professor Richard Hoggart saw himself as 'a *grammar* school boy'. For Hoggart this implied someone who all his life has to jump hurdles, which he places for himself, in order to retain a sense of self worth.

Even primary schools have reunions, as people feel a need to re-experience the comradeship and spirit of community of their youth. No matter how old people are, school is where they acquired their first long-term friends, developed their social personalities and gained a deep and lasting sense of communal identity.

Employment

Education and work are linked at least inasmuch as an individual's success at school often determines the kind of job he or she goes on to do. The relationship is not always this straightforward, but often there is a connection between upward and downward trajectories at school and in the workplace. An important effect of the many divisions in British education – between state and private, Oxbridge and Redbrick, vocational and academic – is that the workforce experiences ideas of stratification which have been superseded in many other countries. Thus the British workforce is distinguished by its divisions rather than its cohesiveness. Remuneration replicates social division. Process or factory workers have always received (weekly) wages, while predominantly middle-class managers have received (monthly) salaries. There are still quite separate ladders of achievement in numerous workplaces and it is almost impossible for people to cross from one to another. The case of John Major, someone who did not attend university, let alone Oxbridge, rising to become prime minister (1990–97), is the exception that proves the rule.

Further examples of the continuing stratified nature of Britain unfortunately abound. British company reports still append names to photos of directors while referring to technical processes beneath photos of workers. The civil service is divided into administrative, executive and clerical grades; industry into management and shop floor; banks into directors, managers, clerks and cashiers. These divisions may not be in all cases watertight, but very few people at the top of British industry have risen from the bottom and this both reflects and determines a British cultural identity based on the social and economic divisions which separate groups of people from one another.

Tables 2.1 and 2.2 show, respectively, the distribution of workers between different industries and the national unemployment rate in recent years. Unemployment currently stands at 8.1 per cent of the workforce: 2.75 million, the highest level since 1994. In 2011 the total number of people in employment among men was 15,160,000 and women 13,142,000.

Attitudes to work are determined culturally and in general work has always had a low cultural profile. If we 'read' British society through literature, we can see that most works of fiction for example either don't refer to work or, if they do, disparage it. In Jane Austen's novels in the early nineteenth century, people who are in trade are not quite respectable, and the correct thing to do is to own land and to live off one's rents. Neither Elizabeth Bennet's Mr Darcy nor Emma Woodhouse's Mr Knightley works

TABLE 2.1 Labour force by occupation

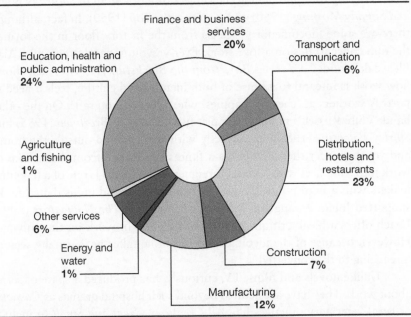

TABLE 2.2 Unemployment levels 1991–2011 (%)

1991	8.0	2002	3.1
1992	9.7	2003	3.1
1993	10.3	2004	4.8
1994	9.4	2005	4.6
1995	8.0	2006	5.5
1996	7.2	2007	5.7
1997	5.5	2008	5.6
1998	4.7	2009	6.8
1999	4.3	2010	6.9
2000	3.8	2011	8.1
2001	3.3		

Office of National Statistics

for a living. Bulstrode in George Eliot's *Middlemarch* (1871–72) is a banker, and thus in a profession that is not yet entirely respectable. In Dickens's novels people try to separate their public (working) selves from their private (domestic) lives in the belief that everybody wants to escape from work. Wemmick, the law clerk in *Great Expectations* (1860–61) pulls up a drawbridge when he goes back to his home where his 'aged parent' lives. Home is sacrosanct. Work is a necessary evil.

Work is rarely portrayed seriously or in detail in British films. Karel Reisz, Tony Richardson and others of the 1950s New Wave cinema were seen as daring for approaching the subject of work at all in *Saturday Night and Sunday Morning* (1960) and *Room at the Top* (1959). In fact, although there are some 'documentary' scenes from the factory floor in the former, the film concentrates on a love story. Even 'revolutionary' drama like Alan Bleasdale's lauded TV series *Boys from the Blackstuff* (1991), which shows how work is integral to a sense of both identity and culture, feels a need to portray workers as 'cheeky chappies' who avoid 'hard graft'. On the other hand, Willy Russell's popular escapist films *Letter to Brezhnev* (1985) and *Shirley Valentine* (1989) deal directly with work in and outside the home, and yet they offer their audiences a fantasy of escape from the tedium of work into romances with 'exotic' foreigners. Ken Loach is one of a few film-makers with a hard political edge both in his films and in his daily life: he supported Julian Assange of Wikileaks in court. In *The Navigators* (2001) Loach offers a bleak critique of the privatisation of work on the railways. However, because of the ideological position he takes he is usually seen as 'preaching to the converted'.

Unlike novels and films, TV, curiously, has produced a spate of series about work. They have accelerated beyond such hospital dramas as *Casualty* or rural veterinary practices like *All Creatures Great and Small* to include the military (*Soldiers*), fire-fighting (*London's Burning*) and many others. TV comedy series set in workplaces include *The Brittas Empire, Drop the Dead Donkey* and *Dinner Ladies,* set in a leisure centre, a newsroom and a canteen respectively. Ricky Gervais's series *The Office* was an extremely popular treatment of the dysfunctional aspects of twenty-first-century work, management culture and office politics, while *The Thick of It* cruelly satirised office life at Labour headquarters, revealing the changes in political approaches since the incisive but comparatively genteel *Yes Minister* of the 1980s. *The I.T. Crowd* offers a further bizarre critique on life at work, which rings true with many people because of its surreal sense of a world in which political correctness and managerialism sit uncomfortably alongside the frailties and foibles of human behaviour.

Unlike a film of working-class reality and fantasy such as Ken Loach's *Looking for Eric* (2009), with its hapless postman hero coached by his own hero, footballer Eric Cantona, a mainstream movie which offers a snapshot of British middle-class life and which did very well at the box office is *Four Weddings and A Funeral* (1994). It is a useful case study and may be seen to reflect common British aspirations and values. The story pursues some friends around Britain and examines their social lives in the context of the ceremonial rituals of the title. The whole is placed in the context of an Anglo-American 'special relationship', which is part shared cultural history and part wish-fulfilment designed to appeal to different agendas on both sides of the Atlantic. As in other films such as *Remains of the Day* (1994), *A Handful of Dust* (1988) or *The Shooting Party* (1984), it adds social comment to a familiar recipe of stately homes in a timeless, upstairs/downstairs England peopled with fascinating eccentrics and nameless servants. This has been called a 'Merchant/Ivory' version of Britain (from the names of the director and producer who made A *Room With a View* in 1985 and *Howards End* in 1992, among others. *Four Weddings and a Funeral* offers a version of Britain which contains a mixture of traditional and new clichés. Bohemianism, the gay community and monarchy are all contained in the non-threatening frame-work of British compromise. Meanwhile there is absolutely no mention of work. The film comes from the same mould as *Chariots of Fire* (1981) and *Another Country* (1984), which ultimately praise the leisured Britain that they depict and steadfastly ignore the means of getting a living. In such pointedly socially divided worlds, work persists in its cultural representations as something the upper classes do not do and the working classes wish not to do. Contrast can be made with the 2010 films *The King's Speech*, about royalty's *noblesse oblige*, and *Made in Dagenham* about the spirit among working people in Britain, here fighting for women's equal pay.

To illustrate further British culture's negative representation of work, we can look at one or two examples from the Britpop phenomenon of the 1990s. The 1995 Blur album is called *The Great Escape*. Its front cover has a picture of someone diving from a motorboat into a beautiful Mediterranean sea. Its back cover has the four members of the group dressed as urban professionals huddled around a computer. Here, as with most popular culture aimed at the country's mass population, the dominant British view is that work is a treadmill from which people dream of escaping (Blur's other album titles also suggest this: *Leisure, Modern Life is Rubbish, Parklife*).

The possibility of a life of leisure is also a fantasy indulged in every week as the National Lottery winning numbers are announced on television and millionaires are literally 'made' overnight. It is assumed the winners will give up work without regret, but many have to be counselled by therapists to cope with (partly their wealth but largely) their position away from the community and working life they have known.

People establish and share identity at work through participation in such incidental 'social' aspects as car pools, coffee clubs, office sweepstakes (betting on horses), company sports clubs and celebrations for engagements and birthdays. More people meet their future spouse through work than in any other way.

On leaving the office or the factory, there is often a shared drink with workmates and nights out to celebrate new jobs, retirements and weddings. (The latter are known as 'hen' and 'stag' nights for women and men respectively.) They take place in nightclubs, pubs or Working Men's Social Clubs.

FIGURE 2.3 A mixed-gender police unit integrates with the local community at a folk festival

Many relationships carry on outside work and workers do jobs ('foreigners') for one another.

Despite the widespread taboo against cultural representations of work (except on TV), in practice British society is constructed so much around employment that those who are cut off from it are also isolated socially. Britain was the first country to industrialise and is one of the first to have to devise programmes for coping with the problems of post-industrial and even post-agricultural society (in 1950, 25 per cent of the workers in Britain still worked on the land – the figure today is under 2 per cent). It has to supply redundant workforces with wide-ranging help, from counselling to setting up small businesses, from make-work schemes to volunteering.

Unemployment and economic change

The work ethic is very strong in the UK and for a majority of the British population their identity is shaped by the notion that they *work*. However, one of the main features of the working classes in the post-Thatcher period in Britain is that a greater proportion of them than of either the middle or upper classes is *not* working. Loss of work to a class that defines itself as *working* is traumatic and will be dealt with further in Chapter 5 on class and politics, as well as changes in the nature of class itself. It is hard for outsiders to appreciate the trauma of growing up in an unemployed household. Yozzer Hughes, a chief character in Alan Bleasdale's *Boys from the Blackstuff* became a cult figure with his catchphrase of 'gizza job', partly because so many people could empathise with him. This has also been a major theme in soap operas such as *EastEnders*.

Women in employment have fared less well than men, though there are now more women in the workforce than men. However, for a number of reasons, including prejudice and part-time working, women have often failed to gain promotion to posts of greater responsibility. The term 'glass ceiling' is applied to this consequent upper limit of women's progress in company careers. Their rate of unemployment is lower than that of men but their average pay is only 79 per cent of men's in similar occupations. However, unemployed ethnic-minority women and men are even more disadvantaged than mainstream workers, with rates of 17 per cent and 24 per cent respectively. The traditional situation of higher rates of employment for women than men is itself in flux. For example, while graduate unemployment worsened sharply for both male and female graduates from 11.1 per cent in December 2008 to 14.0 per cent in December 2009, the unemployment position appears to be far worse for males than for females: in December 2009 17.2 per cent of young male graduates were unemployed compared with 11.2 per cent of female graduates. By October 2011 there were 2.57m unemployed or 8.1 per cent of the workforce in Britain.

Unsurprisingly the above climate has led to a decline in a sense of job security. According to government reports, unlike previous generations middle-aged people now do not feel secure about their financial prospects. When the chairman of a major bank in the wake of the global financial crisis predicted job losses in his industry of 20,000, others saw *their* jobs as precarious, and people became cautious about spending – thus exacerbating the downturn at a time when the country was anyway ill prepared to cope.

The amount of disposable income that people saved in 2010 was 5.4 per cent compared with the 9.2 per cent saved in the 1990s. Karl Marx's predictions about the 'casualisation of labour' and the imminent implosion of capitalism appear to some people to be coming to pass and certainly many more people are being employed on temporary or part-time contracts. But instead of seeing this as the apocalyptic end to our system, some business analysts prefer to see it as following the pattern of the United States and supplying a more flexible productive base which ultimately regulates more efficiently the balance between supply and demand in the labour market.

For the last hundred years the south-east of England has been the most prosperous part of Britain and for a time in the 1980s, people there enthusiastically endorsed the concept of corporate Britain. To those in less privileged parts of the country, it seemed as though only those in and around London were enabled to participate in company share purchase schemes and take advantage of the under-priced privatisation sales of utilities such as electricity, water and telephone companies. The majority of small shareholders (they were known as 'Sids', because of a British Gas privatisation advertising campaign with a character of that name) took their profits and sold out, in the spirit of the entrepreneurialism which was being recommended to them by government. Some did sense themselves for a time as empowered and as part of corporate Britain. Other people felt that, because the industries were owned by the country, *their* national assets were being sold to those sufficiently well off to have money to invest in them. So this was seen as yet another way of shifting money from the regions to the well-to-do south.

People on the political right argued that Britain had become a poor country because it had created a climate of dependency: Its citizens lacked initiative, relied on the 'nanny' state to look after their every need and thus avoid their personal responsibilities. This hard-edged Thatcherite view led to a situation where in the interest of industrial efficiency, jobs were being axed at precisely the time when council tenants were being encouraged by the government to buy their state-owned homes ('council houses') on very good terms. Some individuals simply couldn't cope and returned their house keys to their mortgage providers. At one point in the early 1990s, homes were being repossessed at the rate of 1,000 per week, and even among the more affluent there were up to one and a quarter million people in Britain with 'negative equity'. That is, the loan they had taken out from the bank was greater than the value of the house they borrowed it for. As the global financial crisis developed, by August 2011 the number of homes worth less than their outstanding loans was 800,000, and unemployment and personal indebtedness were ominously on the rise.

Attitudes to work in Britain have also undoubtedly been affected by the decline in religious observance. Protestantism has had a particularly close relation to work. A belief in the moral importance of work (*laborare est orare* – to work is to pray) was especially notable in the late eighteenth century, with the growth of commerce in London and in the early nineteenth century, with the start of the Industrial Revolution. The popularity of Daniel Defoe's *Robinson Crusoe* (1741) shows how ingrained in the culture was the idea of the 'self-employed' individual who, out of a sense of religious duty, struggled against odds to succeed. He 'justified his existence' through work. This ideology appealed to a population which until recently had been largely rural and self-employed, but who, because of the 'division of labour' was now forced to do single unsatisfying city-based jobs.

In *Religion and the Rise of Capitalism* (1926), R. H. Tawney drew attention to the link between people's religious beliefs and their relative wealth. He attributed Britain's economic well-being to the Protestant work ethic. The idea is that we are put on earth, not just to live and to eat, but to work hard (partly as descendants and inheritors of the sin of Adam and Eve: work as 'punishment'). People who believe in the sanctity of work become rich. Conversely, the more unworldly the religion the less likely the religious congregation is to become rich. The situation is undoubtedly circular – economic decline may test religious commitment, which in turn limits adherence to the work ethic. The latter is based on a religious belief, but in practice, people of all persuasions have come to believe in work as a good thing and as a defining characteristic of being British. Again this has increased psychological and social trauma for those unable to find jobs.

If both culturally ingrained commitment to work is eroded and opportunities are taken away and replaced with the mentality induced by enforced dependency upon the state, people have to find outlets elsewhere. Their energies have been channelled into leisure, and this displacement has taken place in Britain progressively throughout the years of unemployment and the move to casual work. Shopping as a leisure pursuit has been encouraged because it fills people's time and is good for the economy. The graph of the decline in the number of permanent jobs is crossed by the ascendant one of ownership of satellite TVs and DVD players, the practice of sports and other indoor and outdoor leisure pursuits.

Leisure around the home

In dealing with leisure we are concerned not just with how people occupy themselves but with the cultural significance of their hobbies and practices. This applies to group and individual activities. We may divide the leisure pursuits which British people engage in into private and public. These are crude designations, but they do offer a way in to understanding how leisure affects cultural consciousness and identity.

As mentioned in the Introduction, the dominant medium for cultural exchange in Britain is television, though for teenagers the Web is taking over. It is difficult to pinpoint the moment at which TV became a significant part of the national cultural consciousness, but many oral histories of older people refer to the novelty of watching the June 1953 Coronation of Queen Elizabeth II on TV. This they did in company with friends, relations and neighbours. The move from listening to the FA Cup Final on 'the wireless' (radio) to watching it on TV marked a further important change. Particularly since the 1960s, daily consumption of TV has risen as broadcasting expanded from evenings only, to daytime, to the mornings – so-called 'breakfast TV'. TV watching is now available 24 hours a day, especially with numerous cable and satellite stations. The average time spent watching TV is more than three hours a day – much more than the internet's hour and a quarter per day. The young and the old watch more, the middle-aged a lot less. TV is a powerful social adhesive in Britain. Following stories on TV provides people with topics of conversation, allows them to get to know one another's tastes and preferences, and enables them to explore the current social and cultural pre-occupations that TV directs them towards. Workmates and friends are bonded together by their responses to the news, sitcoms, dramas or soaps that they have seen on TV.

It is clear that the change in the importance to their lives that people attach to TV had come about by 1974. At that time Edward Heath, Britain's prime minister, made two mistakes in devising strategic responses to the emergency of the oil crisis. In order to save electricity, he brought in a three-day working week, and he made the TV companies finish broadcasting each evening at 10.30 pm. In other words, he prevented people from working and he interfered with their watching of television. They were not prepared to put up with either of those changes. There was widespread opposition to the government and undoubtedly the above measures were factors in Heath's loss of the General Election in 1974.

Television's place is very much in the home. So, for example, when pubs introduced large-screen TVs for specific sports events and promotions in order to increase custom, their success was limited, because pubs are more places for social interaction than for 'watching the box'. Many people prefer to go out and attend football matches than watch them on television. They get much more of a sense of shared identity from their support for the same team. There is a 'family' atmosphere at some of the big clubs, despite the fact that there are 40,000 people present. Such large attendances indicate a wish for a shared sense of community, which TV alone can't provide. Anecdotally, attendance at football matches is increasing and watching it on TV is declining, though events like the World Cup see huge audiences in bars and pubs for the communal atmosphere.

However, in a country with all sorts of signs of social breakdown, from child murder and random knife attacks in the cities to rural suicides and abduction, it is electronic expressions of community that people cling to. They watch their own society through TV dramas such as *Casualty* or *The Bill*, which offer excitement set in an everyday context, or soap operas like *Emmerdale* or *Heartbeat*, which invoke an idealised rural past. Young people especially relate to soap operas. By far the most popular soaps followed by people in the age group 14–25 are the English *Hollyoaks* and the Australian serials *Neighbours* and *Home & Away*. An older age group watches *EastEnders* and *Coronation Street*. Given the success in numerous areas of British life of US culture, there is a surprising lack of interest in American soaps. More popular are high-adrenalin shows such as *24* and *CSI*, or light dramas like *Charmed* and *Desperate Housewives*. Characters in these programmes supply viewers with topics of conversation which provide the potential glue for their own social community. Table 2.3 shows the relative popularity of TV programmes.

Besides television and the ever-proliferating use of the internet, the major leisure activity of many British people is their hobby. The hobbies or minority interests pursued by Britons are numerous, wide-ranging and

TABLE 2.3 Most popular TV shows (October 2011)

	Millions
Emmerdale	40.8
Coronation St	39.8
EastEnders	34.3
Strictly Come Dancing	29.94
The X Factor	20.7
Downton Abbey	10.16
Deal or No Deal	8.56
Merlin	7.04
Neighbours	5.67
Midsomer Murders	5.67
BBC NEWS	4.54
ITV NEWS	3.25

Source: BARB 2011

passionately indulged in. They are part of the people's identities. Such minority activities include philately, train-spotting, ferret-keeping, fishing, pigeon-fancying, bird-watching, scouting, swimming, cycling, fell-running – just counting along a scale of physical activity. Most of these hobbies will have magazines to accompany them, or at the very least a newsletter. The number of browsers in high-street newsagents evidences the range and diversity of Britain's leisure interests and perspectives, as do Tables 2.4–2.6.

Table 2.4 shows how, over the past twenty years there has been a significant shift particularly in men's magazine reading habits, as illustrated in Table 2.5. *FHM*, the lifestyle magazine, *Nuts* a 'lads' mag', two car magazines and a television guide may characterise men's current reading and accurately record a move from interest in active leisure and general topics towards TV watching. The magazines that sell best to women are almost exclusively gender-specific: *Take A Break*, *Woman and Home*, *Woman*, *Bella* and *Woman's Weekly* (source: Press Gazette 2011).

Reading of books, the other major domestic leisure-time activity, has held up well. Book buying, ironically, is stimulated by television. *Brideshead Revisited* (1945), *Pride and Prejudice* (1813) and *Bleak House* (1853) sold many times more copies after their TV series than they ever did previously.

TABLE 2.4 Most popular magazines read by men (1990, 2000, 2010)

1990	%
Reader's Digest	20
What Car	7
Classic Cars	6
Golf Monthly	4

2000	%
FHM	20
Sky Customer	9
Cable Guide	6
Loaded	6
Skyview TV Guide	6

2010	%
Sky Magazine	9
Auto Trader	4
BBC Top Gear	3
FHM	3
Nuts	1

Source: NRS Readership Estimates 2011

TABLE 2.5 Readership of selected newspapers/magazines (2011)

	Thousands	*% of potential readership*
The Sun	7,683	13.4
Daily Mail	4,622	9.6
Daily Mirror	3,997	5.5
The Daily Telegraph	1,688	3.2
The Times	1,486	2.4
Daily Express	1,457	2.9
The Guardian	1,143	2.1
Financial Times	344	0.3
What's on TV	3,289	8.5
Take A Break	2,715	9.1
Radio Times	2,334	4.8
OK	2,201	7.2
TV Choice	1,930	4.9
Cosmopolitan	1,537	3.0
TV Times	1,516	3.6
Woman's Own	957	3.5
Private Eye	729	0.9
The Economist	582	0.7
The Big Issue	475	1.0

Source: National Readership Survey 2011

eReaders may also stimulate the purchase of books. Of course much time previously devoted to reading is now spent, particularly by the young, on social networking. The Web is part of young people's psyche. Facebook, Twitter and Google+ are the current UK favourites. Such virtual 'communities' are efficient and satisfying for now. The future will decide, when some global outage occurs, whether people will 'miss' social networking beyond the need for such tools as Skype to stay in contact, or whether it will be their fellow participants they are missing.

Table 2.6, which covers which books people buy for themselves, is divided along gender lines. Table 2.7 shows how rapidly people's leisure activities are changing – especially with the rise of the internet.

Public entertainment

Pubs and cinemas

We will now look at some entertainments outside of the home which British people use to occupy their free time. The principal place of entertainment

TABLE 2.6 [A survey of] reading which impresses the opposite sex

Top ten reads to impress a man

1) Current affairs websites
2) Shakespeare
3) Song lyrics
4) Cookery books
5) Poetry
6) Nelson Mandela autobiography *Long Walk to Freedom*
7) Jane Austen
8) Facebook/Myspace
9) Religious texts
10) Financial Times

Top ten reads to impress a woman

1) Nelson Mandela autobiography *Long Walk to Freedom*
2) Shakespeare
3) Cookery books
4) Poetry
5) Song lyrics
6) Current affairs websites
7) Text messages
8) Emails
9) Financial Times
10) Facebook

Source: National Year of Reading 2008

TABLE 2.7 Percentage of time spent online in April 2007 (536 million hours) and April 2010 (884 million hours; a rise of 65%)

Activity	2007	2010	+/−
Blogs/social	8.8	22.7	+159
Email	6.5	7.2	+11
Games	5.9	6.9	+15
Instant messaging	14.2	4.9	−66
Classifieds/auction	5.0	4.7	−6
Portals	3.7	4.0	+10
Search	4.1	4.0	−3
Software info	5.3	3.4	−36
News	1.5	2.8	+84
Adult	2.8	2.7	−3

Source: UK Online Measurement Company

outside the home that people automatically think of in relation to Britain is the public house, or 'pub'. In the past, pubs have performed different social functions. Traditionally they were a male preserve. Various sociological studies have suggested that until the 1950s the British pub was a more welcoming place for a man than his home. It was familiar and cozy (small bar rooms were called 'snugs'), with a fire and games such as darts and dominoes. This changed when houses in the 1950s, a period of increasing affluence, were brought up to date and made more attractive with higher standards of draught-proofing, labour-saving appliances, new furnishings and even central heating in some cases. The 1950s were a 'home-centred society'. It was then less acceptable for a woman to go into a pub on her own than it was for a man. Some city centre pubs specified 'men only' and many covertly discouraged single women. Today they are much more welcoming to people of both sexes, but few older women will say they feel comfortable going into a pub on their own.

Among 'outside' entertainments, pubs and cinemas have been through periods of boom and bust in English social life. Cinema attendance in Britain reached its peak in 1946 with 1.6 billion cinema visits. It bottomed in 1984 with 54 million. Over the last five years it has plateaued above 150 million. A report from the Film Council said that 27 per cent of the £775 million spent on 176million cinema visits in Britain was for humorous films. (The percentages in Germany and Spain were 23 and 18 respectively.)

There were more than 140 million cinema attendances in 2002 (largely thanks to *Harry Potter* and *The Lord of the Rings*), despite the competition of television. However, the majority of all cinema-going is still done by under 5 per cent of the total population and the range of films on offer has not widened, despite the increase in the number of multiplex screens, which are owned by large multinationals and which show mainly Hollywood films. So cinema attendance, as a cultural practice, has yet to regain its 1960s popularity, but its importance should not be underestimated as a cohesive social force, particularly for young people.

Cinema appears to be resilient at the moment because it is a communal activity. Margaret Thatcher famously said 'there is no such thing as society', but in fact people yearn, if not for 'society', then for community. They want to share collective entertainment, whether through street carnival, clubbing, attendance at football matches and so on. Cinema is a good illustration of such communal activity. Iconic popular films that have coincided with previous editions of this book are *Four Weddings and a Funeral* (1994), *Bridget Jones's Diary* (2001), *The Queen* (2006) and *Harry Potter and the Deathly Hallows* (2010). All of these deal with ceremonial or ritual events or practices. They are about public shared experience and are chosen in their recreation time by people who view them not in the 'privacy' of the DVD or the iphone, but in the collective experience of cinema. A film which has caught the contemporary mood for our present edition is *The King's Speech* (2010) with Colin Firth and Helena Bonham Carter. The canny launching of the film's publicity campaign on Christmas Day, before the annual Queen's Speech watched by about ten million people, certainly helped its subsequent success. Those who were looking forward to the 29 April royal wedding of William and Kate were also given in the movie something to fuel their pleasurable anticipation. So, going out to the cinema is still a staple part of British life.

Pubs, on the other hand, are struggling, with the percentages of men and women who never drink alcohol at 15 and 20 respectively, and rising. Breweries find it hard to get tenants, who are reluctant to work the unsocial hours required and pay high costs for the beer. In 2009 52 pubs a week were

FIGURE 2.4 The 'family hostile' Albion Pub caters to adult customers only

closing. However, with the churches in Britain in decline, as congregations age and Sunday attendances fall, some pubs are finding a new role. They fill the social vacuum created by religious decline and perform the function of community meeting place, and so are still, in the new century, very much central to British life. That this is the case is shown by the many pubs in soap operas, including 'The Vic' in *EastEnders*, 'The Rover's Return' in *Coronation Street* and 'Y Deri' in *Pobol y Cwm*.

Pantomimes and theatre

At Christmas time, pantomimes form an important aspect of British cultural experience. Unknown on the Continent, they are staged in theatres, village halls and community centres of all sorts, amateur and professional. Well-known TV personalities or even politicians often appear in them. Parents attend with children and in a controlled dramatic environment pantomimes offer a 'safe' form of initiation into the adult world. They contain a number of standard ingredients: cross-dressing (the 'Principal Boy' is always a woman; the 'Dame' is a man); *double-entendre* (parents can understand lewd meanings which pass over the heads of their children); contemporary reference (current politicians, or aspects of daily life like public transport or the NHS are guyed); ritualised audience participation, where children get to shout: 'He's behind you', or 'Oh yes it is'/'Oh no it isn't'. They very often involve reworking of myths as in *Babes in the Wood*, or *Cinderella*, where the badly treated individual gets justice and their rightful place in the world.

When London theatre was suffering during the post-9/11 tourist absence in 2001, pantomime there and elsewhere in Britain was booming. Thousands of people flocked to pantos which earned millions of pounds of profit. At a time of military intervention in Afghanistan and global uncertainty, people sought out traditional family entertainment. To assuage their fears of the bogeyman Osama bin Laden, a character with his name was incorporated into the year's most popular panto, *Aladdin*. Other perennial favourites doing well then and since include *Cinderella, Beauty and the Beast, Puss in Boots, Snow White and the Seven Dwarfs, Peter Pan* and *Dick Whittington*.

Theatre, ballet and opera give Britain a high cultural profile particularly with overseas tourists, even though they may remain minority pursuits in Britain. London West End theatre productions such as Andrew Lloyd Webber's *Cats*, Willy Russell's *Blood Brothers* or Agatha Christie's *The Mousetrap* have always attracted large tourist numbers. In 2010 there were 14.1 million attendances at London theatres. Perhaps because the largest concentration of these cultural resources is in London with its National Theatre, Royal Shakespeare Company, English National Opera and Royal

Ballet, they tend to be seen as 'elitist', and indeed theatres generally are patronised by older, well-to-do people. However, theatres are in fact dispersed around the regions. Liverpool has The Playhouse. Manchester's Royal Exchange Theatre offers high quality drama. Leeds-based Opera North is thriving and Scottish and Welsh Opera companies are well received on their countrywide tours. Despite a difficult financial climate, several concert halls were either built or refurbished in the 1990s including Manchester's £42 million Bridgewater Hall, Birmingham's Symphony Hall and Liverpool's Philharmonic Hall. These all have a devoted local clientele. In addition, there are an estimated 1,300 youth theatres catering for 65,000 participants.

Sport

The major outdoor leisure outlet in Britain is sport. People in Britain spend a great deal of their leisure time either participating in sport or watching it. This widespread interest is illustrated in the fact that 250,000 people applied to be volunteers for the 2012 Olympics. However, the main sports practised in Britain are rugby and football (soccer) during the winter. Rugby is controlled by the Rugby Union, soccer by the Football Association. The traditional division between lower-social-status professional soccer players (who need to be paid) and higher-social-status rugby players ('gifted amateurs') has been eroded by the Union's decision in 1995 to relax its rules to allow professional rugby clubs. Soccer is known as 'a gentlemen's game for roughs' and rugby as 'a roughs' game for gentlemen'. One of the many paradoxes of British society is that although most of the public (that is private) schools in Britain play the middle-class game of rugby as their main sport, both Eton and Harrow, Britain's most exclusive schools, still field more soccer than rugby teams. Nationwide attendances at soccer matches in the 2008/9 season totalled 29.9 million. This compares with the peak figure in 1954/5 of 34 million.

There are two major groups of professional clubs who play in either the Premier League or the Football League. There are also two main competitions: the League Cup and the FA Cup, both knockout competitions. Going to a football match between major clubs such as Arsenal, Liverpool or Manchester United can be a powerful experience. Supporters of rival teams are segregated at football matches and often ritually taunt one another. For example, supporters in Liverpool's Kop (a terrace named after a lookout hill from the Boer War: Spion Kop) used to sing: 'See them lying on the runway . . .' to Manchester United supporters – to remind them of their team's plane crash in Munich in the late 1950s. Most of the chanting is not so vicious; a milder taunt nowadays is to sing the *Monty Python* song 'Always look on the bright side of life' to your rivals, when your team has just scored a goal. Much debate centres on whether football supplies a safety valve to avoid violence, rather than an encouragement to it, and it is argued that aggression is harmlessly released in the above ritualised exchanges between supporters. Supporters are thought to feel a necessary sense of shared community through loyalty to their team and local pride when it wins. A measure of the seriousness with which supporters take their soccer is contained in the Liverpool manager Bill Shankly's famous remark: 'Football isn't a matter of life and death. It's far more important than that.'

In summer, the game of cricket is played widely on village greens, as well as at the professional level and is a genuinely popular 'grassroots' game about observance of rules, fairness and a pitting of wits and talent between equally matched teams. However, there are class associations to all British sports and in the case of cricket there is a history of contention for 'ownership' of the game. For example many British stately homes have an adjacent cricket pitch and pavilion and over the years encounters have taken place there between 'gentlemen and players'. This again underlines the British distinction between the upper classes (gentlemen), who are leisured and admirable, and the lower (players), who work and are disparaged.

This may also be seen in rugby. Rugby league was founded as a break-away from Rugby Union famously at the George Hotel in Huddersfield in 1895. Basically the players were impoverished northern working men who wanted to be paid for giving up their precious Saturday afternoon to play a game of rugby. For the next 100 years Rugby Union remained a middle-class game, played by amateurs who could afford to do so.

Significantly, professional soccer is associated with Britain's cities while cricket, which may well be played in urban centres such as Old Trafford (Manchester), Headingley (Leeds) or Lords (London), is associated with rural Britain. So while football clubs are named 'Leeds United' or 'Manchester City', professional cricketers play for counties, such as Kent, Somersetshire and Gloucestershire.

Variations occur in the terminology used to describe people watching leisure entertainments. Those who watch soccer, rugby, cinema, TV, theatre or opera are known respectively as 'crowds', 'spectators', 'audiences', 'viewers', 'theatre-goers' or 'opera buffs'. These terms form part of a spectrum of cultural snobbery. Soccer fans are traditionally working class and are called 'crowds', suggesting they are amorphous. Middle-class people who watch rugby are 'spectators' – they are dispassionate onlookers. 'Audiences' are more sophisticated again because they listen. 'Viewers' is a euphemism which denies the passivity of the TV 'couch potato'. 'Theatre-goer' implies some form of dynamism and the word 'buff' comes from the uniform (made of buffalo hide) worn by smart regiments.

There are many other outdoor sporting events in Britain, particularly in the summer, which attract national and international interest. However,

FIGURE 2.5 Village road runners pose after the Lake Vyrnwy half marathon. Photo ©
T. Clixby

there are many more less publicised ones, which supply the high point in
individual enthusiasts' years. Surprisingly, local events can sometimes be
better patronised than national ones. For example, until recent years, the
50,000 runners in Gateshead's annual Great North Run, compared with the
34,806 who took part in the London Marathon, received far less publicity.
The Great North Run was hardly alluded to in the national news media with
their metropolitan emphasis, but the latter was hyped and televised. That
situation has only gradually changed to more local coverage and publicity.

Impressionistically, the degree of health consciousness, fitness and
dietary awareness is higher among the British young than the Americans.
But young Swiss, Germans or Canadians are much more likely to swim or
ride bikes than the British. There is no British equivalent to the Continental
'parcours' (outdoor fitness areas in national parks) and facilities such as the
National Rowing Centre at Nottingham or the Manchester Velodrome (for
cycling) are over-stretched and of no help in keeping the generality of
people fit. Most exercise takes place indoors for women and increasingly
for men. Health and fitness clubs or gyms have become very popular
throughout the country in recent years (cynics say because they are dating
agencies) and large numbers of people regularly attend aerobics or 'step'
classes.

In a study published by the Office for National Statistics, the following
sports were most popular among the four-fifths of men, randomly inter-

FIGURE 2.6 Land yachts prepare to race at Hoylake

viewed, who took part in at least moderate physical activity: walking (48 per cent), snooker (18 per cent), cycling (15 per cent) and swimming (13 per cent). This compares with the 10 per cent who played football. Despite this focus on fitness, however, cigarette smoking, particularly among young women, has risen slightly.

Festivals

Arts festivals take place annually in most large cities, and smaller places like Glyndebourne and Buxton have their own opera festivals. Pop and rock festivals in particular have become a feature of youth culture, now often with green, chill-out or family angles. The best known are at Glastonbury and Reading. Entrance fees are relatively expensive at £200 for two or three days, but they are extremely well attended with upwards of 20,000 people.

Museums

In this survey of communal leisure activities, we can also say that a traditional version of British culture is nurtured in a range of public institutions:

TABLE 2.8 Most popular places to visit

Free admission	Visits (millions)
Blackpool Pleasure Beach	5.9
British Museum	4.5
National Gallery	4.2
Tate Modern	3.9
Natural History Museum	3.0
Science Museum	2.0
V&A Museum	1.9

Charged admission	Visits (millions)
London Eye	3.2
Tower of London	1.9
Kew Gardens	1.5
Edinburgh Castle	1.1
Eden Project	1.1
Chester Zoo	1.0
Canterbury Cathedral	1.0

Source: Association of Leading Visitor Attractions (2005)

mainly museums and art galleries. In the past it has tended to be high culture which is conserved here and they were places of obligatory pilgrimage for schoolchildren, who in the course of their subsequent lives never returned. In recent years, this has changed. The institutions have become much more imaginative and their collections have been partially devolved to the regions. There is a Tate Gallery in Liverpool and a branch of London's National Portrait Gallery at Bodelwyddan Castle in north Wales. Instead of a single unchanging stock, museums now tend to stage more 'thematic' exhibitions, such as Liverpool Maritime Museum's slavery exhibition, or its new water-front Museum of Liverpool which deals with the material conditions of people's lives rather than high culture and was opened by the Queen in 2011. Responding to public interest, London's Victoria and Albert Museum rearranged its collection to offer 'British Galleries'. Manchester has excellent new museums: the Lowry and Imperial War Museum North. Leeds has the Royal Armouries.

Holidays

Leisure was originally the preserve of the upper classes. Only they had the time and money to tramp their own grouse moors in Scotland, or sail their yachts with professional crews at Cowes. For example, the industrialist

Sir Thomas Lipton was able to finance his own Americas Cup yachting challenges and pay his crews in the 1930s. So when leisure became available to ordinary people through decreased working hours and paid annual leave, by and large in the 1950s, it gave social status to those benefiting from it. This soon changed, as catering for larger numbers of leisured people on a year round basis turned into an industry. Treatment of holiday-makers became more systematic, more professional, less deferential and less status-aware.

Since the 1960s the two-week annual holiday is more likely to be spent abroad. Package holidays were introduced to Britain in the 1950s by the Russian entrepreneur Vladimir Raitz, founder of Horizon holidays. The beneficiaries became the hoteliers of France, Spain and Florida, and those losing out were British seaside landladies at traditional resorts. The most popular overseas holiday destinations for Britons in 2009 and the numbers going to them were: Spain (10.7 million), France (8.9 million) and the US (2.7 million). British people have become obsessed with holidaying abroad and make 58 million trips per year. David Lodge suggests in *Paradise News* (1992) that tourism is the new world religion. The Hoover company so underestimated the demand for a holiday scheme it was promoting in 1993 that it lost £50 million.

New patterns in leisure

Gambling

Betting on the sport of the rich, horse racing, has always been practised by the working rather than the middle class, whose puritanism in regard to gambling has been tempered only by government-sponsored Premium Bonds and the National Lottery. The latter has become a major national talking point in Britain, which was the last country in Europe to introduce one, in November 1994. As a social and cultural phenomenon it is especially interesting. It generates comment in the media, between politicians and among people in general. It has brought a whole new clientele into gambling. Tickets are sold through newsagents and post offices – where everybody goes – whereas other forms of gambling such as horse-racing are contained within betting shops where passers-by may not even see in through the windows and where the family is virtually excluded. Many people, once a year, will place a bet on the Grand National or the Derby, but with the Lottery and its sequel 'Instants' scratch cards, everyone has a 'flutter' (a bet) week by week. Online betting has become a major industry.

The National Lottery has become an important social and cultural phenomenon. Its revenues, at £65 million per week, are well above initial estimates of £14–35 million, and nine out of ten adults are claimed to buy tickets on occasions. It is clearly a financial success. This is especially striking since the bookmakers Ladbrokes have likened the chance of winning the jackpot to that of Elvis landing a UFO (unidentified flying object) on the Loch Ness Monster. The odds are about 14 million to one. George Orwell, writing in his 1948 novel *1984*, imagined it with quite uncanny accuracy:

> The Lottery, with its weekly pay-out of enormous prizes was the one public event to which the proles [workers] paid serious attention. It was probable that there were some millions of proles for whom the Lottery was the principal if not the only reason for remaining alive. It was their delight, their folly, their anodyne, their intellectual stimulant. Where the Lottery was concerned even people who could barely read and write seemed capable of intricate calculations and staggering feats of memory.

It is tempting to say that TV programmes like *Deal or No Deal* or the Lottery itself are really about the possibility of social change. The latter certainly has caused social upheaval and division. Predictably some people have not been able to cope with huge winnings. Many legal cases have centred on breaches of trust among workmates, within families and between friends.

The weekly TV programme on Saturday nights where the draw is made has 12 million viewers for its mixture of orchestrated hype and celebration of greed. The proceeds are devoted to 'good causes', many of which are associated with heritage or 'high' culture like Sadlers Wells ballet, or the Royal Opera Company. It has introduced the word 'rollover' (unwon prizes carried forward) into the dictionary. It has increased the number of what were previously (football) 'pools winners' (in its first year it produced more than 100 millionaires) and so raised their profiles as social and cultural phenomena.

A number of lobbies have predictably come out against the Lottery: church leaders, directors of charities helping the poor, other charities whose revenues have fallen and the companies who previously received the money gambled on football, via their weekly 'pools coupons'. They raise the following main objections: people are spending money they can't afford; revenues are being diverted from the poor to the rich; the state is encouraging gambling; less money is going to charity overall.

Public acceptance of the Lottery and people's enthusiastic identification of themselves as prepared to take a risk may, however, represent a sea change in Britain's attitudes to gambling, entrepreneurialism and the new rich. In much British middle-class culture and entertainment – from the novel to plays to TV sitcoms – the most reviled characters have been the *nouveaux riches*, whether as individuals or as a class. Mrs Malaprop, Josiah Bounderby and Hyacinth Bucket are examples of people whose wealth and pretension exceed their level of cultural attainment, sensitivity and good manners. A series like *Fawlty Towers* probes the inter-relationships between class, snobbery, deference, respectability, good manners, money and service, in the crucible of a home-*cum*-'guest house'.

A lot of the criticism of the Lottery is based on the fear that one class will be subsidising another's pleasures. A major complaint about the disbursement of funds is that places of entertainment for the rich have benefited. What irks many people is that winning the Lottery goes against their idea of 'natural justice', as defined by the middle classes, in terms of the work ethic we discussed earlier: 'unearned' money is frowned upon. Also, when someone with a criminal record won several million pounds, *The Daily Telegraph* expressed its readers' sense of outrage that such 'undeserved' luck should happen. But the paper itself is caught in the bind of accepting and promoting such aspects of capitalism as free enterprise and entrepreneurialism yet not liking one of the inevitable consequences.

Shopping

The growth of consumerism has made a great impact on people's leisure lives. Esther Rantzen's TV programme *That's Life* (1973–94) represented a major turning point in Britain. It helped the development of a consumer culture. Hitherto, corporate Britain could afford to ignore disgruntled customers. But Rantzen held up such arrogance to ridicule and 'empowered' the wronged consumers. A shift occurred in the relative balance of power. Now the consumer is king. Redress is demanded and forthcoming. Trading Standards officers are feared. America's litigious consumer culture has spread to Britain where customers can sue McDonalds for spilling coffee over them or making them fat.

Because of this apparent liberation of the common man via spending, shopping has become one of Britain's major leisure pastimes. Many shops, particularly supermarkets and high street stores, are open seven days a week. This has had a significant impact on many people's lives. The work–life balance of those in the retail industry has obviously been adversely affected, as their low wages entail them working longer hours. For others, Sunday has become a day for shopping, like any other, and the demise of the traditional work pattern where even lowly paid workers were off on Sundays has meant that fewer people are guaranteed the 'community' time on Sunday, which might originally have been spent in church, but which is now spent shopping, pursuing leisure activities or watching football on TV.

Trends in entertainment

There is now a noticeable preference by young people for inanimate over animate sources of entertainment. This is evident not just in the decline of such live arts as theatre or home pastimes like card playing or in the preference of nightclubs with DJs over live gigs. Technophiliac 'Generation X' (from Douglas Coupland's 1991 novel of that name) often prefer things to people: cash machines to bank cashiers (US: tellers); computers to socialising; cyber cafes to coffee houses; virtual reality to reality; the internet and technological gizmos such as ipods, mobile phones and tablets, to live individuals. Nor do people just prefer TV and cinema to live entertainment. Within electronic media they prefer cartoons to 'real' representations of people. Technology has proved that it can deliver the 'real world' yet people want less 'real' images than are contained in traditional representation. They prefer their TV adverts to contain animated characters rather than real ones.

Another notable change in the pattern of people's leisure is a move away from socialising at home to frequenting public places of entertainment: 'fun pubs', multiplexes (containing cinemas, bowling allies, fruit machines and night clubs). There are regional variations, but generally the fact that British socialising took place in the pub or club made it difficult for new people to integrate into post-war British society. Asians in particular preferred to socialise at home, and this exacerbated cultural differences and separated people. In time, however, as in so many aspects of culture referred to elsewhere (body piercing, casual clothing, rap music, use of marijuana), while young mainstream people adopted immigrants' practices, young people from minority backgrounds joined the move to socialise outside the home. So young people of all ethnic origins now mix in places of public entertainment. McDonalds has had a universalising impact here. Their premises, balloons, party poppers and so on are supplied free of charge for children's parties, and draw in all comers. Operators of multiplex cinemas, bowling alleys and nightclubs (many of them multinationals, such as Time-Warner) benefit from this groundwork and cater to a young population brought up on 'canned' culture and dedicated to Britain's consumer society. Most Britons are unaware that the owner of the greatest number of pubs in Britain (4,867) is the Japanese company Nomura – or that the following famous British brands are now foreign-owned: Walkers Crisps, HP Sauce and Cadbury (American), Jaguar and Land Rover (Indian), Thomas Cook and Rolls Royce (German), Rowntree (Swiss), Hamleys Toys (Icelandic). They are, however, only too well aware that several Premier League football clubs, including Liverpool and Manchester United, are now in overseas ownership.

The older generation. meanwhile, which saves 13 per cent of its disposable income (v. the national average of 5.4 per cent), continues to opt for home entertainment. Eighty-four per cent of British households have video or DVD recorders and are catered for by an estimated 2,000 video shops – supplying a market that didn't exist 30 years ago, and which has expanded with DVD-by-post services.

Irish pubs

Lastly in this section on leisure, a revealing debate has been taking place about the introduction of Irish pubs into the British high street. This trend, a 'simple' commercial phenomenon, is seen to have all sorts of other implications. Irish pubs are financially successful, but people ask: 'What are they saying about Britain? Do they suggest it is a soulless place which needs an infusion of Celtic culture?' CAMRA, the Campaign for Real Ale, resists the trend as part of a commercialising of the English institution of the pub – a dilution of authentic English values. Others are unhappy about the ideological implications of this raising of the profile of a 'minority' culture in the war for hearts and minds in relation to an Ulster political settlement. Others again are concerned that national identity is being exploited for purely commercial ends. Some see the trend as just one more illustration of a postmodern phenomenon that uses elements of the past and elsewhere as a vocabulary with which to write the new Britain. In that respect, Irishness has only a surface significance – it could as easily be an American influence like McDonalds, or a Japanese one like karaoke – and they suggest that the trend should be welcomed as more evidence of tolerant multicultural Britain.

However, perhaps the most significant thing is that the forum in which this nationalistic venture is being played out – the high street – is a more democratic one than parliament, whose legislation cramps and controls people. (The post-war Labour administration, which produced 1,000 pages of legislation per year, was seen as 'interventionist'. The present government produces 3,000 pages per year. The UK's tax code has increased from 4,998 pages in 1997 to 11,520 in 2009.) People want to liberate themselves through culture and feel that cultural change will bring about a better world than legislation will. They suspect that *laissez-faire* capitalism will produce stampedes of commercial developers to out-of-town shopping centres or a situation where all high streets have more or less the same shops: Halfords, Boots, Marks & Spencer. In other words, a homogenising commercial process will take place which will ultimately dilute rather than enrich culture and cultural identity. In order to counter these forces they have only the cultural practices listed above. By exercising individual choice, they can wrest control over their lives away from commercial or government agencies.

Conclusion

To sum up this chapter: the cultural ambience is not neutral, it is a plain on which warring factions contend. Education, work and leisure are defining aspects of British cultural identity. Schools place a distinctive stamp on their pupils – a past pupil will be defined both in society at large *and* by the individual him or herself as a *grammar school* boy or girl, or more specifically as a product of Shrewsbury School or King Street primary. This pattern is repeated in the work arena when society labels people 'owned' by particular industries or by the state as a *Ford* worker, a *civil* servant. People acknowledge these descriptions of themselves, because they also define themselves by their schools and their work functions. The rhetorical question 'How do you do?', on being introduced to people, is very shortly followed by 'What do you do?', and soon thereafter by 'Where did you go to school?'. So education and work are significant defining aspects of identity. As we have seen further, people will always try to take control of their lives and define their own identities through the exercise of individual choice in their leisure activities. Finally we have highlighted a number of debates which arise in relation to these issues.

 ## Exercises

1   Reading checklist:
- Why are public schools so called?
- What is the origin of the word 'education'?
- What is the difference between wages and salaries?
- Are average female earnings the same as those of males?
- What are 'hen' and 'stag' nights?
- What is the Protestant ethic?
- What is a 'glass ceiling'?
- Where is the Kop?
- How are soccer and cricket teams differently named?
- What is a Merchant/Ivory representation of Britain?
- Who plays the Principal Boy in a pantomime?
- What is CAMRA?
- Which was the last country in Europe to have a National Lottery?

2   What kinds of schools are more likely to be portrayed in films? Why is this? You might consider viewing on DVD some of the following films: *Kes, The Belles of St. Trinians, Another Country*. How do these representations differ from the school in (say) *Dead Poets Society*?

3   Why are portrayals of work so rare in British novels/plays? Is American writing more likely to deal with work? Are British cultural forms more or less escapist than American ones?

4   Discussion questions:
- What is the effect on individual identity of pupils attending state or private schools?
- Does education always involve the imposition on one group in society of the values of another?
- Is it healthy or unhealthy to watch soap operas?
- How is unemployment related to identity?
- Does self-employment confer more dignity on workers?
- The chapter refers to the presence in Britain of McDonalds. Are overseas influences in a culture to be welcomed or resisted?
- Should the state fund culture? If so, should it aim to encourage high or popular culture? If not, why not?
- How important are tradition and traditional ways in a culture?

Reading

Hill, S. *et al. Managing to Change?: British Workplaces and the Future of Work.* Palgrave, 2004. Conclusions drawn from a study of 2000 British workplaces.

Abercrombie, N. *et al. Contemporary British Society.* Polity, 2000. Third edition of popular textbook.

Storey, John. *An Introductory Guide to Cultural Theory and Popular Culture.* Harvester, 1993. A very accessible book set in a British context.

Room, Adrian. *An A to Z of British Life.* OUP, 1992. A mine of information. Comprehensive and well illustrated, a useful reference source.

Giles, J. & Middleton, T. *Writing Englishness 1900–1950.* Routledge, 1996. A very useful sourcebook of traditional material relating to the construction of the concept of Englishness.

Cultural examples

Films

My Summer of Love (2004) dir. Pawel Pawlikowski. Intense prize-winning drama about a naïve Yorkshire girl and her wayward brother, when a sophisticated young woman enters their lives.

Notes on a Scandal (2006) dir. Richard Eyre. School-based drama about a lonely teacher who exploits her knowledge of a younger colleague's relationship with a pupil to gain power over her.

Educating Rita (1983) dir. Lewis Gilbert. A working-class woman, unfulfilled by life at home with her husband, tries an Open University English course and develops a strong relationship with her tutor.

Another Country (1984) dir. Marek Kanievska. Speculative drama about the claustrophobic
    public school life of two future British spies, Guy Burgess and Donald MacLean,
    played by Rupert Everett and Colin Firth.
The Browning Version (1995) dir. Mike Figgis. Remake of the Terence Rattigan play about
    a boarding-school teacher's realisation that he and his wife have led empty,
    unloving lives.
The Navigators (2001) dir. Ken Loach. Drama about privatised railway maintenance
    workers. Mocks the jargon and short cuts of the enterprise culture.
The King's Speech (2010) dir. Tom Hooper. Won best film Oscar. Typical light-hearted
    and class-ridden British period drama. An account of King George VI's struggles
    to get over his stammer.

Books

Muriel Spark *The Prime of Miss Jean Brodie* (1961). Powerful story of the effects of
    education on susceptible young people.
J. K. Rowling *Harry Potter and the Philosopher's Stone* (1997). Start of the most successful
    novel and film franchises ever produced from Britain, with numerous insights into
    British prejudices in the family and the setting of a boarding school (NB: Snape
    was the name of a famous headmaster at Eton).
Bill Bryson *Notes from a Small Island* (1996). Idiosyncratic but informed view of Britain
    offered by a then-resident American journalist with experience of British work and
    leisure.
Stuart Maconie *Pies and Prejudice* (2008). A humorous search for the 'real' north of
    England.
Shappi Korsandi *A Beginner's Guide to Acting English* (2009). The very successful Iranian
    stand-up comedienne pokes fun at culture.
Richard Askwith *Feet in the Clouds* (2005). In praise of the amateur sport of fell-running
    and its obscure heroes.

TV programmes

Boys from the Blackstuff. Sympathetic portrayal of unemployed people who work on the
    side, and their encounters with officialdom. Written by Alan Bleasdale.
Porterhouse Blue. Series set in Cambridge academe with David Jason and Ian Richardson
    – from the novel by Tom Sharpe.
Drop the Dead Donkey. Award-winning weekly comedy series set in a newspaper office.
    Written by Andy Hamilton.
Dragon's Den. Popular reality show in which entrepreneurs pitch their ideas to
    multimillionaires in hope of funding.
The Royle Family. Written by Caroline Aherne and starring Ricky Tomlinson. A couch-potato
    Salford family watch TV, eat, drink and entertain. Has won numerous awards.
The Office. Ricky Gervais's acclaimed sitcom portrays the trials of everyday white-collar
    life.

The I.T. Crowd. Written by Graham Linehan, who wrote *Father Ted.* A study of the
   workplace in the computing age.
Downton Abbey. Written by Julian Fellowes, this is the most successful British costume
   drama since the 1981 television serial version of *Brideshead Revisited.*

Websites

www.nc.uk.net
   Official site of the National Curriculum, with information about what attainment levels
   are required in each of the subject areas.
www.knowhere.co.uk
   This is an informative youth and leisure-oriented site – the antidote to Tourist
   Information.
www.stats.
   Football365.co.uk Lots of facts here for the football-obsessed.
www.its-behind-you.com
   Gives an account of the evolution of pantomime through *commedia dell'arte*, mystery
   plays and Elizabethan masques.
www.efestivals.co.uk
   An online agency containing information and booking for many UK festivals.
www.liv.ac.uk/IPM
   Institute of Popular Music at Liverpool University. Has collections and sound clips.
www.league of gentlemen.co.uk
   Website devoted to the cult television programme. Has a scrapbook and downloads
   from the first and second series.
www.youtube.co.uk
   Snapshot of people's tastes – contains invaluable footage of what is really important
   in people's cultural lives.
www.telegraph.co.uk/news/uknews/1542634/Cameron-as-leader-of-the-Slightly-Silly-
   Party.html
   Article, with photograph, about the exclusive Bullingdon club that spawned the Prime
   Minster and the Mayor of London.

Gender, sex
and the family

Roberta Garrett

Timeline

1831	Infant Custody Act
1848	Factory Act
1861	Abolition of death penalty for sodomy
1882	Married Women's Property Act
1928	Vote for women over 21
1967	Abortion made legal
1969	Divorce Reform Act (divorce by mutual consent)
1975	Sex Discrimination Act
1987	Clause 28
1993	Child Support Agency
2000	Age of gay consent lowered to 16
2004	Civil Partnerships Act
2006	Age Discrimination Act

Introduction

SINCE THE INDUSTRIAL REVOLUTION, rapidly changing employment patterns coupled with demographic and social movements have challenged the beliefs, laws and customs governing notions of family and gender. As the timeline indicates, there has been a long series of legal reforms affecting sexual behaviour, kinship structures and the social status of women.

On the one hand, these reforms were the result of progressive, humanitarian social movements such as feminism, which, in less than two hundred years, has secured rights of guardianship, property ownership, political representation and reproductive control for British women. On the other hand, protective legislation – such as the 1848 Factory Act limiting women and children to a ten-hour working day – countered the exploitation of women workers in the newly developing manufacturing industries primarily in order to ensure their allegiance to motherhood and wifely duties. In this sense, nineteenth-century parliamentary reforms went hand-in-hand with a gradual acceptance of the state's right to directly intervene in and regulate the domestic sphere. During the 1960s and 1970s 'permissive' legislation such as the legalisation of abortion, the introduction of the no-fault divorce and the decriminalisation of homosexuality have reversed this trend, reflecting the higher priority awarded to personal choice and freedom as opposed to public morality and duty. In recent years, the pendulum appears to be swinging back again, with legislation such as the Child Support Act, which enforces parental responsibilities by law, and calls to reintroduce more restrictive divorce laws.

In the twenty-first century, there will undoubtedly be further contentious reforms in legislation concerning sexual discrimination, abortion, divorce and sexual practice. All of these affect, and are in turn affected by, social attitudes and cultural activities. Their strongest impact, however, will be perceived in terms of the British family unit, and so, when looking at trends in attitudes towards gender and sex, it is here that we must begin.

The family unit

Alongside the effects of migration, there are factors pulling in opposite directions in terms of the size of the British population. While the average lifespan has increased in the UK, the British fertility rate – the expected number of children born per woman in her child-bearing years – has been steadily declining since the population boom of the immediate post-war years (Britain's was 1.82 between 2005 and 2010 according to the UN). A higher number of couples do not have children and those that do generally have smaller families. This is largely attributed to both improvements in female education and career prospects, and greater social acceptance of contraception. The average age of a first-time mother is now 29, and 32 for first-time fathers (the average age of first-time brides is now 30, and bridegrooms 32). The majority of women work outside of the home both before and after having children, regardless of marital status. Consequently, the traditional twentieth-century average British family with 2.4 children has now dwindled to 1.8: a trend which reflects the overall decline in the proportion of 'conventional' family units. The number of British households which fall into the 'two adults plus dependent children' nuclear model is only around 36 per cent and this figure includes not only married couples, but the increasing number of long-term cohabitees (who may decide not to marry for personal and ideological reasons, but also for financial ones as the average 'white' wedding in 2012 costs over £20,000).

Perhaps one of the most significant shifts over the last thirty years has been in attitudes towards marriage, which, though still popular (around 75 per cent of people marry at least once), is less so than at any previous time in British history: according to the Office of National Statistics there were a total of 231,490 marriages in 2009 (the lowest total since 1895), down from 232,990 in 2008 and continuing a downward trend since the peak of 426,241 in England and Wales in 1972. The decline in registered marriages has also been mirrored by increases in marital breakdown over the last few decades, though divorce figures have fallen every year since 2003. Divorces per thousand marriages were at an average figure of 10.5 in 2009 and UK rates are among the highest in Europe.

As a result of these changes, the number of single parent families (90 per cent of which are headed by women) has risen dramatically, comprising in 2009 one in four of all family units and generating the latest in a long line of perceived threats to the fabric of British family life. It is also feared by some that this number will increase as childbirth out of wedlock rises. The percentage of new mothers aged under 20 has also given risen to concern, standing at 44,690 (26.2 per 1,000 women) in England and Wales in 2008, while the number of girls under 16 having an abortion reached a record level of 4,376 – 4.4 per 1,000 women – during 2007.

FIGURE 3.1 Changing attitudes to motherhood (Damien Hirst's 'Virgin Mother')

If the statistics indicate a sustained decline in those living in traditional family units, these figures need to be balanced against other inter-related changes in life experience and cultural norms. For example, while the liberalisation of the divorce laws and the (albeit limited) possibility of female economic independence has undoubtedly done much to make divorce a realistic option for greater numbers of unhappy couples, the extended life expectancy of both partners is also an important contributory factor. A couple who marry in their twenties are now committing themselves to stay together for the next fifty or so years (average life expectancy is now 80), but even in 1980 the average marriage lasted only 37 years, and by 2010 that figure had fallen to 24.

Ethnicity is also an important factor in accounting for different British family structures. For example, many Vietnamese and Bengali families retain an extended family structure, while a higher than average proportion of Afro-Caribbean families are mother-led. More significantly, the relatively low proportion of 'normal' British families does not reflect the symbolic or ideological importance of the conventional family unit, which remains extremely strong despite its minority status. The two-parent, patriarchal family continues to be regarded by many as the most important of all social institutions, bearing the brunt of responsibility for producing well-adjusted, law-abiding citizens. And although the Conservatives have traditionally assumed the role of 'the party of family values', the family has increasingly occupied an elevated position within the rhetoric of all major political parties. Labour leader Tony Blair, one of Britain's longest-serving recent prime ministers, promoted himself as a family man. At 43, the youthful Prime Minister brought his school-age children to Number 10 and was the first prime minister in 150 years to father a child while in office. Blair's popular image as a relaxed, 'ordinary' dad was adopted by subsequent prime ministers Gordon Brown and David Cameron. The Labour government also established the Institute of Family and Parenting, a government-funded research body that influenced policy decision on family welfare and childcare provision. Many would argue that there has been a deliberate 'politicisiation' of family life since the late 1990s and that parents have been increasingly subject to state scrutiny and intervention. This has been accompanied by an onslaught of media stories concerning child welfare and issues such as poor diet, obesity, child neglect or over-lenient parenting. Despite the state and media preoccupation with poor parenting and the problems of family life, public discussion of the family is generally concerned with the best means of defending it and ensuring its continuation, as opposed to whether other forms of socialisation – such as communal child-rearing – might prove to be a healthier or more practical model for most people. In short, while parents are subject to much criticism, the overall desirability or legitimacy of the family itself is rarely questioned, at least within mainstream political debate.

But as with any social institution, notions of what constitutes a healthy, normal family unit vary according to contemporary cultural practices and social concerns. In the 1970s, the 'teenage bride' became the subject of much moral concern, whereas such debates since the 1990s have instead focused on the growing numbers of single mothers. It would seem that, whether young women are for or against marriage, their marital status constitutes an on-going cause of anxiety (the continued resistance to the use of Ms instead of Mrs and Miss illustrates this). In this sense, shifting conceptions of gender identity and, in particular, women's greater participation in public as opposed to domestic life, have been a key factor in generating fears about the collapse of the family throughout the last two centuries. In a similar manner, notions of the family are closely linked with debates over national identity and cultural cohesion; at all points of the political spectrum, commitment to 'the family' is frequently invoked as a source of national unity.

In attempting to understand the symbolic importance of the contemporary nuclear model, it is useful to examine its historical development. This is usually traced to the late Victorian period, when, as religious influence declined, the family took up the mantle of moral guardianship. It was expected to provide both moral guidance and social stability, or as early twentieth-century social anthropologists put it, to function as a 'nursery of citizenship'. Despite being more of a cosmopolitan dynasty than a cosy nuclear group, the British royal family swiftly came to symbolise the ideal British family unit. Even today, the Queen is sometimes referred to as 'the mother of the commonwealth', just as England, the imperial centre, was once viewed as 'the mother country'. The ideological importance of the royal family goes some way towards explaining why the spate of acrimonious partings and scandals blighting the Queen's children have been such a cause of consternation within the UK, and why the wedding of Prince William to the commoner Kate Middleton in 2011 was not only socially significant for many people, but symbolically important for the status of marriage.

Given this weight of expectations, it is not surprising that the family, as an institution, seems always to be in crisis. Nevertheless, while fears of its erosion are often exaggerated and vary according to cultural context, there is no doubt that the last forty years have been a particularly turbulent period in the history of family structure and gender roles. To consider these transformations in more detail, this chapter will next examine the changing status of British women and then move on to look more broadly at attitudes towards marriage, parenting and sexuality.

Gender and British institutions

Despite the strength and longevity of the British women's movement, many traditional British institutions remain remarkably male-dominated, although this is slowly beginning to change. We can start to examine both institutionalised sexism and the attempts to challenge it, by looking at predominately male institutions such as the political and legal systems and the Church of England. The culture of Westminster is often likened to that of a boy's public school, and this perspective was reinforced when, in 2010, 16 out of 29 Cabinet members appointed in the new Conservative–Liberal government had attended public – also known as 'independent' – schools, even though more than 90 per cent of people in the UK have attended publicly funded state schools (despite the name, English and Welsh 'public schools' are privately funded). In 2010, there were also only four female appointments to the Cabinet (home secretary Theresa May, environment chief Caroline Spelman, Wales secretary Cheryl Gillan and Conservative Party chairman Baroness Warsi) and for the first time in 13 years there were no openly gay Cabinet members.

Not only are there very few female Members of Parliament but the House of Commons thrives on an atmosphere of masculine combat. Heckling, jeering and the routine exchange of insults are part of the daily proceedings, such that there are regular calls for a ban on name-calling and an emphasis on 'mature' debate (only a very few insulting words, such as 'liar', are not allowed, and so not heard, in the House).

For aspiring female members, the macho culture of Westminster is a minor problem compared with that of getting elected, or even selected to stand, in the first place. Not surprisingly, local constituency executives nominate the candidate with the best chance of getting elected, which, given the age-old prejudices of both sexes, is less likely to be a woman. Of course, there are always notable exceptions. Margaret Thatcher's eleven-year reign proved that a female leader could be quite as confrontational and bloody-minded as any man. During her years in office, Thatcher was frequently described as both 'the best man for the job' and 'the Iron Lady', perhaps indicating the degree of unease and confusion produced by the presence of a female leader in a traditional male enclave (the satirical puppet show *Spitting Image* emphasised this by always showing her using a men's toilet). As it made her the first female British prime minister, Thatcher's election was of symbolic importance, although it may be noted that the overall number of female MPs fell during her term in office and that she herself was outspoken in her opposition to women's rights. Thatcher's appointment was shortly followed by another, no less historic female appointment, when Betty Boothroyd was made the first woman to occupy the powerful position of House of Commons Speaker – the arbiter of Commons debate.

Of the major political parties, Labour has the strongest commitment to, and historical identification with, feminist politics. Recent party initiatives have aimed to counter discrimination by promoting a high number of women to power-positions within the party (such as the shadow cabinet) and devising all-women electoral shortlists for some constituencies. These policies have aroused much controversy, for while many think it necessary to take positive action to achieve equal political representation, others have argued that the policies undermine the achievements of the women they favour. Furthermore, Labour's pro-feminist sympathies have never guaranteed the largest share of the female vote. In fact, the Conservative Party's endorsement of strong law-and-order policies, combined with a commitment to traditional family values appeals to a higher proportion of (particularly older) female voters.

The British legal system is one of the country's oldest, most traditionalist institutions. As such, it is often accused of gender bias in terms of proceedings, sentences and professional opportunities. Although women are now entering the legal profession in ever increasing numbers (half of all British law students are female), they are less likely to reach the top of their profession, more often becoming solicitors than higher-ranked and (generally) better-paid barristers. There are few British female QCs (senior barristers, members of the Queen's Council) and even fewer female judges. It is therefore less surprising that the judiciary has come in for particularly harsh condemnation regarding its attitudes towards sexual assaults and other forms of violence against women. British judges have been accused of letting rapists off lightly and apportioning an inexcusable degree of blame to female victims. Indeed, one of the main reasons that so few sexual assaults are reported in the UK is that women feel anxious that they, and not their attacker, will be made morally, if not legally, culpable for the crime. This fear is exacerbated by well-publicised comments made by prominent members of the judiciary concerning the clothing style and sexual history of victims. Another contentious issue has been that of domestic violence. Again, the judiciary have been condemned for showing leniency towards men who perpetrate it and little sympathy with women who retaliate. In response, women's groups have mounted lengthy campaigns for the release of women convicted of killing violent, abusive husbands arguing that even in cases in which the death was premeditated, years of persistent abuse amounted to provocation, and thus could not be regarded as cold-blooded murder. Interestingly, these campaigns have proved largely ineffective, and in 2011 when he appeared on radio to defend government plans to halve sentences for criminals who pleaded guilty early, the justice secretary Ken Clarke faced calls to resign after suggesting that date rape is not always 'rape'.

On 11 November 1992 the General Synod of the Church of England voted in favour of the ordination of women priests. This decision was the result of over a century of struggle on the part of women's rights campaigners, and ended a lengthy and divisive battle within the Church. The initial demand for female ordination began in the late nineteenth century as part of the first wave of the British feminist movement. As a result of this pressure, the Church of England created the somewhat ambiguous order of 'deaconess', which entitled women to preside over certain rituals, but was not regarded as part of the holy triumvirate of bishops, priests and deacons. The Church of England did not permit women deacons until as late as 1987, by which time Anglican churchwomen in Canada and the US had been taking the priesthood for around ten years. In this respect, the Church of England was somewhat out of kilter with other branches of the Anglican Church, and indeed the British public at large, 80 per cent of whom had been in favour of the ordination of women for some time. The fiercest clerical opposition to female ordination came, not surprisingly, from the Church's influential Anglo-Catholic wing, many of whom either renounced the priesthood altogether or converted to Catholicism when the decision was announced.

However, in 2006, researchers claimed that the Church of England would struggle in the future without women priests, when English church census figures showed that half of priests ordained in recent years were women.

Women and employment

Probably the most important factor in the transformation of British gender identities has been the long-term and seemingly irreversible trend towards female participation in the paid labour force.

Women continued to enter the labour force in ever-increasing numbers in the last 100 years, but many fears have been voiced about changing gender roles and a perceived deterioration of family life. Women's paid employment may be an accepted fact of modern life, but it is still regarded by many as an undesirable one. In the first half of the twentieth century, government policy reflected the widely held view that the female population constituted a reserve labour force, only to be drawn on in times of dire necessity. During the First World War, the vast numbers of women who were encouraged to enter the labour force had to fight bitterly to achieve the same wage as their male counterparts, a privilege granted to women workers during the Second World War, in which, for the first time, state-run nurseries were also provided. But, like the previous generation of women war workers, they were expected to relinquish both their jobs and their state childcare facilities during peacetime.

The immediate post-war period saw a forceful reassertion of traditional roles; women were enticed back into the home as sociologists and psychologists warned of the dangers of maternal deprivation caused by the working mother's absence. Fears concerning the welfare of so-called 'latch-key kids' (those who had no mother to greet them from school) reinforced the notion that children could not be properly cared for without a home-based mother, heightening public hostility towards such women. From then on there have been many media scare stories about the poor treatment of children in daycare or the negative effects on the behaviour of young children in nurseries (such as increased aggression), but evidence is rarely consistent or conclusive, and surveys that find positive, rather than negative, effects attached to childcare for young children tend to receive far less publicity, indicating a continuing social prejudice against working mothers. In the 1980s the emerging stereotype of the high-earning, confident 'career' woman fuelled a new wave of antagonism towards working mothers. Maternal employment, something that has always existed, tends to be more

FIGURE 3.2 Memorial to the role women played in the war

FIGURE 3.3 The annual Poppy appeal

easily accepted if it is associated with poorer, less educated women doing unskilled work out of necessity. As women's educational and employment possibilities have increased, female aspirations have been raised, and there is greater acceptance of the idea that married women, even mothers, might choose to work because they wish to be financially independent or seek to contribute to society and find fulfilment in activities that aren't confined to the traditional feminine sphere of home and family. However, this is still disapproved of by many, who accuse such women of greedily wanting to 'have it all' rather than choosing between a career and a family. As many women have pointed out, such attitudes expose a continuing double standard whereby the normal male expectation of enjoying both a career and a family is viewed as selfish and unreasonable if desired by a woman. Allison Pearson's comic novel *I Don't Know How She Does It* (made into a film in 2011) addresses the theme of a high-earning professional woman attempting to 'juggle' family and career. Although the novel is sympathetic to the problems of working mothers, heroine Kate Reddy resolves the difficulties of combining these roles by abandoning her banking career to focus more energy on her family rather than questioning the unfairness of the double standard. The idea that women must adapt and compromise rather than calling for a fairer distribution of childcare and housework is also reflected by the growing numbers of what the media have approvingly dubbed 'mumtrepreneurs': mothers who give up professional jobs to start a home-based business in order to cause the least disruption to family life. The few mumtrepreneurs that succeed are applauded for being economically productive while still being available for the school run – but the reality for most is less rosy. The failure rate for all small businesses is extremely high and the energy and commitment required to make them succeed equals or exceeds that of any demanding career, thus putting even greater strain on mothers. The fantasy of the successful mumtrepreneur brings together the celebration of enterprise culture fuelled by television shows such as *The Apprentice* and the new emphasis on intensive parenting, but it still leaves most women struggling to balance contradictory roles, and it seems likely that the demand for greater participation from fathers and better, cheaper childcare will resurface with even greater force and urgency as the long-term increase in women's employment continues to rise. This began in the late 1950s and has continued to increase in every decade since, though with a much greater emphasis on part-time work in comparison with men. Shifts in patterns of employment, particularly the expansion of secretarial, administrative and clerical occupations in the 1960s and 1970s, and the rapid growth of the service sector since the 1980s, have opened up new areas of female employment. Today, over two-thirds of women aged 15–64 in Britain are in work, and in 2010, an analysis of official figures revealed that the number of men of working age with jobs had slumped from 92 per cent in 1971 to 75 per cent, while the number of employed women had risen from 56 to 69 per cent as the service sector had flourished.

Coupled with the demise of heavy industry, and a subsequent drop in the male-dominated areas of unskilled manual work, for the first time ever, the balance has tipped towards an almost evenly divided male and female British labour force. Moreover, there is a marked difference in the composition of the female labour force: in the first half of the twentieth century the majority of working women were either young and single or middle-aged with grown children, whereas the greatest increase in recent decades has been amongst those with partners and dependants. Also, in the last 15 years the proportion of mothers working part time has remained fairly constant, but the proportion working full time has risen from 23 per cent in 1996 to 29 per cent in 2011.

But these statistics can be misleading: British women are still far from achieving equality in the workplace. Despite the legacy of hard-won women's rights legislation, such as the Equal Pay Act (1970) and Sex Discrimination Act (1975), women are still earning just under 80 per cent of men's pay (e.g. a 2007 report found that three times as many male as female graduates earn top salaries within three years of leaving universities). In practice, equal-pay legislation is difficult to enforce and discrimination hard to prove. Women are still much more likely to be discriminated against on grounds of age or physical attractiveness, although, clearly, employers are no longer able to openly specify gender in a job description. The affix 'man' – as in postman, salesman, fireman – has either been replaced by 'person' (salesperson) or dropped completely (firefighter).

It is also the case that a number of women are now working in previously male-dominated areas, but sex segregation persists. Female employees tend to be heavily concentrated in non-unionised, unskilled areas of work, with an overwhelming majority (81 per cent) working in service industries (e.g. as cleaners, waitresses, bar and hotel staff). The catering industry, for example, relies largely on part-time and casual labour; precisely the kind of low-paid, low-status, 'pink collar' occupations, that women with small children and limited childcare assistance are often forced into accepting. But even predominantly female skilled occupations – such as secretarial or administrative work – tend to command less pay and status by virtue of their 'feminine' associations. Probably the most serious example is that of British nurses, who earn less than those in most other parts of western Europe, chiefly because nursing is still viewed in this country more as an extension of woman's natural 'caring' role than as a skilled profession. In addition, there is little evidence to suggest that women's increased participation in the labour force has been accompanied by a corresponding shift in domestic responsibilities. Working women continue to do the major share of housework, child-rearing and caring for elderly relatives. Surprisingly, this rule often applies in situations where women are the primary earners. Studies of areas of high male unemployment, such as Wearside in the post-industrial north-east, show a rise in stay-at-home husbands and working wives. But they also indicate that while husbands are prepared to perform 'light' domestic duties (such as shopping and cooking) they still draw the line at cleaning and other 'menial' domestic tasks. In 2011 a survey of housework and childcare patterns conducted by Oxford academics reported that on average women spend over four hours a day on housework and childcare while for men it was only around two and a half hours; this figure persisted regardless of how much the women and men worked. In short, although the gap in male and female childcare and housework duties is narrowing, traditional gender identities are proving hard to change.

As we might expect, female employment opportunities are also heavily influenced by other factors, such as region, class and race. For example, although a higher than average number of Afro-Caribbean women go on to further education, levels of unemployment within this ethnic grouping are significantly greater than among their white female counterparts. Predictably, the greatest career gains have been made by white, middle-class, university-educated women, who are now beginning to make significant inroads into previously male-dominated professions such as law and medicine. But the gender pay gap exists across the piece and in 2007 the

Office of National Statistics (ONS) reported that the percentage gap between the average hourly pay for men and women stood at 17.2 per cent, and the Institute of Directors reported that pay for female directors was 22 per cent lower than their male counterparts.

All in all, employment opportunities for British women certainly exceed those of previous generations, but they are still far from equal with those of British men. Nevertheless, if the reality of women's employment opportunity is not as progressive as it is often assumed to be, this does not diminish its impact in terms of cultural representation and notions of female identity. British advertising and television now represent women in a much wider spectrum of roles than just girlfriend, wife or mother. Since the 1980s, there has been an abundance of television programmes featuring women in traditionally male or 'high-powered' professional jobs. These can be seen as presenting new role models or as adding a new twist to well-worn fictional formulas such as the police procedural or hospital drama series.

Perhaps as a result of these images, young women now have far greater expectations than ever before. A recent study of British teenage girls revealed that many now confidently expect to have both a successful career and a family, although given present working conditions, they are unlikely to achieve both these aims.

Marriage and divorce

Prior to the implementation of the 1969 Divorce Reform Act, a legal separation required a guilty party. Adultery was by far the most frequently cited reason and the 'wronged' wife or husband had to provide evidence that an affair had taken place. Not surprisingly, this emphasis on moral culpability heightened any existing bitterness between parties, as lurid details were dragged out in court. In fact, when divorce became available through mutual agreement (albeit after a five-year separation, later reduced to two years) the majority of British private detective agencies went out of business as a result. From that point onwards divorce rates have soared, causing many to argue for stricter divorce laws.

This view was widely endorsed by the Conservative government in the early 1990s, who launched a 'moral crusade' popularly known as the 'back to basics' campaign. This initiative implored the public to stand firm in their commitment to marriage and family life, but was discredited by the disclosure of a string of sex scandals involving prominent MPs. From then on the phrase 'back to basics' became almost synonymous with sexual hypocrisy and corruption. The new Labour government, in office between 1997–2010, abolished tax breaks for married couples, but the current

Conservative-led coalition government is planning to reintroduce financial incentives to stay married, to reflect their commitment to the institution.

Those who uphold the sanctity of marriage view Britain's divorce rate as an indictment of its commitment-shy national culture: divorced people are sometimes castigated as selfish and fickle, putting their needs above those of their children. On the other hand, while few regard it positively, many agree that it is unfair to force miserable couples to stay together. From whichever viewpoint, it is clear that while a high percentage of the population continue to marry, people's expectations of what this entails are vastly different from those of their parents.

Until the late nineteenth century, British women, unlike those in Islamic or Hindu societies, were required to relinquish all property rights upon marriage. Divorce was virtually unheard of among anyone except the upper classes. Nevertheless, it was still more easily accessible to men, who had only to establish that adultery had taken place. A wife needed proof of adultery plus desertion, bigamy, incest or cruelty to divorce her husband. It was not until 1923 that women and men could bring a divorce suit on the same grounds, and women were denied a share of the ex-husband's income until as late as the mid-1960s. Given that many had no independent means of support, divorce was clearly not an attractive or realistic prospect for large numbers of women. Even today, a woman's credit rating usually drops following a divorce while the reverse is true for her ex-husband. But in spite of this disparity, by far the majority of divorces are instigated by women, who are also much less likely to marry again. In part, the higher divorce rate is therefore an inevitable consequence of women's increased financial autonomy, but it also corresponds to more general shifts in the structure of the family and the relative importance attached to the heterosexual couple.

At least until the mid-twentieth century, the dominant form of family structure was extended rather than nuclear, with parents and even grandparents, uncles and aunts living in close proximity to their grown-up children. It was also considered normal for women and men to inhabit quite different worlds in terms of both work and social activities. Due to the increased geographical and social mobility of the population, this often romanticised family unit has gradually disappeared and is now found mainly in soap operas based in traditional working-class communities: Albert Square in 'cockney' soap *EastEnders* is a good example, although there is some indication that rising house prices and childcare costs are reintroducing some aspects of the extended family, as many young people cannot afford to buy property until they have worked for a considerable number of years and couples with young children struggle to afford childcare, many adults are becoming dependent on their relatively prosperous 'baby boomer' parents for accommodation in young adulthood or free childcare when they start their own families.

One consequence of the decline of the extended family has been the emergence of stronger adult friendship networks, a development explored in popular British films and television shows such as *Peter's Friends*, *Four Weddings and a Funeral*, *Bridget Jones's Diary* and *Happy Go Lucky*, and television shows such as *Cold Feet* and *Coupling*. Another has been the emergence of a more 'companionable' idea of marriage. Within the contemporary companionate model, mutual respect, emotional fulfilment and shared 'quality time' have, at least in theory, replaced the old model, which assumed separate spheres and female dependence.

But if higher expectations and better alternatives have done much to increase the divorce rate, the financial incentives to marry are also not what they used to be. Over the last 15 years, tax relief for married couples has been gradually reduced. Meanwhile, unemployed married people are disqualified from certain state benefits if their partners are in work. This also applies to cohabitees, but clearly it is rather more difficult to establish their domestic arrangements. As one in two children is now born out of wedlock, several proposals have been put forward to further extend the legal rights of long-term cohabitees, though plans for no-cause divorces met with stiff opposition.

FIGURE 3.4 Families eat out

Parenting

There has undoubtedly been a rejection of the often harsh child-rearing methods favoured in the UK a century ago. Indeed, the emotional and physical wellbeing of children is a constant source of political and media concern. Despite this, a UNICEF survey in 2011 found British children to be the least happy in the developed world. This was largely related to the economic pressures placed on parents and the culture of long working hours in the UK, although the disintegration of the extended family and the trend towards 'micromanaging' children's lives, with little independent outdoor play and much pressure on parents to provide a full programme of extra-curricular activities, also seems a likely causal factor. Childcare is also among the most expensive in Europe. The Labour government expanded state-funded nursery provision in the late 1990s and all three-year-olds are now entitled to either a morning or afternoon session five days a week, but this still leaves parents funding childcare for much of the working day (and all week for younger infants). Although the current prime minster, David Cameron, launched his election campaign with the idea of the community-oriented ' big society' the reality for British parents is a double-whammy of little state provision and social support coupled with higher expectations of their role in educating and providing for their children. Yet, at the same time, the family is revered and the popular media are dominated by debates about the falling standard of British parenting. We can begin to consider this paradox by focusing on two particularly contentious issues: first, the increase in single parent households and second, children's exposure to violence both within the family and as depicted in forms of popular entertainment.

In the 1990s, arguments raged over Britain's high proportion of single-parent families when a government minister claimed that an over-generous state benefit system was encouraging young, single mothers to 'marry the state' and embark on a 'benefit career'. This controversial statement came shortly after suggestions that teenage girls were becoming pregnant chiefly in order to secure scarce local authority housing. At the heart of this issue was not only the assumption that many young women preferred not to work, but the fear that rather than becoming single mothers through male abandonment – and thus becoming worthy recipients of state support – young women were actually choosing to live without men, in communities of single mothers. In order to lower the tax burden and reinstate traditional family values, the Conservative government considered developing a system (already operating in some parts of the US) whereby single mothers are penalised for the birth of a second or third child.

The stereotype of the benefit scrounger mother is commonly invoked in the media. For example, the popular comedy show *Little Britain* fleshed out this derogatory 'pramface' stereotype in the figure of Vicky Pollard, a

FIGURE 3.5 Ice skating at Christmas is a communal and family activity

workshy, obese and confrontational teenage girl who swaps one of her many offspring for a *Westlife* CD. A more disturbing example of this prejudice was manifested in the coverage of the case of Shannon Matthews, a 10-year-old girl who disappeared from her home in the Dewsbury, a poor area of West Yorkshire, in 2008. The case followed the high profile media campaign to find missing toddler Madeleine McCann, but it was later revealed to be a hoax concocted by Shannon's mother, Karen Matthews, with the help of her boyfriend and his brother (who had been concealing the missing child). Although the local parenting community knew nothing of the crime and did everything to assist the police search, the case was viewed as indicative of the cruel treatment of children among communities of workless single parents. In response to these attacks, groups such as the Association of Single Parents swiftly pointed out that although many single parents rely on state subsidies, this results from difficulties in finding a decent enough job to cover childcare expenses, rather than a disinclination to work. In addition to this, it was revealed that two-thirds of lone parents had become so through divorce or separation rather than choice, and that far from enjoying a high standard of living at the tax-payers expense, as many as 75 per cent were surviving below the official poverty line (by 2010 this had reduced to 50 per cent as half of all people in lone parent families were reported as receiving a low income, still more than twice the rate for couples with children). Due to these and other criticisms, plans to cut benefit for single parents have been shelved.

On the whole the behaviour of fathers is subject to much less criticism and scrutiny than mothers. While single mothers are stereotyped in a number of unflattering ways, the few men who take on primary care of their children are regarded with intense admiration (a good example of this in popular representation is the 2011 television series *Single Father*, which sympathetically depicted a man struggling to cope after he is widowed and left with young children).

However, fathers who become estranged from their children after divorce are a very different matter. Another explosive parenting debate arose over the establishment of the Child Support Agency (followed by the more aggressively named Child Maintenance and Enforcement Commission). This government-funded body was set up to fix maintenance payments and pursue absent fathers after the discovery that fewer than one in three were supporting their children. The agency soon came under fire for fixing payment rates at an unrealistically high level, often destroying amicable agreements in the process. Critics also argued that the agency was more concerned with raising the payments of those who were already contributing rather than finding those who were not. The furore intensified after the occurrence of two well-publicised suicide cases, in which financial stress caused by the agency's demands was thought to be a contributory factor. Eventually, a House of Commons Select Committee was formed to review the workings of the agency. Stricter guidelines were introduced to ensure that fathers were left with sufficient funds to live on and, as was often the case, support second families.

While the single parent and Child Support Agency controversies highlighted the financial responsibilities attached to being a parent, there has also been a growing awareness of the widespread extent of child abuse and the long-term psychological effects on its victims. This has led to much debate concerning the difference between legitimate expressions of parental authority and malicious ill treatment. For example, many thought that a poster campaign run by the Royal Society for the Prevention of Cruelty to Children went too far in emphasising the damaging effects of verbal as well as physical abuse. Questions have also been raised as to how far the state is entitled to intervene in family life, leaving the social services to tread a dangerous path between accusations of unnecessary and disruptive interference and negligence.

One of the most serious debates about British parenting arose in 1993, after two-year-old James Bulger was abducted from a shopping centre in Bootle, Merseyside and murdered by two 11-year-old boys. Not surprisingly, the horrifying case caused a national outcry and much attention was given to seeking an explanation for the boys' behaviour. While a good deal of blame was apportioned to the two boys' parents, questions were also raised as to what extent the murder reflected a rising tide of British violence and how far this could be traced to the corrosive influence of violent, American 'video nasty' imports. A study authorised in the wake of the Bulger case by the Commission on Children and Violence found that the key determinants linking young, violent offenders were parental abuse and poverty rather than excessive exposure to television or cinema violence. One of the more positive results of debates on child abuse was the organisation of a twenty-four-hour free-of-charge phone counselling service for distressed children and teenagers – the national Childline – which began in 1993.

The Bulger case remained high profile, and the release from prison of the two boys in 2001 was met with howls of protest from, among others, the family and friends of James Bulger. The vehemence of the reaction from sections of the community meant that the boys were given new identities and police protection once they returned into society, but the furore returned when one of the boys was re-imprisoned for possession and distribution of indecent images of children in 2010. Also introduced that year was a Vetting and Barring Scheme, requiring the registration by law of anyone who has 'regular' or 'intense' contact with children or vulnerable adults. This followed recommendations after the high-profile inquiry into the murders by college caretaker Ian Huntley of Holly Wells and Jessica Chapman in 2002. The requirement to sign up to the new scheme caused an outcry among children's authors who regularly attended schools to read to pupils. Philip Pullman, author of the 'His Dark Materials' series, complained 'Why should I pay £64 to a government agency to give me a little certificate to say I'm not a paedophile? Children are abused in the home, not in classes of 30 or groups of 200 in the assembly hall with teachers looking on.'

In the first decade of the new century, the issue of paedophilia had become the subject of major concern from the moment the government came under pressure in 2001 to release its published list of 'sex offenders,' as many parents demanded the right to know if paedophiles were living in their area. The issue was brought to a head when many ex-offenders were attacked in their homes and the assaults spread to the extent that a paediatrician was attacked by a group of people who misunderstood the meaning of the word. Subsequently, in July 2001, an edition of the satirical Channel 4 mock news-programme *Brass Eye* called 'Paedogeddon!' caused a national debate over media representations of paedophilia, liberals defending the show as an attack on glib 'investigative' reporting that in fact sensationalised issues such as paedophilia and titillated viewers, while reactionary quarters, especially *The Daily Mail*, demanded that the programme's maker, Chris Morris, be prosecuted. Because the programme focused on what is currently the most controversial aspect of contemporary British morality, it met with almost hysterical responses from the press, charities, politicians and also sections of the media, its target. A home office minister, Beverley Hughes, was com-pelled to condemn the programme on national radio, even though she had to admit she had not seen it. As a result of increased public concern, the Sexual Offences Act was introduced in 2003 to replace older sexual offences laws and contained more specific and explicit wording, as well as adding new offences such as non-consensual voyeurism and causing a child to watch sexual activity. It also created the 'sex offenders register', a database of offenders and others required to register with the police, officially called the Violent and Sex Offender Register (ViSOR).

Philip Pullman was also one of the 200 teachers, academics, authors, charity leaders and other experts who wrote a letter to the *Daily Telegraph* newspaper in 2011 calling for measures to 'interrupt the erosion of child-hood'. This was a follow-up to a letter the group had written to the news-paper in 2006 berating the way in which they perceived early testing in school, advertising, bad childcare, and a reliance on computer games and television to be enticing children into growing up too quickly. The 2006 letter led to an investigation into the state of childhood by the Children's Society, but the group of 200 experts argued that the process has proceeded apace since 2006 rather than abated in any way.

Sexuality and identity

The British are famed for both their prurience and their sexual reserve, a stereotype which, though exploited within many British cultural forms (Merchant–Ivory 'heritage' cinema, for example), probably derives less from contemporary cultural attitudes than from England's former role in the global imposition of repressive middle-class norms and values. It is true that British censorship laws are still stricter than many other European states, and that the UK is one of the few countries in which a government minister will be forced to resign over a minor sex scandal. But in other respects attitudes are fairly liberal. The shift towards so-called 'permissiveness' is associated with 'swinging London', the explosion of British youth culture and the legalisation of homosexuality, abortion, birth control and divorce reform in the 1960s. The Obscene Publications trial of 1960, in which it was finally decided that D. H. Lawrence's sexually explicit but critically acclaimed novel, *Lady Chatterley's Lover*, would be made available to the British public, is generally regarded as something of a watershed, dividing prudish 'Victorian' Britain from permissive, contemporary Britain.

However, while the majority of permissive legislative reforms date from the 1960s (when registered marriages actually increased) the social effect of this legislation was not really felt until the 1970s, and even 1980s, by which time permissiveness had begun to acquire a pejorative meaning, denoting the collapse of moral authority and the traditional family unit. Aside from concerns about single mothers, absentee fathers and rising divorce rates, the backlash against permissiveness was given a new impetus by the AIDS crisis, with much attention focused on the British gay community.

Britain's first official AIDS-related death, that of Terrence Higgins, occurred in 1982 and led to the establishment of what remains Britain's biggest AIDS/HIV education and advice service, the Terrence Higgins Trust. The early years of the crisis produced a wave of anti-gay hysteria, exacerbated by the popular press, who were quick to wrongly identify AIDS as an exclusively homosexual 'plague'. Many British newspapers actually went so far as to support such draconian measures as the recriminalisation of sodomy or the forced quarantine of those suffering from the disease. For example, speculating on the predicted growth in HIV infection, Auberon Waugh's knowingly provocative 1985 *Daily Telegraph* column asked why 'No one has mentioned what might seem the most obvious way of cutting down this figure (of one million by 1990) – by repealing the Sexual Offences Act of 1967 and making sodomy a criminal offence once again.' British rates of infection have not reached these initial predictions, and in the twenty-first century such attitudes as those implied by Waugh's speculation are less common, though this is perhaps because the discussion of AIDS has been in the background in recent years, not least because sex has become the essential ingredient of any marketing campaign. Surveys continue to indicate that while 'safe' sexual practices have been widely adopted within the gay community since the mid-1980s, the majority of heterosexuals do not regard themselves as significantly at risk, despite the fact that new cases of HIV remain higher than they ever were in the twentieth century and reached a high of 7,837 in 2005 (double the figure for the year 2000). Furthermore, the climate of homophobia created by the initial burst of AIDS scare-stories did much to undermine growing acceptance of the gay community. In

Britain, it has never been illegal to actually be a homosexual, only to participate in homosexual acts, while lesbianism has not been recognised by the law, supposedly because Queen Victoria refused to acknowledge its existence.

Following the 1967 Sexual Offences Act, which decriminalised homosexual activities in England and Wales (extended to Scotland in 1980 and Northern Ireland in 1979), a lively gay and lesbian subculture flourished in urban areas of England. Soho, for example, famous for its gay-owned shops, pubs, clubs and cafes, has become one of London's biggest nightlife attractions. Moreover, the widespread media adoption of the word 'gay', a term denoting positive self-identification, as opposed to 'homosexual' or more pejorative terms, suggested a growing acknowledgement of gay identity as an alternative lifestyle choice, rather than just a sexual preference. The growing acceptance of gay lifestyles has been apparent on television, from the first 'lesbian kiss' broadcast in *Brookside*, through the huge popularity of the drama serial *Queer as Folk*, to the winning of the second series of Big Brother by a gay man in 2001 and the ubiquity of the catchphrase 'I am the only gay in the village' from *Little Britain*. More importantly, in September 2001 the first ceremonies for gay couples were begun in London, which started a civil register of gay partnerships. These 'pacts' had no legal status but were ceremonies conducted by an approved Greater London Authority officer. Gay rights groups hoped the ceremonies would lead to legislation to confer on homosexual couples the same legal rights as married people and in 2004 the Civil Partnership Act gave same-sex couples rights and responsibilities identical to marriage. The Gender Recognition Act 2004 of the same year finally allowed transsexual people to change their legal gender after gender reassignment.

The Gay Pride march, now so well established that it is referred to simply as 'Pride', has helped to make London one of the gay capitals of the world. This is supported by the tourist industry, which is less concerned with gay rights than with attracting the 'pink' pound. Ranging from 'professional' pressure groups like Stonewall to more militant organisations such as Act Up (Aids Coalition to Unleash Power) and Outrage (who sometimes adopt the term 'queer' to distinguish themselves from more moderate, assimilationist gay groups), there has been a resurgence of British gay activism. Two specific issues – that of the age of gay consent, and that of the forced exposure or 'outing' of homosexuals and lesbians – have commanded particularly high levels of public interest and will be examined in turn.

Initiatives to bring the gay age of consent (which was 21) in line with that applied to heterosexuals (16) was part of a broader gay equality package drafted by the Stonewall group, and inspired by the European Union's social charter commitment to ending all forms of discrimination. An uneasy compromise was reached in February 1993 when the homosexual age of consent was changed to 18, but it was finally lowered to 16 in November 2000. At the other end of the spectrum, groups such as the Faggots Rooting Out Closet Sexuality Group (FROCS) adopted the more controversial tactic of outing allegedly gay public figures – specifically those perceived to have lent their support to discriminatory practices. Outing is often associated with the exposure of pop stars and media celebrities, but in Britain (if not in the US), gay outing groups tend to target more establishment figures, such as eminent clergymen or members of Parliament. This has to be distinguished from the routine exposure of gay media celebrities more commonly practised by the tabloid press, who are also, ironically, almost unanimous in their opposition to 'political' outing. For example, in 2001, Michael Portillo was undermined by press and politicians when he ran for leadership of the Conservative Party: most people believed him to be the front runner for the office but his campaign was perhaps damaged for some members of the party by allegations of homosexual acts. However, Portillo was in no sense politically ruined by the allegations, as his career would once have been, and a particularly vicious, homophobic press campaign can often generate a good deal of public sympathy for its victim. Britain has a long tradition of camp male entertainers, joined in recent years by television 'personalities' such as Gok Wan, Graham Norton or Alan Carr. Such entertainers both exploit and critique gay stereotypes, but the relative lack of openly gay figures who do not embrace their 'novelty' status indicates that the British public still struggle to accept gay men and women as a normal part of everyday life.

British attitudes towards homosexuality and lesbianism have to be considered in relation to the overall political climate. The AIDS crisis increased prejudice, but current attitudes appear to be much more tolerant than before. Among younger age groups in particular, the distinctions between gay and straight culture are more blurred than ever. Gay male dress codes have been widely adopted by heterosexual men, and gay clubs are now more mixed in terms of both gender and sexual orientation.

If gender roles are learnt first and foremost within the family, they are reinforced or challenged in our choice of social activities and leisure pursuits. Indeed, if the family is less central to most people's lives today, these may provide a greater source of identification. One of the clearest indications of the collapse of polarised gender identities is the slow decline of exclusively male or female British institutions such as the Women's Institute (WI) or the working men's club. Although it is often dismissed as a backward-looking, traditionalist organisation, the WI was formed in 1915 with the intention of informing and broadening the horizons of housewives, many of whom, at that time, received little or no conventional education. In fact, many of the Institute's early philanthropic patrons, such as the first chairperson, Lady Denman, were inspired by the first feminist movement. But as women's educational and career opportunities have increased, the Institute has come to be associated with one particular aspect of its work: the appreciation and preservation of traditional 'feminine' crafts such as cookery and needlepoint. Clearly, as the majority of women now work, not only do they have less time to devote to pursuing home-based crafts, but these have become less important as an indication of gender identity. Consequently, membership has fallen from 500,000 in its heyday in the late 1950s and early 1960s to the contemporary figure of 207,000 in 2011. The WI is still involved in raising awareness of contemporary women's health issues, such as breast cancer, or environmental risks to children, but as membership is largely drawn from the over-50s age group and the institute has little appeal for younger women it looks set to fade away in time. Its most high-profile moment this century came when Tony Blair was given a slow handclap in 2000 by a WI meeting because he used the occasion to discuss general policy issues, which the largely conservative gathering believed were not addressed to them but to members of the press in attendance. The television sitcom *Jam & Jerusalem* is centered on a local WI and takes its title from the hobby and hymn most associated with the movement.

Like the Women's Institute, the formation of working men's clubs harks back to a period in which male identity (particularly that of working-class men) was primarily constituted through the kinds of manual trades and blue-collar occupations which have receded in the post-war period. With 2,200 affiliated working men's clubs in Britain, working men's clubs are still popular, mainly for group and leisure activities. But most have evolved into mixed social clubs and are now only tenuously linked to the workplace. Only 2 per cent exclude women from the premises, although they are barred from participating in organisational responsibilities in many more and like the WI the clubs now appeal to older people.

The health and fitness culture that has flourished in Britain over the last 20 years has also opened up a new range of cross-gender leisure activities. Women are still less likely to compete in team sports and tend to favour fitness classes, but activities such as running, swimming and weight training are becoming increasingly popular with both sexes. The gym, once a strictly male domain, is now frequented by almost equal numbers of men and women. Furthermore, while it is often maintained that women's participation in fitness activities is motivated by vanity and men's by health concerns, there is much evidence to suggest that British men are becoming increasingly preoccupied with appearance, styling and body-shape. This can be understood as part of a more general shift in perceptions of British male identity. British men have often been characterised, perhaps unfairly, as badly dressed and proudly indifferent to common standards of style, taste and personal grooming. In the 1980s, the expansion and diversification of the menswear retailing industry, coupled with a growth in men's skincare products, revolutionised attitudes towards British masculinity that in the new century have created a new norm in which moisturising and man bags seeming entirely normal male metrosexual behaviour to the majority. The new ranges of fashion and beauty products targeted at men have led to more sexualised male images circulating in advertising and in what is now an established market of men's fashion and lifestyle magazines, such as *Esquire*.

At other times such images may have carried distinctly gay connotations, but their contemporary appeal is ambivalently cross-gender. As a result of these developments, British men have finally been cajoled into spending a greater proportion of their leisure time engaged in that most 'feminine' of activities, shopping, which now takes up a fair proportion of leisure time for both sexes, augmenting more traditional male activities, such as Saturday afternoon football.

Conclusion

Today, the British population comprises 51 per cent female and 49 per cent male subjects. However, the higher numbers of women are heavily concentrated in the over-65 age group and do not reflect the gender composition of the population as a whole. Recent studies also suggest that male life expectancy is catching up (it is currently about five years lower) and that over the century this imbalance is likely to be reversed in favour of men. Such predictions may be altered if all parents in the future are allowed, as some argue they should be, the right to choose the sex of their children. Either way, the gender composition of the population will undoubtedly affect attitudes towards age, marriage, children and women in paid employment.

However, the overall picture that emerges at present is one in which gender roles are becoming somewhat more flexible and the two-parent, patriarchal family is gradually becoming less dominant. This has produced a variety of responses. Right-wing politicians and many prominent Church leaders tend to blame permissive legislation and the legacy of the permissive social movements of the 1960s and 1970s (such as feminism and gay liberation) for the decline in traditional family life and conventional gender roles. From this perspective, the nuclear family unit is evoked as a symbol of social cohesion, and its break-up is regarded as the root cause of many contemporary social ills, from drug addiction to vandalism. For example, in summer 2011 many right-wing commentators blamed family breakdown for the wave of riots that spread across London and other inner cities. Yet fears about the future of the family cross traditional party lines, and while the more conservative sectors of society tend to blame liberal reforms, others have argued that if permissiveness weakened the family, it was Mrs Thatcher's right-wing revolution that really killed it off. The rampant individualism and consumer greed which has flourished since the 1980s is viewed as responsible for undermining the moral values necessary to sustain family life.

Lastly, we must consider whether the decline of the traditional family has actually led to a more atomised, alienated society. There is also evidence to suggest that new, more flexible family structures and systems of community support are beginning to take its place. Single mothers, for example, often rely heavily on one another for both childcare assistance and emotional support. Similarly, while children of divorced parents are generally regarded as disadvantaged, it has also been suggested that many actually benefit from drawing on a wider support network of two families. It is also important to recognise the new range of identities that the decay of the traditional British family has opened up. For women in particular, the evolution of the family unit clearly coincides with greater social freedom and status, and increased financial autonomy.

 ## Exercises

1   What is the difference between a nuclear and extended family? Do you know or can you think of other kinship structures? How do family structures vary according to (a) class and (b) ethnic background? Which, if any, is most commonly represented in popular television film?

2   What is the meaning of the following popular phrases: 'Victorian values', 'family wage', 'the Big Society', 'work/life balance', 'white wedding', 'lie back and think of England'? How did they originate, and in what sense are they specific to British culture?

3   The British blockbuster film *Four Weddings and a Funeral* featured three traditional English weddings and one Scottish wedding. What do you think are the staple ingredients of a British wedding? What is the significance of each?

4   In recent years there has been much debate about non-sexist language. Can you think of gender-neutral alternatives for the following occupational titles: seaman; ombudsman; dustman; craftsman; fisherman; postman; signalman? What about phrases such as 'working mother', 'career woman', 'pramface' or 'yummy mummy'? Why is there no male equivalent for these terms? Is this likely to change in the future? Do you think it is important to adopt non-sexist language?

5   Do you think 'outing' is a fair practice? Under what circumstances? Consider arguments for and against.

6   What does it mean to say that children are growing up too fast? To what extent might this viewpoint reflect an older generation's wish to see childhood remain similar to their own experience?

Reading

Asher, Rebecca *Shattered: Modern Motherhood and the Illusion of Equality.* Harvill Secker, 2011. An analysis of how attitudes towards parenting and gender continue to disadvantage women economically and socially.

Banks, O. *Faces of Feminism.* Basil Blackwell, 1981. An introductory guide to the development of nineteenth- and twentieth-century feminist politics in Britain.

Walter, Natasha *Living Dolls: The Return of Sexism.* Virago, 2010. Popular book that discusses the recent resurgence of older forms of male objectification of women.

Jeffrey-Poulter, S. *Peers, Queers and Commons: The Struggle for Gay Law Reform from 1950 to the Present.* Routledge, 1991. An examination of the British legal and political system in relation to its treatment of homosexuals and lesbians.

Barnyard, Kat *The Equality Illusion: The Truth about Women and Men Today.* Faber, 2011. Following the gender split throughout a typical day, Barnyard explains how women are still treated by society more as bodies than as people.

Cultural examples

Film

Fish Tank (2009) dir. Andrea Arnold. Film about a teenager growing up in a single-parent family on a London council estate who finds her release through hip-hop dance.

Four Weddings and a Funeral (1994) dir. Mike Newell. Courtship and marriage rituals among the English middle-class.

Made in Dagenham (2010) dir. Nigel Cole. Film about the strike for equal pay led by female machinists at the Ford car plant in London.

Me Without You (2001) dir. Sandra Goldbacher. Charts the relationship between two teenager girls as they progress through their student days into maturity.

Morvern Callar (2002) dir. Lynne Ramsey. Samantha Morton plays the Scottish adolescent coming to terms with the death of her boyfriend. Based on Alan Warner's novel.

The Queen (2006) dir. Stephen Frears. Dramatic portrait study of the Queen, and her relationship with Tony Blair, in the period after Princess Diana's death.

Raining Stones (1993) dir. Ken Loach. Gritty view of male unemployment and its effects on two working-class families.

To Die For (1994) dir. Peter Mackenzie Litten. London-based exploration of AIDS and its aftermath among the gay community.

Vera Drake (2004) dir. Mike Leigh. Drama that depicts the life of a kindly wife and mother, who risks arrest by performing illegal abortions in the 1950s.

Young Soul Rebels (1992) dir. Isaac Julien. Alternative view of punk and the Silver Jubilee year, focusing on black disco and gay subcultures.

Books

David Nicholls, *One Day* (2009) Charts the 'will they, won't they?' relationship between two 1980s graduates by looking at one day in their lives over the course of two decades.

Alan Hollingshurst, *The Line of Beauty* (2004) Booker-winning novel about Thatcherism, consumerism and the growing AIDS crisis, seen through the eyes of an ambitious young gay man.

Adam Mars-Jones and Edmund White, *The Darker Proof: stories from the crisis* (1987) A collection of short stories exploring the AIDS crisis in the UK.

Alan Warner, *The Stars in the Bright Sky* (2010) Follow up to the author's much admired novel *The Sopranos* about the bonding rituals and the tensions among a group of young women.

TV programmes

The Trip. Bittersweet midlife crisis comedy about a fictional tour of gastropub hotel eateries in the Yorkshire Dales by friends Steve Coogan, best known as Alan Partridge, and Rob Brydon, best known from *Gavin and Stacey*.

The Hour. Period drama set at the BBC in the 1950s, depicting the developing career of one of Britain's first female current affairs producers.

Fresh Meat. Post-feminist situation comedy exploring ideas of gender and sexual identity at university.

Miranda. Offbeat hit comedy about the life of an accident prone, single, joke shop owner in her thirties.

Mistresses. Drama series about affluent women and their complex sexual and romantic entanglements.

My Family. Popular situation comedy featuring an 'average' British family.

Peep Show. Cult comedy about two flatmates' dysfunctional lives and relationships.

Queer as Folk. First major explicit gay serial on British television.

Vera. Television series about a hard drinking, middle-aged female detective, which inherits the tradition established by Lynda la Plante's *Prime Suspect* series in the 1980s and 1990s.

The Vicar of Dibley. Richard Curtis's comedy about a female vicar in an English village. Complemented by *Rev*, a more recent comedy about an inner-city male vicar.

 # Websites

www.theory.org.uk/ctr-que1.htm
   Site devoted to explaining and exploring queer theory.
www.mumsnet.com
   Influential website that seeks to be the country's most popular meeting point for parents.

www.disgruntledhousewife.com

Humorous and irreverent pro-feminist site on how to conduct a male–female relationship.

www.queeruk.net

Guide to UK gay culture and online community.

www.childrenssociety.org.uk/news-views/press-release/nation-urged-join-uks-first-inquiry-childhood

In 2006, the Children's Society launches the UK's first independent national inquiry into childhood.

www.fathers-4-justice.org/about.php

Website campaigning for better child access rights for divorced fathers.

Youth culture and style

Jo Croft

Timeline

Age

16 ——— Leave school
Sex legal in UK except in Northern Ireland
Buy cigarettes
Average age at which virginity is lost for both sexes
Marry with parental consent

17 ——— Drive a car
Sex legal in Northern Ireland

18 ——— Buy alcohol
Watch adult films
Marry without parental consent
Vote

29 ——— Average first marriage age for women

31 ——— Average first marriage age for men

41 ——— Average divorce age for women

43 ——— Average divorce age for men

60 ——— Retirement age for women

65 ——— Retirement age for women (from 2010)
Retirement age for men

76 ——— Average age of death for men

81 ——— Average age of death for women

Introduction

WHEN WE ATTEMPT TO DESCRIBE somebody else, or when we are required to describe ourselves (on an official form, for example), age almost always seems to be a crucial component to such descriptions. Age shapes and sets limits upon the way we live our lives in a way that we take for granted. As the timeline shows, age dictates such things as when we can leave school, when we can legally have sex, when we can drive, when we can marry, when we can start work, when we can drink alcohol, when we can retire and when we can vote. In an obvious sense, age is a 'fact' we cannot alter because it literally describes how long we have been alive: however much advertising campaigns for beauty products, vitamins or health foods might try to convince us otherwise, age is something that fixes our position in society as much as, and often more than, other factors such as race, gender or class.

Nevertheless, once we begin to consider the different ways in which age underpins the identity of any given individual, it emerges as a category that is far from a biological given. The social effects of age have implications far beyond the explicit classification of how old someone is. Age, consequently, is an aspect of identity that powerfully reflects the particular character of life in any national culture and we can learn a great deal about a nation's values and cultural practices by paying attention to the significance it attaches to certain life stages. It is worth noting, for example, that – unlike the United States and many European countries – Britain has no specific legislation governing 'age discrimination'.

As the timeline demonstrates, the official landmarks of age in Britain seem to become fewer and further apart once someone reaches the age of 18, though there is a slight reversal of this trend during old age (driving licences, for instance, have to be reapplied for when you reach the age of 70). In any case, the period between the ages of 11 and 21 is a time when life is most punctuated by changes in status – when the rules about what you can do and where you can go are shifting most dramatically. Therefore, in terms of understanding British cultural identities, the age groups that fall broadly within the category of 'youth' offer some of the most interesting insights –

not least because British institutions seem to subject young people to such close scrutiny. It is almost as if young people in this country are – consciously or unconsciously – regarded as guarantors of not just the nation's future but its soul, for whenever anxieties surface about moral or social decline, the first target for concern is youth.

Britain is a nation that seems to attach particular importance to 'tradition'. 'Britishness' in both the upper class and the working class tends to be characterised by an adherence to 'old values', and it could be argued that the British see themselves, and are perhaps viewed by the rest of the world, as having an 'old' (established, traditional or even ancient) culture. In consequence, it might also be claimed that, precisely because of this British conservatism, young people are regarded as both threatening and vulnerable. One of the issues which will be explored in this chapter is the extent to which British notions of social stability are explicitly associated with the stability of relationships between generations. A claim, after all, might be made that the massive changes in people's lifestyles in post-war Britain have been felt most acutely in terms of 'age relations'. 'The genera-tion gap', juvenile delinquency, loss of community, the fragmentation of the nuclear family and disappearance of the extended family: all these much-debated social phenomena seem in one way or another to be associated with a perceived shift in relationships between different age groups.

Along with the rest of Europe, Britain will soon have to cope with some drastic changes in the age distribution of its population. Over the next twenty years, the average age will increase considerably. By the year 2025 the number of pensioners is predicted by a European Commission report to rise by 43 per cent while the working population remains roughly the same. The number of young people under 20 will also fall, by 8 per cent. Additionally, along with many other European countries (France, Holland, Denmark), Britain's fertility rate has fallen over the past twenty-five years, so that now it is not sufficient to maintain the current level of population and only mass immigration can maintain population levels.

These changes have profound implications. At the simplest level, when a workforce has to support more people it can easily lead to inter-generational tensions. Also, as the proportion of people in retirement grows, the strain on state social and health services grows. The effect of these additional expenses will be to lower people's spending power, which will in turn threaten industries that produce or sell goods. The decline in the numbers of young people may also significantly disrupt the housing market which depends on new entrants at the bottom to enable others to move up. Such changes and their likely implications will probably add to the impor-tance attached to youth and its conduct. For example, one modern phenom-enon is the way in which young adults live longer at home, delaying marriage and child-rearing (over half of men aged 22–24 live with their parents). One view of this sees them as living off their parents, the result of decades of softening Western affluence, while another claims young people now use time at home to gain qualifications and save money for a secure future, while parents have become more involved in helping their twenty-somethings get a foot on the economic ladder.

It could perhaps be argued that in earlier epochs of British history less emphasis was placed upon youth as a time of crisis because there was less legislation governed by age, and hence fewer official turning points or transitions in a person's life. In other words, age is a component of identity which is very much tied to cultural factors such as the education system, health or marriage practices.

In this chapter, while other aspects of age in Britain will be touched upon, the focus will be on late childhood, adolescence and youth culture, because it is in these fast-changing periods of life that British people absorb and challenge accepted cultural identities. It is also here that the direction of present and future British identities can be apprehended, as a range of new ideas and beliefs are added to those associated with the traditional social values attaching to work, class and the family: the staple ingredients sustaining cultural identity for older British citizens.

Youth, teenagers and adolescents

At first glance, the terms 'adolescent', 'teenager' and 'youth' seem to mean exactly the same thing. They all refer to young people who are not children, and yet who are also not quite adults: inbetweeners. However, there is also a sense in which these words suggest different forms of identity, different groupings of the British population. For example, 'youth' is generally used to refer to young people operating in the public sphere, as part of a social group, and most typically it is associated with boys rather than girls. We talk about 'youth clubs', 'youth training schemes', 'youth unemployment' and of course 'youth culture'. 'Adolescence', on the other hand, is a term which is more likely to be used in connection with an individual's identity – to refer to a private, psychic realm of experience, as in such common expressions as 'adolescent angst', 'adolescent diary' or 'adolescent crisis'. The term 'teenager' first emerged in the 1950s when young people were newly identified as a distinct group of consumers, and since then it has typically been associated with certain kinds of products or markets: for example 'teenage fashion', 'teenage magazines' and 'teen pop idols'. With respect to gender, we should note that the expressions 'teenage pregnancy' and 'gang of youths' suggest that 'teenage' is feminine and 'youth' is masculine. More recently, the term 'tweenager' has been coined to describe eleven- and twelve-year-olds who aspire to the lifestyle of their older siblings, and nowadays have the pocket money to do so. While they shop for the fashions aimed at teenagers, another term, 'kidult', has arisen to describe adults who dress in the style of children. Both terms are predominantly applied to females rather than males, and there is also concern expressed about the way even younger children adopt adult habits too early, with six-year-olds attending make-up parties and seven-year-olds wearing crop tops and fake tattoos. Fashion is clearly no longer restricted by any age limits, with pre-teens shopping for themselves at Gap, Topshop and Miss Selfridge, their tastes dictated by pop bands like One Direction and The Saturdays as well as magazines such as *Sugar* and *Bliss*.

The three fundamental natural events, birth, procreation and death, offer the most succinct summary of the human life cycle. However universal these events may be, though, there are inevitably massive differences in the ways that they are experienced by people from one culture or community to the next. In the contemporary context of Western capitalist societies, patterns and levels of 'consumption' best illustrate some of these differences. Whenever statistics are sought on the details of people's lives (to answer the question 'How do people live?'), the most plentiful and perhaps scrupulous sources of information are provided by market research. In other words, the way in which money is spent and the kinds of things that people choose to buy tell us quite a lot about the identities of British people and cultural formation is partly reflected in modes of consumption. The British may not be a 'nation of shopkeepers', but, as a nation of purchasers, 'we are what we buy'.

In order to gauge how age shapes patterns of behaviour, it is important to read between the lines of facts and reports which detail how people spend their money and their time at different stages of their lives. The term 'lifestyle' itself seems to have become inextricably linked to the notion of choices over spending. The phrases 'lifestyle politics' or 'lifestyle magazines' therefore tend to be used (often derogatively) to refer to middle-class preoccupations with 'consumer choice', and Britain today, where the phrase 'everyone is middle class now' is increasingly common (if still inaccurate), seems to be characterised as a 'consumer culture'. In this context, the typical British teenager is viewed as the consumer 'par excellence', and is seen by some, often older commentators, as a 'fashion victim' driven by larger forces than personal expression. But others see the teenager as a supple negotiator of the minefields both of contemporary style trends and of technology. Knowing the price of a 'Big Mac' from McDonalds is sometimes the limit of an older person's familiarity with youth culture, which is more often about empowerment than victimisation.

Famously, the 'teenager' is considered to have been an invention or symptom of shifting consumer markets in the 1950s, both in Europe and in America. Many studies of British youth that have been carried out since then have focused, in one way or another, upon the way young people characterise themselves through the clothes they wear, the music they listen to, the films they watch and the places they go to. When Richard Hoggart wrote (rather apocalyptically) about the state of the nation's youth in his well-known book *The Uses of Literacy* (1957), he summoned up an image of the British teenager being almost literally consumed by a 'mass culture' which in turn was linked to the saturating effects of 'Americanisation'.

More recently, social commentators have argued that it is precisely through their role as consumers of popular culture that British young people express themselves most powerfully and creatively, not least because they feel excluded by the more traditional realms of the arts. There is a widening gap between the officially sanctioned practices of 'high art' and the forms of self-expression and creativity that young people choose to explore in their everyday lives. An acute example of this is young people's use of graffiti in the UK, an art form initially borrowed from the inner-city subcultures of black Americans. From the mid-1980s onwards, complex, brightly coloured designs produced with spray-paints became a common sight on 'spare' bits of wall in many towns and cities, especially along railway tracks and under motorway bridges. Typically, these motifs would be based around a single word, name or phrase, with obscure connotations, and an important element of the appeal of graffiti within British youth culture is that you have

FIGURE 4.1 Graffiti from the school of 'Banksy' has increased some house prices

to know *how* to read its messages, and above all to recognise the 'signature' of the artist. For many young people, the explicit association between British graffiti and urban America seems to imbue this art form with the power to 'glamorise' mundane environments such as housing estates or shopping malls – to make these spaces both more exotic and more hard-edged. Perhaps this accounts, then, for the particular prominence of the graffiti scene in new towns such as Crawley, just south of London, where (generally) white working-class youths became minor celebrities and where police would regularly search teenagers for incriminating spray cans.

In the following sections, we will focus on the way that British young people spend their money and their time, both when 'going out' and when 'staying in'.

Going out: 'dressing up and dressing down'

It may seem a bit too straightforward to characterise British youth cultures in terms of fashion styles. Nevertheless, dress codes are obviously crucial keys to understanding how the lines are drawn between different identities in Britain. After all, the way that we dress can serve either to confirm or to subvert various facets of our identities, such as our gender, ethnicity, class and age. Clothes also reflect our perceptions of the historical epoch in which we live – how we relate to the cultural mood of the day. The postmodern preoccupations of the last decades of the twentieth century, for example, were linked to nostalgia, pastiche and what might be better described as kinds of 'fusion' or as cultural hybridity (mixing different styles of fashion, music or anything else). Contemporary fashions constantly play upon these cultural styles from previous decades to evoke the spirit (or *zeitgeist*) of contemporary Britain. 'Now' is in many ways a recycling of previous *zeitgeists*. The spectrum of subcultures is enormously wide and Britain has produced a high number over recent decades. Consequently, *The Guardian* newspaper ran an article in 2011 listing the 'top ten' British youth sub-cultures according to the influential designer Red or Dead and founder Wayne Hemingway: dandies and flappers (from the 1920s), teds (from the 1950s), mods (1950s/60s), skinheads (1950s), hippies (1960s), glam rockers (early 1970s), punks (late 1970s), goths (late 1970s), new romantics (1980s) and dance movements from the 1970s on: disco, rave, soul and acid.

One way of thinking about different subcultural groupings within young British fashion is in terms of class identities. Subcultures such as punks, hippies, crusties, bikers and goths have tended – in one way or another – to challenge the traditional values of smart and respectable dress. On the other hand, mods, soul boys (and girls), teds, skinheads and home-boys have usually emphasised a 'sharper' style of dress, though of course in diverse ways. This opposition between 'smart' and 'scruffy' clothes bears some relation to class allegiances insofar as dress codes which place greater value on clothes 'looking new' are more often adopted by working-class young people, while scruffier 'bohemian' styles are more likely to have middle-class wearers. But often, subcultural styles of dress confront and confound mainstream expectations about people's position in the social structure, especially in the cities.

The above is too simplistic a formula to apply to all UK youth sub-cultures, especially as these styles in themselves are not necessarily mutually exclusive, and most young people, in any case, are likely to draw on a range of possible influences. The enormous increase in the student population, for instance, has affected the class delineations of subcultural style, as many more working-class young people enter a terrain which had previously been a middle-class preserve.

As Dick Hebdige points out in his book *Subculture: the Meaning of Style*, black subcultures have been a central factor in the formation of many white working-class subcultural styles such as that of mods (short for moderns). Both Afro-Caribbean and Afro-American influences have been critical in shaping British youth culture since the 1950s, not least because more and more young people in this country are growing up in multi-ethnic, cross-cultural environments. In 2011, the Institute for Social and Economic Research (ISER) estimated that 2 million Britons were mixed race, twice the official figure based on self-declaration. Self-reported data has 2.9 per cent of children described as mixed race, but the percentage living with parents from different ethnic groups or in a mixed-race household is shown to be 8.9 per cent, suggesting that among under-16s this is now the largest ethnic population group after 'white'.

In the late 1970s and 1980s, the Afro-Caribbean Rastafarian style influenced both black and white youth subcultural fashion, with red, green and gold Ethiopian colours commonly featuring on T-shirts, hats, badges and jackets. Today, more than ever, black subcultural styles tend to lead the way in British street fashion, especially those derived from the Afro-American Rap scene: the 'home boy' look of very baggy jeans, big hooded jackets and baseball caps is very common among teenage boys, especially the under 16s. 'Clubwear' styles (for example tight lycra, shiny fabrics and bright colours) also seem to be influenced strongly by black street fashions. Perhaps most significantly, Asian youth culture in Britain seems to draw very much on Afro-American and Afro-Caribbean subcultural styles (the Asian Underground movement draws on electronica). The influence of the European club scene has also affected British styles, as clubs in the UK often try to recreate the atmosphere of Ibiza or Ayia Napa, and the ambient sounds of European bands such as Air (amid the electic Anglophone Euro sounds of Phoenix, The Amazing, Daft Punk or Kings of Convenience) have eroded the deep-seated British aversion to pop music from the Continent, previously denigrated as 'Europop' (the title of a parodic song by the Divine Comedy). Identifications and cultural allegiances in Britain are now much more complex, in other words, than is suggested by traditional models of assimilation.

When considering what people wear, we need also to think about where they go, as the two are usually connected. To begin with, pubs still have a unique status in British culture as places where people of different ages and, to a lesser extent, different classes, are likely to socialise together, particularly for quiz nights or screened sports matches. British soap operas such as *Coronation Street* and *EastEnders* have long played on the pub's function as a place where lots of different kinds of people could plausibly meet up. This, in turn, has led to complaints from TV monitoring groups that soap operas might encourage viewers to drink more alcohol, because characters are so often portrayed having a drink in their 'local', and subsequently prices have risen to make pub drinking expensive for most young people. Consequently, many young people now drink at home before heading out and government policy is increasingly aimed at a perceived British drinking culture in which alcohol is thought to be too cheap in supermarkets. The more traditional activity of 'pub crawls' – on which lots of different pubs are visited in one evening – also persists in Britain, particularly among students and groups of 'laddish' young men (such as the members of a rugby team or the groom and his mates on a 'stag' party). The pub remains *the* primary leisure institution for white British culture but is generally much less popular among Afro-Caribbeans and Asians. It could be argued that pubs are bound up with British ideas of 'rites of passage', insofar as a young person's first legal drink in a pub is treated as a landmark. Growing concern about under-age drinking has meant that more attention is paid to young pub customers providing proof that they are over 18, and the major companies that run pubs have introduced their own ID cards.

Bars and clubs rather than pubs are the focus of many young people's social lives. The growth of the 'rave' scene in Britain (which began with 'acid house' parties in the late 1980s) has meant that dancing has again become a central activity, as it had been in the 'dance halls' of the 1950s and early 1960s, and the discos of the 1970s. In contrast to these earlier dance scenes though, alcohol has tended to be a peripheral element of contemporary UK dance culture. Instead, rave puts much more emphasis on taking drugs such as 'ecstasy', the effects of which tend to be cancelled out by alcohol. People dancing constantly for several hours are more likely to drink fluids, especially bottled water, to avoid dehydration and to restore energy levels. At most raves music is played by DJs, but occasionally by live performers, and the scene has fragmented considerably to include a wide range of music styles, often differentiated by beats per minute: techno, house, acid, trance, techno, breakbeat hardcore, drum and bass, dubstep and grime.

Though they are now largely accommodated into the mainstream, at the outset a key element in the appeal of raves was their illegality: events where thousands of people would come together were often publicised by enigmatic flyers, and by messages transmitted on pirate radio stations such as Kiss. The counter-cultural status of raves could be compared to 'blues parties' or 'shebeens', which became particularly popular in Afro-Caribbean communities in the 1980s. Like raves, these parties blurred the boundaries between private gatherings and public events insofar as they tended to be held in 'unofficial' or even squatted venues, with entrance by informally sold tickets or invitations. Like raves, blues parties were associated both with a specific type of music (reggae and ragga) played through enormous sound systems, and with drugs (cannabis) more than with alcohol – though cans of beer or other alcohol would usually be sold or included in the entrance price.

In large cities, especially northern ones such as Liverpool, Manchester, Sheffield or Newcastle, there is a whole ritual that revolves around 'going out on the town' on Friday and Saturday nights. Long queues form as hundreds of people gather around the pubs, clubs and wine bars – young women often dressed glamorously in thin-strapped, backless evening dresses, gauzy tunics or very short skirts, and young men in more casual (but nevertheless immaculate) shirts and trousers. In the context of 'a night out on the town', the stereotype of the British love of queuing acquires another significance. The more popular clubs, for instance, sometimes hire 'queue spotters' who look out for particularly stylishly dressed 'punters' – the best dressed may well be allowed to go to the front of the queue, while those guilty of certain 'fashion crimes' (for example wearing white socks or the 'wrong' kind of shoes) may not be allowed in at all. Like the film lines curling around corners in the heyday of cinema-going, these queues of clubbers function as a kind of social scene, a place to meet your friends, to flirt, or to compete with your peers. Young people also might end their evening in another queue, waiting to buy chips or a kebab, or standing in line for a taxi.

This kind of weekend spectacle is not often regarded as being part of any specific subculture, apart from what might be broadly described as 'clubbing', and yet it is still governed by a distinct set of codes – for example, in many cities, Friday night is girls' and boys' night out, but Saturday night is for couples. One of the most striking aspects of these weekly events is the disregard most of the young people appear to have for the weather – the rule seems to be that jackets or coats are not worn even on freezing winter nights (this is also a question of money as it is a luxury to buy an impressive coat or jacket which will only be 'checked' – hung away – at the club). Perhaps most noticeable, though, is the fact that men and women tend to go out not with boyfriends or girlfriends, but with their 'mates' of the same sex. For women especially, this seems to be an important element in the way they choose to dress – the flamboyance and overtly sexual nature of the outfits that many young women wear are apparently in some way legitimated by the fact that they are dressing up 'for fun', rather than explicitly to attract men. Indeed, it is often said that women on these occasions are 'dressing up' for other women, that an integral part of the ritual is be identified as part of a female group and to gain the approval of other members of that social crowd. None of these so-called 'rules' or codes of dress is clear-cut, however.

Staying in: young people and the media

On average, in 2010 people in Britain were recorded as spending nearly four hours watching the television every day, which is more than in any other European country. Despite the rise of the internet and social networking, the television still occupies centre stage in people's evenings, with family viewing centred on shows such as *The X Factor*, *Britain's Got Talent* and *Doctor Who*.

After the weather, it is accurate to say that television programmes provide the favourite topic of conversation for British people (according to market research, 46 per cent of UK population discuss TV programmes with their friends or family). In many ways, television seems to be at the hub of 'the British way of life', offering a structure and rhythm around which people may shape their leisure time. Nowadays, the success or otherwise of major national holidays such as Christmas and Easter is far less likely to be talked about in terms of the quality of church services, than the quality of programmes on television. Among older people there is a mood of nostalgia about the 'good old days' of family viewing on television, especially in connection with Christmas, and weekend nights are crammed with 'top ten' shows and compilation programmes about previous decades. In the 1950s through to the 1970s, there was actually a regular programme broadcast from a theatre in Leeds called 'The Good Old Days' which simulated a night out at the music hall in Edwardian England (complete with audiences in fancy dress Edwardian clothes, singing along with the performers). Today, equivalent viewing slots are more likely to show archive footage of old TV shows, and digital TV stations such as UK Gold are entirely devoted to re-runs of 'classic' British programmes. So, whereas thirty years ago older people might sentimentally reminisce about 'happier' times when the family would make their own entertainment – singing songs around the piano or playing charades – people these days are more likely nostalgically to recall 'the golden age of television' during the 1970s – a time when adults and children could supposedly sit together to watch favourite programmes (such as *The Morecambe and Wise Show, Top of The Pops* or *The Generation Game*) on one of the three available television channels, comfortable in the knowledge that it would all be 'good clean fun'.

A traditional British Christmas has been characterised (or caricatured) through images of the family, ranging across three generations, sitting in front of the television after Christmas dinner, watching the Queen's Speech and then a rerun of a film such as *The Sound of Music* or *The Wizard of Oz*. It is important not to underestimate the status of these televisual myths in relation to the attitudes British people themselves express about national identity, and as a corollary of this, it is often the case that anxieties about social decline are most readily articulated in terms of 'falling standards' on television. The concept of 'family viewing' is a central stake in debates about the role of the BBC, a public-owned institution known to the country as 'auntie' (suggesting its cosy, nanny-like persona). In an attempt to recapture the 'all-round' entertainment of twenty or thirty years ago, the BBC has given rebirth to old favourites like *Doctor Who* while programmes like *Britian's Got Talent* in fact recall the old variety shows of 'The Good Old Days' while reviving the practice of the family 'turns' that television supposedly eradicated. The popularity of a show such as *Downton Abbey* also recalls the past in a way that not only speaks to British people of an older, ordered past but of fondly remembered television programmes like *Upstairs, Downstairs* and *The Forsyte Saga*.

Young people nowadays watch more television than preceding generations. However, as far as television programmers and advertisers are concerned, 'youth audiences' are potentially the most elusive segment of the population in the UK. Although television may play an influential role in the identities of British young people, they generally spend less time watching than people over 25 or under 12 (that the older generation are expected to stay in explains the prevalence of nostalgia shows on Saturday nights). British youth, implicitly, are less likely than any other section of the population to be seen as inhabitants of the domestic environment. The young arguably also watch television in a different way: less as a central activity than as a backdrop – more akin, say, to having the radio turned on than watching a film at the cinema. This is reflected in the success of reality TV shows, especially those that can also be 'watched' on the internet 24 hours a day, such as *Big Brother*. The rise in reality TV (*I'm A Celebrity Get Me Out of Here* or *The Edwardian House*) has been perceived in numerous ways, from 'dumbing down' to the fulfillment of Andy Warhol's prediction that 'in the future everyone will be famous for fifteen minutes', but its main effect has been to place more 'ordinary' people on television, and so to encourage young viewers (participants are rarely over 35) to make assessments of themselves and their peers in relation to a set of 'real personalities' they might themselves easily know or even be. The late afternoon schedules are also stocked with innumerable quiz shows, such as *Pointless*, *Countdown* and *The Weakest Link*, which can appeal to anyone wishing to unwind from the day, and arguably reflect the traditional British love of games.

However, whereas youth television seems to anticipate an audience caught up with the demands of a hectic social life, other activities such as computer games, reading or listening to music suggest a more solitary vision of the teenager at home. Uncommunicative adolescents playing with their gameboys or listening to their Ipods acutely exemplify this. However, social networking and its pitfalls in the twenty-first century seem to have replaced the previous range of concerns about the state of the nation's youth focused upon the dangers of children and adolescents inhabiting private fantasy worlds through their computers. Not only are predatory adults feared, but parents are known to check on their children through sites such as Facebook in order to discover details about their private lives, both confirming and complicating commonplace anecdotes about the technology 'generation gap', whereby children are deemed to be more adept than their parents at computers. Computers certainly threaten parents with a potential loss of control. Above all, fears seem to centre upon the fact that the Internet enables children to communicate not only with other children but also with adults, without supervision. This has added a mood of parental caution over what is otherwise greeted more optimistically as a communication network that encourages the breakdown of traditional boundaries, including those between different ages and generations. In terms of computer games, violent action franchises like *Grand Theft Auto* and *Call of Duty* retain a cultish popularity, particularly with teenage boys.

Increasingly played by adults, computer games have a close relationship, aesthetically and thematically, to comics and magazines that parents grew up with. Since the mid-1980s, comics – especially 'graphic novels' – have spawned a whole subcultural scene, and most British towns now have a specialist comics shop (Forbidden Planet, for instance, are a nationwide chain of shops). HMV, which used principally to serve as music and DVD outlets, also sell comics, books and magazines aimed at this cultish readership, thus suggesting further subcultural cross-overs between computer games, music, movies and comics. However, when people in Britain talk about 'teenage magazines', they are most likely to be referring to publications such as *Sugar* aimed at girls. This is significant in that adolescent femininity in the UK tends to be associated – more than any other aspect of youth culture – with stereotypical consumerism. Young women are more explicitly identified as a 'market' than as a series of subcultures. The point to make here, perhaps, is that the cultural activities of British young women are interpreted less positively than young men, in that women are more likely to be stereotyped as passive consumers (of clothes and magazines about celebrities) than as creative participants in a subcultural scene.

In the twenty-first century, there is some concern over what is perceived to be a kind of female vulgarity, whose hedonistic lifestyle is driven by increasing levels of financial independence. The consequence is that some hotels and restaurants refuse to accept bookings from all-female parties, where once they would have thought twice about all-male groups. Some pubs now ban 'hen' parties and, reportedly, holiday companies claim that Britain's new wave of ladettes, young women with a love of binge drinking and brazen behaviour, are exceeding the antics of male 'yobs' in terms of noise, abuse and violence.

On the more sober side of youth culture is the growth in focus on employability and entrepreneurialism. For example, TeenBiz is the UK's first business start-up initiative for young people aged 18 and under, founded by a finalist from one season of the extremely popular BBC television series, *The Apprentice*. The scheme aims to provide teenage entrepreneurs with the tools needed to start their own businesses, and on its opening in 2011 to coincide with Global Entrepreneurship Week, the scheme said it was 'launching in a climate of high teenage unemployment and social disengagement, as demonstrated by the summer riots which took places in cities across England'. The figure of disaffected youth threatening the moral fabric of society is present once more here, but instead of calls for national service, or similar, the emphasis here is on business start-up in an era when there are fewer jobs in the public and private sectors. In 2011, youth unemployment reached an 18-year high, standing at 991,000, after 300,000 public sector jobs were axed in response to the economic recession. With unemployment nudging towards 10 per cent, one response to this in the private sector came from Hallmark, who for the first time introduced a range of unemployment sympathy cards.

Overall, the crucial point to make about youth culture is its speed of change and its difference from more mainstream representations of British identity, whether those of children at school or adults at work. Youth identities are more commonly associated with pleasure and leisure, but they are crossed by other crucial factors in cultural positioning discussed in this book: gender, ethnicity, region and class.

Sex and drugs and rock'n'roll

It is both clichéd and true to say that the lives of young people in the UK in the post-war era have been characterised on the basis of the rather unholy trinity of 'sex and drugs and rock'n'roll'. This section will therefore focus on these three aspects because they are associated more closely and apprehensively with British youth culture than any others.

Although the poet Philip Larkin suggested that 'Sex began in 1963', anxieties about the sexual mores of the younger generation certainly preceded the so-called sexual revolution of the 1960s. Nevertheless, sex is undoubtedly a realm of contemporary British life where the mythical 'generation gap' is felt particularly keenly, and this is no doubt exacerbated by a perceived difference between what is sexually common now and what was acceptable fifty years ago. Nostalgia is now expressed with peculiar intensity in relation to notions of childhood innocence, whereby today's children and teenagers are regarded as both more vulnerable and as more sexually 'knowing', as growing up too fast and not experiencing the innocence of the adult world their parents had.

Whereas a hundred years ago fears were rife about the social dangers of adolescent masturbation, now the key areas of concern surrounding British young people are the sources and timing of sex education, teenage pregnancy and sexual abuse. In Britain's increasingly secular climate, on the other hand, the issue of 'sex before marriage' or cohabitation is no longer hotly contested, and nearly 80 per cent of women now cohabit before marriage (and one in four children is born to parents who are cohabiting). More than anything, carnal knowledge seems to be the central stake in debates about young people's sexuality. UK campaigns and initiatives such as 'Childline' and 'Kidscape' have increased public awareness of bullying and childhood sexual abuse.

Until the 1980s, the general perception in Britain had been that sex would inevitably be subject to fewer and fewer restrictions for each subsequent generation. However, concern over HIV and AIDS temporarily put paid to that vision of an unstoppable machine of sexual liberation, and this has been compounded by wider knowledge about sexually transmitted infections such as chlamydia. It could even be argued that many young people today have quite different relationship expectations than their parents had as teenagers because many things are now commonplace rather than cause for comment: living together, children outside of marriage, women-headed households, inter-racial marriages, civil marriages, commuter marriages between individuals who live apart, childless marriages and smaller families. Still, there are more fears about sex, and unwanted pregnancy no longer necessarily represents the worst possible scenario for sexually active teenagers. Campaigns to educate people about 'safer sex' have meant an increased openness about referring to sexual practices that fall outside the scope of 'straight sex' (for example, dressing up or using 'sex toys'), and the idea of conventional sex as being the only kind has ceased to dominate.

Glossy media representations of sex are far more likely nowadays to play on fetishistic imagery, and where earlier advertising used to appeal to men almost exclusively along the lines of 'buy the car, get the girl', marketing now seeks to associate products with erotic experimentation. Contemporary British youth culture seems to place a premium upon the idea of imaginative sexual practices, and is perhaps less ready to equate 'experience' (that is of penetrative sex) with sexual pleasure and knowledge. Teenage magazines like *Just 17* are littered with slogans such as 'to be sussed is a must', and most young people in this country over the age of eleven (and often younger) now know what a condom is. It seems that sex, for British young people today, is double-edged. Talking about sex, listening to other people talking about sex, reading about sex and even watching sex on the television or video has become progressively easier, but it is the proliferation of sex on the Internet that has created a supposed 'porn generation' that is challenging to parents who grew up in the 1980s. For some people, childhood is in danger of becoming entirely eroded, while for others, young people can never know too much.

Drugs are another area of life where the 'generation gap' appears to be wide. In post-war Britain, youth subcultures have always been associated with the use of particular (usually illegal) drugs: mods with amphetamines ('speed'), hippies with cannabis ('dope', 'pot', 'blow', etc.) and LSD ('acid'), ravers and clubbers with 'ecstasy'. Today though, drug use has become fairly mainstream among the UK youth population, and it is estimated that more than 50 per cent of young people will have tried at least one illegal drug by the time they are eighteen (while more than half of all students say they are regular users of cannabis, according to the Office of National Statistics in 2001 only 30 per cent of all 15-year-olds in England have tried the drug).

The drugs scene has now been characterised, rather ambiguously, as being about 'recreational drug use', rather than as a small alienated enclave of drug addicts, as in the past. This is a shift indicated by the increasing calls to legalise soft drugs, at least: a wave of pressure which resulted in the experiment in 2001 of police being officially told in Lambeth, which includes

TABLE 4.1 Children in NHS drug treatment, 2009

Number	%	Drug
547	2	Heroin and other opiates
229	1	Amphetamines
745	3	Cocaine
110	1	Crack
210	1	Ecstasy
12,642	53	Cannabis
284	1	Solvents
8,799	37	Alcohol
270	1	Other
23,836	100	Total

Brixton, to turn a blind eye to cannabis use, effectively decriminalising the drug for the first time. An ICM poll at the same time showed that 65 per cent of people in Britain think that prosecution for cannabis possession should be the police's lowest priority (yet, in 2000, 97,000 people were prosecuted for precisely that offence). Cannabis use has been the most common and is associated with the strand of club culture, Chill Out, where rooms are set aside for clubbers who want to relax on sofas and scatter cushions watching cool images on large screens and listening to ambient sounds, by bands like Groove Armada and Zero 7.

While the young criticise their parents for destroying the planet and the economy, an apolitical consumerism appears to have taken hold of British youth for an earlier generation raised on CND marches and anti-Vietnam protests, hippie love-ins followed by punk rock anarchism. However, the young in Britain seem yet again to fulfil their role as 'sophisticated' consumers who make discriminating choices from, in this case, a whole menu of intoxicating substances. In his book *Street Drugs*, for instance, Andrew Tyler argues that 'value for money' influences the decisions young people make about using drugs: 'They will judge a pint [of beer] against, say, the psychoactive clout of a £2 LSD blotter'. This may account for the fact that while overall alcohol consumption has risen considerably in the last forty years, pub and club sales of beer have dropped. Drinks with a relatively high alcohol content seem to be aimed, by and large, at a youth market which appears to prioritise both 'cheapness' and 'coolness' and a guaranteed 'high'. In the twenty-first century, the high-energy fizzy drink has become the staple beverage, alongside bottled water, but with the added attraction that drinks such as Red Bull serve as mixers for vodka, which has become the trendy spirit (as evidenced by the high number of vodka bars, with names like Revolution, that have thrived in British cities).

Set against this image of British youth as adept 'recreational' users of drugs are the media portrayals of young people either as hapless victims or as crazed addicts. Such representations do not offer an accurate overall perspective. Today cannabis and alcohol are by far the two most common drugs but in the 1980s there was a huge increase in heroin (or 'skag') use among British working-class youth, especially in urban areas, and this 'skag' culture was often the target of sensationalist news stories. Heroin was, somewhat exaggeratedly, rumoured to be as easy to get hold of as tobacco in some cities, and was undoubtedly a major cause of rising property crime. In the early 1990s, concern was focused upon the possibility of a cocaine ('crack') epidemic, and numerous stories were run in the press and on TV about crack-related crime in the United States. However, while crack became more common in this country, particularly in inner city areas, the spotlight shifted once again in the mid- to late 1990s to ecstasy (which first appeared on the British drugs scene in 1988), which prompted a number of media-led moral panics based around the widely publicised deaths of teenagers using the drug (the most notable case being Leah Betts's death in 1995 on her eighteenth birthday). National publicity focused on this drug in particular, even though in 2000, 20 per cent of pupils excluded from schools were suspended for drinking alcohol on the premises and one in four deaths of young men aged between 15 and 29 is alcohol-related. One of the most commonly expressed concerns is that British parents no longer 'know what their children are doing', and the focus of concern in the 2010s is far more on abuse than use, with parents less concerned that their children might be sampling cannabis than they might be damaging their livers with binge drinking. However commonplace drugs may be, within the social lives of many young people in this country, they are seen as both alien and threatening to much of the British population over 40.

Most British youth subcultures have been aligned, at some stage, with a particular type of music. Consequently, as delineations, cross-overs and fusions between different styles of pop music have become ever more complicated, so too have the criteria distinguishing one subcultural scene from another. Rock music certainly no longer is (if it ever was) a single unifying symbol of youth rebellion. At one level, it is almost as if British pop music has become so diverse that the differences between music scenes now seem to be blurred and indistinct. The 'tribalism' of the 1960s and 1970s, whereby musical taste was often inextricably bound to much broader allegiances, seems to have largely faded. Music nevertheless still plays a critical part in

FIGURE 4.2 Drug graffiti near to the historic city of Chester

the construction of identities for British youth, but in more fluid ways. In 1978, British 15-year-olds may well have used musical taste as a means of declaring themselves to be punks or mods. Today, 15-year-olds are probably more likely to say that they like 'a bit of jungle, house, techno or garage' than to use music to ascribe a specific subcultural identity to themselves, and the proliferation of music styles means that fashions are changing more quickly than in the past. The phenomenon of Britpop in the mid-1990s is a good example of this historical shift in the constituency of youth subcultures insofar as bands such as Oasis, Pulp and Blur were not closely linked to a fixed subcultural identity, despite their associations with 'mod' style.

The 'serious' end of popular music in the twenty-first century has become far more diffuse, though bands such as Radiohead and Coldplay manage to play songs that would have fitted into airplay lists in the 1970s and are still enormously successful. Now that the first rock stars are turning seventy, there is a tendency to see rock as both 'over', in the sense that 'rock bands' are to an extent passé, and having in some sense 'won' the battle over popular music: to have become a part of the mainstream, such that politicians regularly cite their favourite bands. The music scene more generally has diversified into a battery of trends, such as alt.rock, trance, ambient, garage, trip hop, the new acoustic movement, and so on.

At some level, youth culture in Britain may well still be based around 'sex and drugs and rock'n'roll', but the subcultures have changed over the

FIGURE 4.3 A street band contrasts traditional instruments with contemporary attitude

decades. In the 2010s, there are different groups that align themselves sometimes with music, but sometimes with class, attitude and fashion. A well-
known stereotype is that of the chav, which has become a generic term for
urban youth who behave badly. Anti-social behaviour and coarse attitudes
are associated with a type of demonised underclass that stereotypically
listens to dance music such as the new R&B, and wears Burberry accessories,
track suits and crude styling. These youths may be contrasted with the
dressed-down, dark and furtive look of 'hoodies', often suspected of crime
despite Prime Minister Cameron's infamous 2006 plea to 'hug a hoodie' as
part of his formula for mending 'broken Britain'.

Opportunistic hoodies, associated with the summer riots in England
in 2011, who conceal their identity in order to be anonymous are distinguishable from those with dark music tastes who also wear hoods, often
adorned with the name of a favourite metal or hardcore band. Sometimes
hanging in skate communities, and known as greebos, these youths may
have been emo children a few years back but now favour dyed hair and
baggy trousers, united by heavy rock music tastes and a desire to be
individualistic and anti-fashion, though mainstream clothing shops cater for
their look.

There are also the more familiar music groupings such as goths and
punks and sk8ers, a name given to younger greebos into pop-punk, nu-metal
and ska, but alongside these are myriad other young people who do not
define themselves in relation to music or subcultural styles.

Conclusion

To conclude, we will look briefly at two aspects of culture which are in many
ways opposed to each other: fashion and New Age culture. Both are associated with youth, but both also in fact stretch across the generations and
provide intriguing case studies for analysing the production and consumption of contemporary British identities.

When a morning television programme focused upon the 'street style'
of young people in Britain, the discussion emphasised the flexibility, eclec-
ticism and originality of British fashion and, above all, the refusal of most
stylish British teenagers to be 'slaves' to the dictates of the catwalk or the
high street fashion chains. While the newsagents in this country are filled
with row after row of women's magazines giving the latest tips about 'what's
in this season', the British seem to maintain a rather ambivalent attitude
to the very concept of 'fashion'. There is a sense, of course, in which this
ambivalence can be linked to British conservatism or reserve – to the nation's
reputed resistance to anything new. However, there is another, equally
important, strand to the way in which many British people seem to approach

fashion, which is the almost mythical 'eccentricity' of the British (or perhaps more precisely the English). In fact, the most famous of British designers – Vivienne Westwood, 'Red or Dead', Katherine Hamnett, Alexander McQueen and Paul Smith – are often characterised specifically in terms of their eccentricity and their lack of conformity with the broader trends of the global fashion industry. There is even a clothes company called 'English Eccentrics'. 'Reserve' and 'eccentricity' are attributes associated with 'the British character', and as qualities – albeit stereotypical ones – they possess a particular resonance in relation to British fashion, not least because they seem almost to cancel each other out. 'Classic' British clothing, of course, is characterised by muted colours (especially brown, navy blue and green), sensible/comfortable tailoring, fabrics such as wool or corduroy, and the obligatory, 'understated' string of pearls for women. Above all, perhaps, this style of dress is associated with an upper-class lifestyle of 'hunting, shooting and fishing' (as well as sailing), readily mythologised through media representations of the royal family striding over moors, walking dogs and so on. It is probably not surprising then, that these kind of clothes tend to conjure up conservative, non-urban identities (and often Conservative with a capital 'C'), though they are far from being the exclusive preserve of the aristocratic, landowning echelons of British society. Rather, the 'wax jacket and brogues' way of dressing seems to be identified with what we might call an 'aspirational lifestyle' (cf. 'young fogies', *Country Life*, shops for women like Laura Ashley). Perhaps most significantly, this 'classic' style of British dress has been readily exported and is almost certainly more popular with young people abroad than it is with their British contemporaries. British cultural stereotypes, from bulldogs and pony club rosettes to skinheads and Sloane Rangers, are parodied on the catwalk, not just by British fashion designers like Luella Bartley but by others such as Roberto Menichetti, the Italian ex-design director of Burberry, or the Spanish designer Desiree Mejer of Fake London.

Often, the way people dress in Britain is explicitly informed by distinctions of social class, and yet certain articles of clothing have much more ambiguous class connotations. The 'cloth cap' for instance (which is typically made of woollen cloth, in a small check pattern) is associated both with traditional working-class men (especially in northern working men's clubs) and with upper-class gentlemen (especially out shooting). In a far more specific and self-conscious way, clothes such as Burberry raincoats and even 'deerstalker' hats have crossed certain cultural divides insofar as they were adopted as part of black street fashion – a gesture which seemed both to mock the complacency of white 'Home Counties' style, and to challenge the monopoly of designer sportswear in black Afro-Caribbean fashion itself. In a way, this tendency within British fashion to play with or parody familiar images of British tradition represents a central element in the dress codes of several youth subcultures in this country: for example teddy boys, northern soul, skinheads and punk.

In the last few decades the 'Doc Marten' boot (or 'DM') has probably exemplified the shifting, playful moods of British fashion more than any other single item of clothing. Skinheads in the late 1960s adopted DMs as part of a dress code which seemed to be an exaggerated version of the clothes worn by manual labourers (drainpipe Levis, Ben Sherman check shirts and braces). A particular brand of work boots therefore acquired a significance far beyond the bounds of their initial function, and by the late 1970s the divisions and subdivisions between different subcultures such as punks and rudeboys were marked out not only by haircuts and music but by the way people wore their DMs (the number of holes, the colour, customised versions). As part of a more general impetus among feminists in the early 1980s to reject the trappings of a 'stereotypical' femininity, DMs became more and more popular with young women, especially students, who tended to adopt a kind of 'proletarian' look of baggily practical clothes – overalls and donkey jackets – as a gesture of rebellion against both sexism and the materialistic excesses of the decade. Now, the Doc Marten boot seems to have entered yet another phase, having been adopted, briefly, by the catwalks of international fashion houses at the beginning of the 1990s. The omnipresence of the DM in high street chains of shoe shops has robbed it of much of its potency as a symbol of non-conformity and nowadays it's as likely to be worn to school by a middle-class eleven-year-old (or by a schoolteacher for that matter) as it is to be worn by an 'indie' musician or an anarchic art student. Even the Pope has a pair. You can now buy velvet or silver or brocade Doctor Martens, but somehow they seem to have lost the power to shock, acquiring instead the more dubious accolade of a British 'design classic', which of course is readily exportable and hence less likely to be popular in Britain. The 14-hole black leather DM boot won two awards at the 2010 Fashion Show in New York: 'most popular men's footwear in latest fashion' and 'best counter-cultural footwear of the decade'. At the other end of the spectrum are Jimmy Choo shoes, founded in a workshop in Hackney in London, but bought in bulk by stars like Cameron Diaz and Jennifer Lopez.

Mainstream street looks are today probably most influenced by idolised figures like Katie Price, Wayne Rooney or David and Victoria Beckham. David Beckham's hairstyle changes, from floppy to shaved to mohican and so on, inspire countless imitations, and not just among football fans. Beckham is indeed a role model for many young boys, but there have been countless newspaper articles from the late 1990s onwards speaking out about the downturn in boys' fortunes generally, and their lack of positive role models in particular. Much of this concern is based on statistics such as the following: boys are five times more likely to commit suicide than girls, and four times more likely to be addicted to drugs or alcohol; boys are nine times more likely to be sleeping rough; and girls outperform boys at every level of education, and now outnumber boys at university by a ratio of 3 to 2. The concern over such figures has grown, and the cause of boys' disaffection has been variously diagnosed as a general 'crisis of masculinity', as poorer communication skills and an inability to express feelings, a macho culture that is anti-education, the lack of male teachers in primary schools, and a new 'post-feminist' imbalance between perceptions of girls and boys. The social results are supposedly football thuggery, an increase in violent crime, the spread of drugs and more playground bullying, but there is no consensus over the way to give boys more confidence and a sense of purpose. A related concern is that over the phenomenon of 'dumbing down', a general accusation made by older generations against the shift towards a post-literate visual culture, in which theoretical abstractions and analytical complexities appear less and less in the media. The argument seems to hinge upon whether one considers aspects of culture, from news reporting to summer movie blockbusters, to be more accessible and inclusive than they were, losing their overly didactic and 'improving' elements, or increasingly crass and simplistic.

Finally, we need to note how youth culture can become softened and anaesthetised, but also transformed and diffused. It has now become a kind of truism that more or less every town or even village in Britain is bound to have its resident punk, a figure as much a part of the repertoire of stock British types as the bowler-hatted city gent. Like most myths, though, this scenario of 'a punk in every high street' represents only a very partial truth, one which fails to register the complex differences between particular communities and the constant mutations in the ways different subcultures identify themselves. Elements of punk can be found in various British subcultures, the most notable probably being New Age travellers. Crucially, though, the style of clothes worn by many New Age travellers or the early 1990s phenomenon of 'crusties' also draws very heavily on a hippy aesthetic – ethnic clothes, beads and bangles. New Age hairstyles similarly seem to draw on a range of cultural references such as dreadlocks (Rastafariansim), bright hair dye (punk), shaved (skinhead), mohican (Native American/Hari Krishna/punk) and shaggy, matted long hair (hippy). Any subcultural identity can of course be dissected into its component parts of 'key' motifs and symbols, but the example of New Age/crusty subculture in Britain today also acutely demonstrates how problematic such checklists of cultural identities can be, not least because contemporary British cultural identities seem to be so enmeshed and hybrid – often self-consciously playing with or parodying the styles they adopt. New Age/crusty subculture was perhaps the most recent indication of an extra-social trend that did not react or rebel from within mainstream culture but sought a mode of life outside society, and has consequently been portrayed negatively and ignorantly in most media. People tend to get lumped together according to very superficial criteria, and what is interesting about the phenomenon of New Agers/ crusties is that certain marginalised elements of the population which may have previously formed far more distinct groupings such as hippies, travellers, political activists, the urban homeless and young unemployed people from both urban and rural communities, came to be bracketed together, albeit in an impressionistic way. In fact, the very vagueness of the boundaries which surrounds this subculture suggest that the label of 'crusty' or 'New Age traveller' is more likely to be invoked as a derogatory/ disapproving term in the south of England to describe scruffy youths or homeless people.

In September 2001, the Archbishop of Westminster, leader of 4.1 million Roman Catholics in England and Wales, declared that Christianity 'has almost been vanquished' in Britain and that people now increasingly gain their 'glimpses of the transcendent' in music, green issues and especially New Age movements. Indeed, New Age culture seems to combine spirituality with green politics and music in a way that speaks to the young in a more positive way than any other movement since that of the hippies in the 1960s.

Though many people who identify with New Age lifestyles may originally come from urban areas, there are several reasons why the subculture is generally associated with more rural areas. In the 1980s, a group of

FIGURE 4.4 New Age dancers perform at a party

travellers known as 'The [Peace] Convoy' received a lot of coverage in the British media, partly due to clashes with police over access to the ancient standing stones at Stonehenge in Wiltshire. A festival had been held annually over the summer solstice period at Stonehenge and had come to acquire the status of an 'alternative' to the well-known Glastonbury Festival, which had first taken place in 1970. Whereas Glastonbury has developed into a much bigger, more organised event, with an entry fee and big name bands, Stonehenge remained steadfastly 'unofficial' – a free festival with a greater emphasis upon drugs and anarchism – until in 2000 unrestricted access was allowed for the first time on the solstice, and again on 21 June 2001 an estimated 11,000 crusties, ravers, pagans and others partied peacefully all night to see the dawn. Both Stonehenge and Glastonbury festivals seem to offer strangely powerful conjunctions between modern folklore and the ancient myths of pagan Britain. For this reason English Heritage, custodian of the stones, still allows pre-booked access, including at the summer and winter solstice, and the spring and autumn equinox.

In such a way, the most recent cultural practices, and their representations in the press, will often draw on some of the oldest, and in many ways most powerful, British identities available. However, in this chapter overall, we have seen how Britain's youth since the 1950s continues to generate a varied range of subcultures. The proliferation of ever-evolving fashions and new trends means that, while reinventing the past, teenagers and youths see themselves as original, and today's styles and identities will be absorbed and transformed in a decade's time rather than discarded.

 Exercises

1   How important do you think age is within British culture? Would you say that the differences between age groups are becoming more or less distinct?

2   What kinds of music do you associate with the following British youth subcultures? Name specific bands /artists where possible:
   a)   Hippies
   b)   Goths
   c)   Skinheads
   d)   Crusties
   e)   Bikers
   f)   Rastas
   g)   Rudeboys

3   Why do you think Britain has produced such distinct subcultural styles and groupings? What, if anything, does this tell us about British culture as a whole?

4   What do the following phrases mean? Comment upon the possible insights
     they offer into British attitudes towards age.
     a)   'Mutton dressed as lamb'
     b)   'Put out to pasture'
     c)   'Trying to teach your grandmother to suck eggs'
     d)   'Toyboy'
     e)   'One foot in the grave'
     f)   'Whippersnapper'
     g)   'Wet behind the ears'
     h)   'Darby and Joan'
     i)   'Long in the tooth'
     j)   'Cradle snatcher'
     k)   'Pushing up the daisies'
5   Discuss the implications of the term 'ageism'. Is it possible and/or
     desirable to avoid ageism in contemporary British society?
6   To what extent do you think that young people have more in common with
     the youth of other nations and cultures than with older people from their
     own country?

Reading

Hebdige, Dick. *Subculture: the Meaning of Style*. Routledge, 1979. Influential review of
     youth and alternative culture.
Howker, Ed and Malik, Shiv. *Jilted Generation: How Britain Has Bankrupted Its Youth*.
     Icon, 2010. Stark analysis of how, in contrast to their parents, young Britons today
     have the prospect of the most uncertain future a generation has faced since the
     1930s.
McRobbie, Angela. *Feminism and Youth Culture: From 'Jackie' to 'Just 17'*. Routledge,
     1991. Looks at the effects of the feminist movement on magazine contents and on
     teenagers.
Settersten, Richard and Ray, Barbara. *Not Quite Adults*. Bantam, 2010. Sociological
     analysis of why 20-somethings are delaying adulthood.
Thornton, Sarah. *Club Cultures: Youth, Media, Music*. Polity: Blackwell, 1995. An
     exploration of subcultures across the main areas of youth activity and performance.

Cultural examples

Films

The Inbetweeners Movie (2011) dir. Ben Palmer. Spinoff from cult TV show recognised for its authenticity in the portrayal of teenagers.

Submarine (2010) dir. Richard Ayoade. Coming-of-age drama about the mismatch between self-perceptions and those of others.

The Kid (2010). Film based on a best-selling book about growing up and overcoming adversity. The film starts in the current generic mode of misery memoir then moves through the equally familiar secondary school drama before shifting towards the London gangster movie genre.

Harry Brown (2009) dir. Daniel Barber. In a film that considers the loneliness and isolation of old age, Michael Caine stars as the eponymous pensioner who takes the law into his own hands to address the violence and disrespect surrounding him.

This is England (2006) dir. Shane Meadows. 1980s Britain seen through the eyes of youth, and particularly a group of skinheads in a coastal town. Concerns subculture, gang rivalry and racism.

Human Traffic (1999) dir. Justin Kerrigan. A day in the life of hardcore clubbers in Cardiff.

The Football Factory (2003) dir. Nick Love. Adaptation of John King novel about masculinity and the end of Empire focusing on warring tribes of football fans.

Summer Holiday (1963) dir. Peter Yates. The archetypal sixties British teenager, Cliff Richard, goes to France on a London bus with his friends, singing all the way (worth comparing with the subculture of Nicholas Roeg's *Performance* from 1970, starring Mick Jagger).

My Beautiful Launderette (1985), dir. Stephen Frears. Urban realist film, with touches of magic realism, looking at sexuality and racism in the 1980s 'enterprise culture'. Focuses on the relationship between two youths – one Asian, one white working class.

Jubilee (1977), dir. Derek Jarman. Anarchic, decadent depiction of punk subcultures in Thatcher's Britain.

The Great Rock'n'Roll Swindle (1980) dir. Julien Temple. Portrait of the punk rock group the Sex Pistols.

Scum (1980) dir. Alan Clarke. Brutal portrayal of life for young men in the Borstal system.

Quadrophenia (1979) dir. Frank Roddam. Authentic sixties, London-and-Brighton film about mod culture, featuring Sting and based on an album by *The Who*.

Books

Irvine Welsh. *Trainspotting* (1993) Grim, darkly humorous novel about heroin subculture in Edinburgh. Made into a film in 1996.

Colin MacInnes. *Absolute Beginners* (1959) Cult novel about swinging teenage life in London. Also made into a film in the 1980s.

Richard Allen, *Skinhead* (1970) Teen-novel about violent youth subculture.

Sue Townsend, *The Secret Diary of Adrian Mole 13¾* (1982) Bestselling humour about growing up in Thatcher's Britain through a schoolboy's fictional diary.

Maude Casey, *Over the Water* (1990) Teenage novel about the problems of growing up as a second-generation Irish immigrant girl in the UK.

Leonore Goodings (ed.), *Bitter Sweet Dreams* (1987) Anthology of writings by a cross-section of British teenage girls.

Hanif Kureishi, *The Buddha of Suburbia* (1990) Growing up in and around London, in the 1970s, between different ethnic cultures.

Nick Hornby, *Fever Pitch* (1992) Amusing account of growing up as an obsessive football supporter.

TV programmes

Top Boy. Four-part Channel 4 drama about youths and street gangs growing up on a Hackney housing estate, screened in autumn 2011 after the summer riots.

Fresh Meat. Smart comedy about student life in a shared house. Compare with the 1980s' anarchic humour of the comparatively squalid and all-male household depicted in *The Young Ones.*

Outnumbered. British sitcom about the ways in which children frustrate their parents' attempts to be responsible.

The Inbetweeners. Follows the suburban lives of four teenage friends at the fictional Rudge Park Comprehensive.

Peep Show. Stylistically distinctive comedy show about the lives of two flatmates, foregrounding point of view shots accompanied by the voiceover thoughts of the main characters Mark and Jeremy.

Getting On. Comedy set on a National Health Service (NHS) ward that nicely observes British manners, attitudes and hierarchies.

Websites

www.guardian.co.uk/culture/gallery/2011/jul/10/10-best-british-youth-cultures
    List of the supposed top ten British youth subcultures.

www.thestudentroom.co.uk
    Website devoted to student life and study.

www.sugarscape.com
    Spinoff from Sugar magazine.

www.indiemusic.co.uk
    The Penny Black Music record shop's site provides in-depth knowledge and obscure information.

www.theory.org.uk
    Ultra cool social studies and cultural theory site

www.kidscape.org.uk
    Site about bullying and child welfare.

Class and politics

Frank McDonough

Timeline

1911	House of Lords Reform Act
1924	First Labour government
1940	Churchill, elected prime minister (PM)
1945	General Election: Labour elected
1948	National Health Service
1951	General Election: Conservatives elected
1955	General Election: Eden elected PM
1956	Suez Crisis
1959	Gaitskill fails to reform Clause Four
1959	General Election: Macmillan elected PM (third consecutive Tory victory)
1964	Labour victory
1967	Devaluation of the pound
1973	Britain joins EEC
1979	Winter of Discontent
1979	General Election: Thatcher elected PM
1981	Urban riots
1982	Falklands War
1990	Poll Tax riots
1990	Thatcher ousted from office
1992	Fourth consecutive Tory victory
1994	Police Act
1995	Leader Tony Blair elected PM
2001	Second consecutive Labour victory
2005	Third consecutive Labour victory
2010	Hung parliament: coalition government of Tories and Liberal Democrats

Introduction

CLASS WAS ONCE A CENTRAL FACET of British cultural identity. Each person was defined and graded in terms of their supposed position in this fixed hierarchy. Even the railway carriages were once sub-divided into three classes: first, second and third. It was thought each class had unique characteristics. The 'upper class' had posh accents, went to private schools, lived in stately homes and had aristocratic connections. The middle class were well spoken, lived in suburban houses and valued education. The working class had regional accents, lived in council flats, were members of trade unions, and enjoyed the pub, football and fish and chips.

In recent times, social commentators have suggested there has been a 'decline of class' in British society. Tony Blair, prime minister between 1997 and 2005, famously declared: 'The class war is over'. The term 'classless society' is now used extensively to describe modern Britain. The decline of the old rigid class system is attributed to the period when Margaret Thatcher was prime minister, between 1979 and 1990. Her 'revolution' weakened the influence of key institutions of the upper class – the BBC, the Church of England, the old universities and the monarchy. Her attack on the power of the trade unions and local councils weakened two key sources of working-class power. The group Mrs Thatcher's policies championed was the middle classes, especially those of its members employed in business, banking and the service industries. Under subsequent governments of both parties, John Major (Conservative, 1990–97), Blair (Labour, 1997–2007), Gordon Brown (Labour, 2007–10) and the current David Cameron-led Conservative–Liberal Democrat coalition, the expansion of the values of the middle class has continued.

Very few people speak of 'class' any more as the central focus of British cultural identity. Railways are now divided into just two classes: first and standard. Britain is now more fragmented socially than in terms of class. Society and life now revolve around individual families and are increasingly centred on the home, which usually contains a satellite TV system, CD and DVD players, a computer with internet access and often a large dining area, with a fitted kitchen and a fridge, usually stocked with exotic foreign food and wine. Staying in has become the new 'going out'.

The Irish playwright George Bernard Shaw once wrote: 'It is impossible for an Englishman to open his mouth without making some other Englishman hate or despise him.' This comment emphasises that in Britain, accent has always been an unwritten signifier of class position. Yet the once highly prized 'posh' upper class accent is no longer treated with the deference it once enjoyed. A decidedly 'posh' accent is now associated with being out of the touch with ordinary people. The 'posh' accent of socialite Tara Palmer-Tompkinson is constantly ridiculed by the tabloid press and popular comments. Tony Blair went to great efforts to flatten the vowels of his upper class accent. It's now better, if you have a 'posh' accent, to be a bit silly. Boris Johnson, the Lord Mayor of London, adopts this other-worldly persona with great success. Young people in the middle class, especially in London, have adopted either a more slang-based accent which draws on phrases from US hip-hop music or a more 'Cockney'-sounding London accent that has been called 'Estuary English'.

It cannot be said, however, that class prejudice based on accent has miraculously disappeared. The two regional accents which still suffer stigma and ridicule are 'Scouse', a dialect of the Liverpool area, and 'Brummie', an accent associated with Birmingham. A recent survey of the customers of call centres showed a great many people view both these accents as 'untrust-worthy'. Yet the same poll thought the Newcastle 'Geordie' was 'very attractive and warm'. Indeed, 'Geordie' TV stars such as Ant and Dec (who present the popular programme *I'm a Celebrity Get Me Out of Here*) and the pop star and TV presenter Cheryl Cole enjoy huge popularity and are indeed regarded as 'national treasures'. There is little prejudice against articulate Scottish or Irish accents, but the Welsh accent is often stigmatised in much the same way as Liverpool and Birmingham accents. These changes in how certain working-class accents are stigmatised, while others are admired, shows that a diverse set of cultural and regional prejudices is now evolving, but that a hierarchical view of which are the most desired accents still persists widely.

Cultural taste is an area which can also reveal sharp class divisions. Elite pursuits, such as opera, classical music, serious theatre and modern art, still remain preserves of the upper and middle classes. Even in TV and radio sharp divisions of taste are apparent. The listening audience of BBC Radio 4 is drawn from the middle and upper echelons of society. Hardly any of its presenters have regional accents. ITV 1, on the other hand, has many presenters with pronounced regional accents and draws most of its viewers from the working classes. The holiday destinations of Britons still show sharp class differences. Tuscany is a top destination for the upper middle classes, while Ibiza, famous for its nightclubs and binge-drinking culture, is the chosen destination for working-class young people from urban areas. It would seem cultural taste remains a key determinant of what class you feel you belong to, but there is little doubt that all the classes have undergone change in recent years.

The 'upper' class

Traditionally, the upper class consisted of the royal family, the aristocracy and other titled people. Upper-class status derived more from family background, inherited wealth and land ownership. In such a rigid heredity-based system, it was difficult to move up the class hierarchy. The Edwardian period was the high-water mark for the upper-class aristocracy. By the 1930s Noel Coward in his satirical song 'The Stately Homes of England' was already satirising the decline in power and status of the upper class.

Since the end of the Second World War, the aristocracy has faded economically and politically. In the 1960s there was a general attack against the inherited privileges of the aristocracy, who were derided as 'The Establishment'. The last member of the aristocracy to lead a British political party was the Conservative Sir Alec Douglas Home (1963–65), but he renounced his peerage in order to do so. Of course, aristocrats with titles still exist, but hardly any take part in public life nowadays. The 'stately homes of England' are now tourist attractions, mainly visited by the middle classes. Yet nostalgia for the golden age of the aristocracy has revived through the successful ITV1 drama series *Downton Abbey*, which traces the fortunes of an upper class family in the early twentieth century, and a new up-dated version of *Upstairs, Downstairs* which looks at the relationship between the lives of the upper middle class family and their servants in the inter-war years.

The only visible remnant of the traditional upper class is the royal family. During the 1930s, after the abdication of Edward VIII, who married an American divorcee Wallace Simpson, the monarchy seemed to face the prospect of decline. But the reign of King George VI and his wife Queen Elizabeth led to a revival in the standing of the Royal Family. The coronation of Queen Elizabeth II, the current monarch, in 1953 was the first popular TV event of the post-war era. In 1977 the Queen's Silver Jubilee was equally popular. In 1981, the wedding of Prince Charles, the heir to the British throne, to Lady Diana Spencer was one of the most widely viewed world TV events in the post-war era.

After the 1981 royal wedding things started to go wrong. The decision of Prince Edward to organise *It's a Royal Knockout*, based on a popular TV format during which members of the royal family appeared dressed as cheese and vegetables, was uniformly derided as a 'public-relations disaster'.

The entry into the royal family of Sarah Ferguson (dubbed 'Fergie' by the tabloid press), who married Prince Andrew, led to a series of damaging tabloid stories. These culminated in revelations of an extra-marital love affair in which her ex-lover said the Duchess of York enjoyed 'toe sucking' as an act of sexual foreplay. The excessive use by Prince Andrew (dubbed 'Air Miles Andy') of taxpayers' money to hire helicopters to attend top sporting events aroused further public outrage. The couple were eventually divorced.

Yet a much more deeply damaging crisis for the public standing of the royal family was the messy divorce of the hugely popular Diana, Princess of Wales and Prince Charles in the early 1990s. A litany of love affairs emerged in the tabloid press. In her 1992 Christmas Day broadcast the Queen was forced to admit 'this year has been my annus horribilis'. In a dramatic interview in November 1995 with Martin Bashir on the BBC programme 'Panorama', Diana launched an extraordinary attack on Prince Charles for his infidelity with Camilla Parker-Bowles. She also blamed the entire royal family for making her life a misery.

The story was bound to have a tragic ending. In August 1997, Diana, who had been hounded relentlessly by the tabloid paparazzi since her divorce, was killed in a car accident in Paris, along with her new boyfriend Dodi Al Fayed. The accident was partly caused by pursuing photographers placing pressure on her driver Henri Paul, who was well over the alcohol limit. The outpouring of grief following her death was unprecedented. Tony Blair, the Prime Minister, described her as 'The People's Princess' – and this seemed to capture the public mood perfectly.

The media focus shifted to the apparently 'uncaring attitude' of the royal family towards what was viewed as national tragedy – a sort of British version of the assassination of JFK. As poignant flower-mountains grew outside Buckingham Palace and Kensington Palace (the home of Diana), the royal family remained at Balmoral, their Scottish summer holiday haunt. Blair advised the Queen to return to London and speak to the nation on TV. The Queen bowed to this political pressure.

At the funeral, Diana's brother, Earl Spencer, launched a withering and emotive attack on the royal family and the tabloid press. The pop singer Elton John sang 'Candle in the Wind', originally based on the tragic life of Hollywood icon Marilyn Monroe, but given new words by Bernie Taupin to fit the equally tragic life of Princess Diana. The motorcade of her coffin through the streets of London was witnessed by millions.

It took the royal family many years to recover from damage inflicted by this tragedy. The Queen has abandoned her royal yacht and the royal train, and even pays income tax. The wedding of Prince William, seen by the public as 'Diana's son', to Kate Middleton in 2011 has miraculously restored the popularity of the royal family to a position not enjoyed since the heady days before the Queen's Silver Jubilee in 1977. With her good looks and popular appeal, it seems the Royal Family has in Kate Middleton a public-relations asset seemingly as potent as 'Lady Di'. Let's hope this story has a fairytale ending this time around.

Apart from widely reported events in the lives of the royal family, it is probably correct to suggest that the 'upper class' as previously defined no longer exists. In the USA the expression 'upper class' simply refers to 'the rich' and there is a growing tendency in the UK to see the newly defined British 'upper class' in a similar way. The annual publication of a UK 'Rich List' by *The Sunday Times* is one example of this new emphasis of wealth over breeding as the key entrance requirement to the 'upper class'. The only traditional member of the old aristocracy in the 'Rich List' in 2010 is the Duke of Westminster. In general, wealthy business people now dominate the list and many, such as Roman Abramovich, were not born in the UK. Further down the list come self-made business people such as Sir Richard Branson and Lord Alan Sugar, pop stars such as the ex-Beatle Sir Paul McCartney, writers like J. K. Rowling, and sports stars, most notably David Beckham and Wayne Rooney. The gap between the rich and the poor has never been wider. Recent studies have shown that the richest 1 per cent of the population account for 33 per cent of the nation's wealth. The wealthiest 10 per cent in Britain own over 50 per cent of its property.

It is, however, deeply misleading to think modern successful entrepreneurs are the dominant forces within the rich and powerful new 'upper class' or 'rich' class. Powerful UK business families, whose wealth was acquired more than a century ago, make up the majority of the most powerful FTSE 100 companies quoted on the London stock market. It would be equally wrong to think that a public-school, Oxbridge background is no longer essential to the recruitment policies of these top companies or even to the Cabinet. Indeed, of the current 23-member Conservative–Liberal Cabinet, all went to Oxford or Cambridge. And there are 12 members of the Labour Shadow Cabinet with a similar educational background. Networking still thrives in recruitment to the City of London, the big banks, the law and the media. The extent of nepotism in the media is quite startling with the sons and daughters of previous media figures occupying similar positions. Recent sociological studies reveal there is actually less social mobility in Britain now than at any time since the Edwardian period. The 'upper class' may not exist in exactly the same form it took fifty years ago. It is, apart from the royal family, culturally invisible, but the power and influence of the wealthy and the rich is stronger than ever and more exclusive than for decades.

The 'middle' class

The middle class is normally composed of those who spend more of their income on leisure than on the bare necessities of life. In a recent opinion poll, 70 per cent of the British population defined themselves as 'middle class'. It is the case that even John Lennon, the 'Scouser' who wrote about the virtues of being a 'Working Class Hero' in 1970, attended a selective grammar school and lived in a roomy semi-detached house with a large garden in the solidly middle-class Liverpool suburb of Woolton. His relatives were dairy farmers, teachers and doctors. Yet for the sake of the Beatles 'rags to riches' myth Lennon admitted in one of his last interviews with *Playboy* that he was encouraged by Beatles manager Brian Epstein to hide his middle-classness away.

Lennon's decision to gloss over his middle-class upbringing made sense at the time. In the 1960s and 1970s it was fashionable to deride a middle-class lifestyle as boring and soul-destroying. Being middle class was quite simply not rock 'n' roll. It was far better to pretend to be working class. The popular 1970s TV comedy *The Fall and Rise of Reginald Perrin* outlines the crisis of the middle class in this period quite brilliantly. It features the life of a 'boring' middle-class executive who takes the same route from his semi-detached house in the suburbs to commute to work each day. At work, Reggie grows tired of mixing with equally unadventurous people who speak in hackneyed clichés. At home, he despairs of his boring middle-class relatives whose idea of fun is to drink homemade wine at dinner parties or visit a safari park at the weekend. To break free from this middle-class Alcatraz Reggie fakes his own suicide and disappears. How supremely ironic that the middle-class lifestyle Reggie wanted to escape from has now become, of all things, fashionable. Living in the suburbs and working in an executive job is now seen as part of an aspirational lifestyle. A middle-class hero is now definitely something to be.

The expansion of the middle class numerically has made it much harder to define sociologically. At one time, the middle class could be pigeon-holed into four broad categories. One group was the higher professionals who valued education and training and occupied jobs that laid emphasis on working without supervision. Most held jobs requiring a university degree or a post-graduate qualification – including doctors, lawyers, architects, accountants, engineers and business executives. Family members from this group tended to follow a similar path. Less than 10 per cent of them ended up in a manual job. Such a remarkably low level of downward social mobility suggests shared middle-class values were passed on from generation to generation. A closely related middle-class group were the salaried professionals, including teachers, university and college lecturers, detectives, civil servants and social workers. All had university degrees and post-graduate qualifications. They enjoyed some autonomy, but are not as much as higher professionals. A third group were clerical and administrative staff – the 'lower middle class' in sociological terms. These workers may have had academic qualifications, but they were usually heavily supervised and worked an eight-hour day in close proximity to their co-workers. The final and most expanding group within the middle class was the self-employed. This group had more control over their working lives than say clerical workers, but they lacked the job security and pension benefits afforded to the professional middle class. Some of the self-employed, most notably plumbers, electricians and builders, could earn far more than many salaried professionals, but their income was, and is, directly linked to the general state of the economy. In good times they do exceptionally well, but in hard times they can suffer greatly. However all these groupings have become more fluid.

The philosopher Julian Baggini has cast doubt on whether 70 per cent of the British population is really middle class. 'Culturally this country is still predominantly working-class', he writes. 'Superficially it seems we are middle-class because we have more of the trappings of a middle-class life, but the majority of people are working-class with more money, not middle-class'.

There is one area, however, that reflects a change in the taste of those who lie in that grey zone between the upper edges of the working class and

FIGURE 5.1 Teachers attend a rally to protest against changes to their pensions

solid middle class. This is the huge growth of TV cookery programmes hosted by Jamie Oliver, Gary Rhodes, Nigella Lawson, Gordon Ramsey, Delia Smith, Rick Stein, Heston Blumenthal and others too numerous to mention. These 'classless' TV chefs are really selling a polite middle-class lifestyle, undoubtedly associated with the fine dining principles of France. The rise of the dinner party is one supremely visible example of the cultural spreading of a formerly middle-class lifestyle. One key example is the popular Channel 4 programme *Come Dine with Me*, which brings together four individuals from a variety of backgrounds who each host a middle-class dinner party then grade each other's performance as chefs and dinner hosts. It is usually in the menu choice that sharp class differences come to the surface, especially over traditional issues of correct middle-class table manners and etiquette.

In popular TV comedy series based around middle-class life a more dysfunctional picture emerges. In *Outnumbered*, the middle-class Brockman family have children with very little respect for their parents. In *2point4 Children*, the Porter children go around their suburban home slamming doors, throwing tantrums and running up large phone bills. *My Family* is another comedy based around a middle-class family who are seemingly at war with each other. The overall impression of these TV comedies is that bad parenting is a now staple part of modern middle-class families. The university-educated professionals in these comedies are seemingly incapable of establishing any discipline or order over their assertive, unruly and egotistical middle-class children.

The 'working' class

The working class is the most examined of all the social classes. Working-class people have been extensively portrayed in films, plays, dramas, comedies, novels and documentaries. Endless sociological and government reports have been compiled on the working class. Yet much of what we know of the working class has been written by members of the higher professional middle class. Karl Marx defined the working class or proletariat as people who sell their labour for wages. Such a definition would bring in a wide section of the middle class too. The term was refined in industrial societies to mean those who were dependent on physical labour and spent most of their income on food and shelter.

By the 1950s a stereotypical picture emerged of a typical, usually male, member of the British working class. They left school without any formal qualifications to find a job as a skilled or unskilled manual labourer. They lived in industrial towns and cities in close-knit communities in either landlord or council-owned properties. They were trade union members.

They voted Labour. For leisure, they drank pints of beer in the local pub, had a bet on the horses, enjoyed a trip to the football match. The fish and chip shop was the centre of local cuisine. Every Sunday the family gathered around the table to eat a Sunday dinner (which was actually eaten at lunch-time) and then read the Sunday papers. Working-class women were 'house-wives' and members of the extended family often lived together under the same roof. They increasingly liked to watch the TV together.

Even in the 1950s it was being suggested that this stereotype was breaking down due to improved wages and living conditions, the expansion of secondary education, the growth of consumer-goods consumption and the expansion of credit. As the Conservatives won the 1951, 1955 and 1957 General Elections with steadily increasing majorities it was clear more working-class people were rejecting the traditional 'working-class' Labour Party. A flood of sociological studies appeared indicating that the growth of affluent workers was changing the working class. The most influential study by Goldthorpe and Lockwood on Ford car workers revealed that these workers grasped the idea of social improvement through the means of buying consumer goods. Even so, they concluded this had not led to the working class wanting to become middle class. This was a possibly over-optimistic assessment. A more individualistic and aspiring group had clearly emerged within the working class, and its numbers have grown with the passage of time and changes in the economy. This was particularly true of the grammar-school-educated members of the working class who went on to success in the arts, film and pop culture in the 1960s. Three members of The Beatles (John, Paul and George) attended grammar schools, as did Mick Jagger.

It was the decision by the Thatcher governments of the 1980s to reduce the traditional industrial base in Britain in favour of banking, finance and service industries that led to a massive reduction in coal, steel docks and shipbuilding on which many working-class areas depended. The old working class was smashed economically, politically and culturally by 'Hurricane Thatcher'. The traditional working-class male, popularised in the *Daily Mirror*'s 'Andy Capp' newspaper cartoon strip, is as extinct as a dinosaur. In 1981, there were 13.3 million manual workers, representing over 50 per cent of the workforce, and there were 13 million trade union members. In 2001, the number of manual workers fell to 27 per cent and in 2011 stood at 14 per cent. Trade union membership now stands at just under 7 million, the majority of whom are women.

The de-industrialisation of huge parts of the urban landscape of the UK has dramatically impacted on the former industrial working class and this has particularly affected the working-class male. Working-class women now go out of the home to either full- or part-time work. The rapid expan-sion of service industries such as banking, tourism and insurance has led to

FIGURE 5.2 Unionised public-sector workers protest in Birkenhead

over 35 per cent of working-class households now having a female bread-winner. Working-class women are less dependent on males than ever before.

The 'new' working class in jobs have developed a much more consumer-based lifestyle. Pubs and working men's clubs have closed down in every former industrial working-class area. The new working class view themselves as 'middle class' and their leisure activities of foreign holidays, home ownership, fine dining, wine, exotic food, entertaining at home, at dinner parties or at restaurants are all pursuits that thirty years ago were exclusively middle-class. This new 'working class', who clearly think themselves 'middle-class', are consumer-oriented, aspiring and individualistic. They value education and careers.

We cannot talk of the 'working class' as some homogeneous group with a clear leadership any more. The term 'underclass' has been coined to describe those who remain outside what is a rapidly expanding 'middle class'. This 'underclass' is excluded from the benefits of the consumer society. Street begging, homelessness, drug and alcohol addiction have increased in the poorest sections of society. Long-term unemployment is at record rates. Relative poverty has grown more rapidly in Britain than in any other modern industrial economy, except for the USA.

There has been a sharp change of attitude towards the poor 'under-class' – especially from the growing middle class. The term 'chav' is now in common usage in Britain to describe members of the 'underclass'. It is mainly used by middle-class people to demonise a certain portion of the working class. Lauren, played by the popular comedienne Catherine Tate, is a prime popular cultural example. She attends a comprehensive school in a deprived area of London. She is at odds with traditional middle-class authority figures. Whenever she is criticised for her behaviour, she responds with her classic catchphrase: 'Am I bothered?' She speaks in a rapid US rap style accent and says things such as 'that is well bad'. Another popular 'chav' character of TV comedy is Vicky Pollard. She appears in the comedy series *Little Britain*, played by rotund Matt Lucas. Vicky is a teenage unmarried mother who wears a brightly coloured tracksuit and comes from the ill-defined west-country town of 'Darkly Noone'. She speaks in an incredibly fast, impossible-to-understand dialect. She answers every question with the phrase 'No but yeah but no but yeah but no but'.

The popular ITV *Jeremy Kyle Show* features real life 'chav' versions of these TV comedy stereotypes. Travel companies in the UK now promote 'chav-free holidays'. A popular Channel 4 TV series called *Wife Swap* takes a solid member of the middle class and places her with a 'chav' family. The unwritten moral implication of this programme is clear. The 'chav' house-wife needs reforming into the 'respectable' values of middle-class life. There are many other examples of this demonisation of the 'underclass'. The popular TV series *Shameless* focuses on the lazy, trouble-making Gallagher clan of northern 'chavs'. The website 'Chav Scum' gives numerous examples of the behaviour of this demonised group. Jade Goody, a figure from the popular TV series *Big Brother*, became hugely famous mainly because of her ignorance of history and geography, and her catchphrase 'Am I minging?' is yet another example of the chav archetype. Later she became notorious due to her racist bullying of Shilpa Shetty, a beautiful Indian Bollywood star, on *Celebrity Big Brother*. Goody's brave battle against cancer restored her reputation, however, and her funeral was said to be a chav version of that of 'Lady Di'. A recent episode of The Channel 4 TV reality show *Big Fat Gypsy Wedding*, which focused on the travelling Sinta, a Romany people, was but the latest contribution to the dubious genre of chav bashing.

Perhaps the most prominent real-life example of the demonisation of the 'underclass' was the tragic case of Shannon Matthews, a child who mysteriously disappeared in February 2008, on a council estate in Dewsbury. At the beginning, the story appeared similar to the case of Madeleine McCann, the beautiful daughter of a solid middle-class couple who went missing while on a holiday in Portugal in May 2007. The tragic plight of the McCanns is widely empathised with by the British public. Kate McCann's recent autobiography sold over 1 million copies in hardback. It looked like Shannon might be another Madeleine. Local residents raised money. They searched tirelessly for the young girl around the poor council estate where she lived. The media soon reported the story 24/7. On 14 March Shannon was found – drugged, and hidden under a divan bed – at the home of a relative of her mother. From this point, the story altered quite dramatically. Shannon's mother was dubbed an 'irresponsible chav' who had been party to an elaborate hoax. She was subsequently convicted and sent to prison. The case was highlighted in the press and even by politicians as a prime example of a 'broken Britain' – dominated by the issue of what to do about a 'feral underclass'.

In reality, this disenfranchised 'underclass' is a consequence of policies that have removed so many of the community-based aspects of the older working class from the mainstream. It is in these poor areas of the UK that voting in elections is at its very lowest – and where support for far right groups such as the BNP (British National Party) and the English Defence League are at their strongest.

The wake-up call for the middle class and the 'It's grim up north Islington' set were the London riots of 2011. The bottled-up anger of this portion of the 'underclass' who were excluded from the consumer society flooded out onto the streets on the capital city in scenes of rioting, looting and arson never before witnessed in the UK. Copycat riots spread to Birmingham, Nottingham, Manchester and Liverpool. There were feeble attempts to suggest the rioters were drawn from a cross-section of society, but the reality was that the chief culprits, who appeared in court, were over-whelmingly drawn from previously convicted members of the 'underclass' and the 'chavs' who gave voice to a profound sense of abandonment from the affluent consumer society.

The political system

The transformation of power that has occurred within the classes is also reflected in changes in the political system. The dominant mechanisms of power in Britain still reside at the Houses of Parliament in Westminster in London. The power of central government has never been stronger, in spite of devolved regional assemblies in Scotland, Wales and Northern Ireland. Mrs Thatcher promised to end the 'enlarged role of the state'. In 1979, 43 per cent of the economy was controlled by the state. In 2011, the state is still responsible for 45 per cent of economic activity. Power in Britain is primarily in the hands of the prime minister and the Cabinet.

Through the 1994 Police Act, the police force, previously organised on a local basis, came under the control of the Home Secretary. The National Health Service is controlled by the health secretary. English schools operate a national curriculum and universities have their student fees set by the government. The chancellor of the exchequer has wide-ranging powers to set the rate of taxes over the entire population, regulate the pay rises of public sector workers and set levels of benefit for pensioners, the disabled and the unemployed. This huge concentration of power at Westminster has meant that the London economy dominates the rest of the country in a way that is not true of other major European industrial societies.

Ever since the English Civil War in the seventeenth century, when Parliament ordered the execution of King Charles I, the power of the monarch has dwindled. A British monarch reigns, but does not rule. Today, Queen Elizabeth II is largely a ceremonial figure. The weak power of the monarch is most graphically illustrated in the state opening of Parliament, which takes place each November. At this uniquely eccentric British ceremony a messenger of the monarch, Black Rod, requests that members of parliament listen to the 'Queen's Speech' in the House of Lords, but he has the door of the chamber slammed firmly in his face. This ritual symbolises the independence of the House of Commons from the monarch. Even the 'Queen's Speech' which outlines legislative programme of the government for the coming year is written by the prime minister, in consultation with Cabinet colleagues.

Britain is accurately described as a 'constitutional monarchy' but power resides firmly at Westminster which is made up of two 'houses'. The less important of these is the unelected House of Lords, composed of hereditary and life peers. Until 1911 the upper house actually had a veto over government legislation. Today it can only give advice on government Acts. During the era of the 'New Labour' governments between 1997 and 2010 the House of Lords was radically reformed. The number of hereditary peers, elected by the old aristocracy, was reduced to just 92 and the remaining life peers are nominated by the party leaders.

The dominance of the House of Commons has led to the British political system being described as 'an elected dictatorship'. The House of Commons is elected at general elections, which can be held at any time, but can only run for a maximum period of five years. The growth of the power of the elected House of Commons has been accompanied by the expansion of the electorate through a number of Parliamentary Reform Acts, the last being in 1970 when the vote was given to every citizen aged eighteen or over.

At the May 2010 General Election 650 Members of Parliament (MPs) were elected. Each MP represents one voting area, known as a parliamentary constituency. There is a plan to reduce the number of MPs by redrawing the electoral boundaries so that each constituency is composed of 100,000 electors. Britain operates a 'first past the post' electoral system in each constituency. This means each voter registers a vote for an individual candidate and the one with the most votes is elected as the MP.

The party leader who gains the most 'seats' in parliament is invited by the Queen to form a government. In the event of a hung parliament, it is possible for a minority government to be formed. After the 2010 election no party gained an overall majority, so David Cameron, leader of the party with the most seats – the Conservatives – joined a coalition partnership with Nick Clegg the leader of the Liberal Democrat Party.

It is the prime minister alone who has the power to select the members of the Cabinet. This is composed of his key ministers responsible for different aspects of policy. It used to be said that a British prime minister was merely 'the first among equals' within the Cabinet. However, in recent times both Margaret Thatcher and Tony Blair have cultivated a more 'presidential style' of government. Thatcher's attempt to bypass her Cabinet led to her falling from power in 1990 when the Cabinet effectively forced her to resign. Tony Blair, supported by the Downing Street Press Office, led by Alistair Campbell and his dominant chancellor of the exchequer Gordon Brown, never faced a significant Cabinet rebellion during his period in office. The most controversial aspects of Blair's rule were in the arena of foreign policy. Blair passionately supported British military involvement in Afghanistan as part of the George Bush led 'war on terror', but a vote in the House of Commons on British involvement never took place. Blair was accused of encouraging his all-powerful press secretary Alistair Campbell to 'sex up' documents to prove Iraq had weapons of mass destruction and thereby win the Commons vote to support the US-led war against Iraq. The tag 'President Blair' was henceforth used to illustrate what was seen as a particularly personal style of government, based on the American model. The decision to include televised leadership debates, during the 2010 General Election, placed the focus on the party leaders, as opposed to the political parties, as had been the norm in previous British elections.

Party politics

The three major political parties in Britain are the Conservative Party, the Labour Party and the Liberal Democrats. In reality, the two dominant governing parties since 1918 have been the Conservatives and Labour. Between 1950 to 1970, a staggering 92 per cent of votes went to these two parties. At the May 2010 General Election, the two main parties had a combined vote of 65.1 per cent, with the Liberal Democrats polling 23 per cent. It was frequently said Britain had a class-based political system. There is some truth to this claim. The Conservatives were for a long time the upper-class party, Labour the representatives of the working class and the Liberals the representatives of the middle class.

The Conservative Party first emerged in the 1830s from the old 'Tory' grouping in the House of Commons. It was only in the late nineteenth century, under the leadership of Benjamin Disraeli, that the party gained a modern organisation and a clear political identity. The 'conservative' tag originally meant defending traditional institutions such as the monarchy, the aristocracy and the empire and being a 'national' party that represented all society. Disraeli popularised the idea of 'One Nation' Conservatism, which supported limited social reform to help 'the deserving poor'. The Conservative Party claimed it could rise above class-based politics and represent the people. It was thought that the Conservatives would decline once mass democracy was introduced after 1918, but the party has constantly adapted its policies to fit in with changing social trends and has won extended periods in power between 1931 to 1945, 1951 to 1964 and 1979 to 1997. In the 1930s the party shed its aristocratic image and was led by business figures such as Stanley Baldwin and Neville Chamberlain. In the 1950s under Harold Macmillan the Conservatives accepted Labour policies such as nationalisation and social welfare reform. Under Margaret Thatcher, the party adopted a strong business and consumer-oriented electoral approach, which won four consecutive election victories. Under David Cameron, the party has moved away from the strident free-market approach of Mrs Thatcher. The Achilles heel for the Conservatives, in electoral terms, has been sex scandals. The popularity of the 1957–64 Conservative government was irreparably damaged by the 'Profumo Scandal' – which involved a love affair between a 'call girl' Christine Keeler and the Conservative War minister John Profumo. The government of John Major between 1992 and 1997 was dogged by a series of 'sleazy' sex scandals, including a widely reported love affair between David Mellor, the culture minister, and a little-known actress.

The Labour Party is Britain's second major political party. It was set up in 1900, with support from the trade unions, to represent the interests of the old industrial working class. In 1918, under clause IV of the party's constitution it even made an overt socialist commitment to enact 'the common ownership of the means of production', if it gained power.

It was not until 1945 that the Labour Party won an overall majority at a general election, but the 1945–51 Labour administrations introduced the most wide-ranging series of social reforms, including the National Health Service – something copied around the world – social security, compulsory secondary education and the nationalisation of several industries including coal, steel, gas and electricity. Labour also won two further periods of rule, from 1964 to 1970 and 1974 to 1979. It was its close association with trade unions and high profile strikes that led to a fall in popularity for the Labour Party before 1979. In that era the party was saddled with a 'cloth-cap' image at a time when the middle class was expanding.

It was Tony Blair, portraying the party as 'New Labour', who transformed the image of the Labour Party between 1994 and 2005. He won three impressive landslide election victories – something no other Labour leader has ever achieved. It is ironic that the public school and Oxford back-ground of Blair and his 'posh voice' enabled the Labour Party to attract the widest spectrum of voters in its history. The Blair governments combined support for free enterprise and the City of London with an expansion of the public sector and support for devolution for Scotland, Wales and Northern Ireland. Blair's outstanding electoral appeal was only dented when he gave overwhelming support to the US 'war on terror' against Afghanistan and Iraq and to the press mogul Rupert Murdoch. His penchant for 'media manipulation' by his press secretary Alistair Campbell (whose brutal methods were brilliantly satirised by the film *In the Loop*) also alienated former supporters.

Blair was such a dominant figure that it was inevitable that his departure in 2007 would be a difficult one for the Labour Party as the fall of Margaret Thatcher had been for the Conservatives. His successor Gordon Brown was not helped by the 'banking crisis' of 2007, and the subsequent messy expenses scandal that engulfed members of Parliament in 2009–10. History will conclude that Brown found moving out of Blair's shadow deeply uncomfortable. His abysmal performance in the live TV leadership debates and on the campaign trail contributed greatly to Labour's defeat in the 2010 General Election campaign. Brown's most damaging moment came when Gillian Duffy, a 66-year-old widow, criticised Brown's policy on immigration in a live Sky TV news broadcast. Unaware that his microphone was still switched on, Brown got into his car and described the encounter as a 'disaster', then referred to Duffy as 'that bigoted woman'. Duffy became a tabloid heroine. Brown was forced to openly apologise to her on BBC radio. After the election, Brown was replaced by Ed Miliband as Labour leader, but it will be an uphill struggle to regain the massive popular appeal Labour enjoyed in the Blair years.

The third largest political party is that of the Liberal Democrats. This party evolved from the old Liberal Party, which had been one of the two major political parties before World War One, and the Social Democratic Party, formed in 1981 by the 'Gang of Four' – Roy Jenkins, Shirley Williams, David Owen and Bill Rogers – who were all former Labour Party Cabinet ministers, disenchanted with Labour's move towards the left.

The Liberal Democrats, now led by Nick Clegg, support proportional representation, an even-handed approach to business and labour, the EEC, and policies aimed at supporting freedom of the individual. The outcome of the May 2010 General Election presented the Liberal Democrats with an historic opportunity to participate in a coalition government – something that had not been offered since February 1974 when negotiations with Edward Heath, the Conservative Prime Minister, came to nothing. After the 2010 election, Clegg negotiated with Brown and Cameron, but eventually the Liberal Democrats joined a Conservative–Liberal coalition, in an agreement designed to last five years. However, uncomfortable compromises by the Liberal Democrats on university tuition fees, a vast programme of public spending cuts, defeat in a referendum on proportional representation in 2011 and the use of a veto in controlling the EEC financial problems have led to deep divisions. The Liberal Democrats' standing in the opinion polls has fallen to an all-time low. The major beneficiary of the coalition arrangement has been the Conservative Party.

The other parties represented in parliament are the Scottish National Party and Plaid Cymru. The latter make nationalist demands for Wales. The Ulster Unionists who campaign on Ulster remaining part of the United Kingdom are also represented at Parliament, and have an outlook closer to the Conservatives than Labour. There is also one representative for the Green Party, which campaigns on environmental issues. There are all manner of small special-interest and fringe parties that put up candidates in elections, but have gained no seats in Parliament. The most prominent examples are the British National Party (BNP), which is opposed to immigration, and the United Kingdom Independence Party (UKIP), which is strongly opposed to British membership of the EEC. The Socialist Workers Party advocates socialist policies based on the principles of Marx and Engels. A more bizarre party is the Monster Raving Loony Party, which promises 'free ice cream for all' if elected.

Changing social attitudes

It seems social attitudes have changed dramatically in recent years. The publication of the 2010 Social Attitudes Survey reveals some startling findings. The majority of people now feel gaining a fair reward for talent is more important than equal treatment. In 1983, only 35 per cent believed unemployment benefits were too high. In 2001, this figure had grown only to 38 per cent, but in 2010, 55 per cent think they are much too high. The number who thought the unemployed could get a job if they wanted to was only 27 per cent in 1983, but now stands at a whopping 55 per cent. There is little sympathy for those in poverty nowadays. A staggering 75 per cent of the population feels that it is poor 'shameless' parents who are to blame for the poverty of their families. The idea that the government should act to redistribute income from the rich to the poor has declined quite dramatically too. In 1989, 51 per cent agreed that this should be a key aim of government, but in 2010 this had fallen to a paltry 27 per cent.

Britain is becoming the most secularised of all the key democratic societies. In 1983, only 31 per cent did not belong to a religion, but by 2010 51 per cent did not. The Church of England, the established religion in the UK, is suffering the greatest loss of affiliation, down from 40 per cent in

1983 to 20 per cent in 2010. During the same period there has been a quite remarkable collapse in esteem for bankers – a group championed by both Thatcher and Blair. In 1983, 90 per cent of the population thought banks were 'well run', but in 2010 only 19 per cent thought so. The strong stress on individualism since 1979 seems to have led to a great majority of Britons believing more in self-reliance and less in state welfare. But they are also increasingly disillusioned by the assertion that free-market capitalism provides all the answers.

Conclusion

We are clearly entering a period of deep political and economic flux. The USA, the nation Britain slavishly followed economically and culturally, is seen by many now as in terminal decline. If the twentieth century was the 'American century' then the twenty-first century will be the 'Chinese century'. As so many former certainties are shattering it is hardly surprising that politics and class are altering too. We can no longer categorise people into neat pigeon-holes. These categories are simply not complex enough any more. The low standing of politicians means the public no longer looks to them for answers. The bankers – supposedly the group that would lead us to a new promised land – have merely led everyone down a blind alley.

The key issue facing Britain today is the same as it had been since the end of the Empire: what role will Britain play in the future world economy? No one can yet answer that question. Simply following the USA would now seem foolhardy. Can we simply remain an island separate from Europe? Perhaps the biggest political issue for all parties is: which party will capture the imagination of the vast army of disillusioned young people? A key feature of the Blair–Brown years was the growing apathy of young people to politics. In 2005, more people voted in the final of Channel 4's *Big Brother* reality TV show than in the General Election. In recent times, young people have become more politically active over issues such as student tuition fees, youth unemployment and anti-capitalism riots than at any time since the late 1960s.

There is another simmering and yet critical issue in British society: what will be the fate of the growing 'underclass'? Routinely demonised in the media, and subject to numerous derogatory reality TV shows, this group participated in a quite unparalleled series of riots in Britain during the summer of 2011, which almost placed the army on the streets of Britain. The only certainty, it seems, when looking at the future of class and politics, is uncertainty.

Exercises

1   Offer a definition of upper, middle and working class.
2   To what extent do British people vote along class lines?
3   What is your understanding of the voting systems: 'first past the post' and 'proportional representation'? Which offers the better model on which to base a system for electing a government?
4   How have British class attitudes and styles changed in recent times?
5   Name some British people from a range of occupations. Can you place them in terms of class?

Reading

Bower, Tom. *Gordon Brown*. Harper, 2005. A 'warts and all' account of the Labour Prime Minister.

Jones, Owen. *Chavs: The Demonization of the Working Class*. Verso, 2011. An account of the representation of the underclass.

Oborne, Peter. *The Triumph of the Political Class*. Simon and Schuster, 2007. Charts the rise of a group of people without experience of the 'real' world whose advent threatens the traditional freedoms enjoyed by Britons.

Rawnsley, Andrew. *The End of the Party*. Viking, 2010. An impressively detailed and well informed critique of New Labour.

Cultural examples

Films

In the Loop (2009) dir. Armando Iannucci. Black comedy based on events prior to the 2003 Iraq war. It is a thinly veiled portrayal of Anglo-American machinations partly orchestrated by a 'director of communications and strategy'.

The King's Speech (2010) dir. Tom Hooper. A study of King George VI's working with his Australian speech therapist Lionel Logue to overcome his stammer. A well-received 'heritage' film.

Made in Dagenham (2010) dir. Nigel Cole. Dramatises the Ford sewing machinists' strike of 1968, which led to the Equal Pay Act.

The Iron Lady (2012) dir. Phyllida Lloyd. A biography of the powerful Tory leader. *The Guardian* worried that its empathy with her overlooked the damage she did.

Books

Zadie Smith, *White Teeth* (2000) A portrait of family life in modern Britain where issues of class and race are uppermost.

Alan Bennett, *Untold Stories* (2005) A candid snapshot of life at the grassroots. Working-class family life is exposed and celebrated.

Kazuo Ishiguro, *Never Let Me Go* (2005) A group of young people in a boarding school are being bred to donate their organs. Issues of class, politics, power, obedience and freedom are highlighted.

TV programmes

The Great Offices of State. Dir. Michael Cockerill. A behind-the-scenes documentary of the Home Office, the Foreign Office and the Treasury.

House of Cards. Fictional series about a manipulative Conservative MP seeking power, whose skill at political evasion and double-dealing was compelling, and whose typical hypocritical expressions such as 'You might think that, but I couldn't possibly comment' and 'I have no ambitions in that direction' became catchphrases.

The Fall and Rise of Reginald Perrin. This 2009 remake of the original 1970s sitcom updates the mid-life crisis that the original Reggie was suffering from and illustrates the ennui of modern middle-class life.

Come Dine With Me. Amateur chefs compete against each other in this reality TV series with an acerbic commentary by comedian Dave Lamb.

Outnumbered. A comedy series depicting a slightly dysfunctional middle-class London family in which the kids threaten to dominate the adults.

Downton Abbey. Julian Fellowes's depiction of the upper classes at play. It is the most successful period costume drama since *Brideshead Revisited* (1981).

Shameless. Paul Abbott's comedy drama series set on a Manchester housing estate. It deals with the 'underclass' and working-class culture.

The Thick of It. Armando Iannucci's influential political satire, featuring a thinly disguised Alistair Campbell.

Power of Nightmares. Adam Curtis's documentary series suggesting that politicians strive to be seen as visionaries rather than as managers.

Music

Jamie T. A Wimbledon toff who brings middle-class pride to music.

The Streets. Birmingham white rapper Mike Skinner, who has been called 'Britain's true poet'.

Pulp, *Different Class* (1995) Album of vignettes about class politics, drug culture and British social attitudes.

Blur, *The Great Escape* (1995) A series of comments on British life from the opening track on 'Stereotypes', through a song on the 'Country House' to 'Top Man' (a clothes shop).

Billy Bragg, *Workers' Playtime* (1988) Named after a post-war radio programme broadcast from a factory canteen, this, like all Bragg's albums, is a collection of love
songs and political anthems such as 'Waiting for the Great Leap Forwards', 'Tender
Comrade' and 'Rotting on Remand'.

The Clash, *The Clash* (1977) Archetypal British punk featuring songs like 'White Riot',
'London's Burning', 'Career Opportunities', 'I'm So Bored with the USA' and 'Police
and Thieves'.

Half Man Half Biscuit, *Bisodol Crimond* (2011) The 12th album of the rock band offering
a sardonic commentary on contemporary British life.

Websites

www.news.bbc.co.uk
   Contains in-depth coverage of contemporary issues with lots of links to background
   stories.
www.labour.org.uk; www.libdems.org.uk; www.conservative-party.org.uk
   Web addresses of the main UK political parties.
www.statistics.gov.uk
   These statistics deal with 13 areas of British life (economics, employment etc.).
www.direct.gov.uk
   Portal for all government departments and publications.

Ethnicity and language

Gerry Smyth

Timeline

1066	Norman invasion from northern France
1362	English legally recognised
1603	Death of Elizabeth I
1616	Death of Shakespeare
1707	Union of England and Scotland
1800	Union of Britain and Ireland
1870	Teaching Welsh banned
1947	Gaelic banned on Northern Irish road signs
1955	Churchill argued for slogan: 'Keep British White'
1958	'Race' riots in Notting Hill
1965	Race Relations Act
1968	'Troubles' start in Northern Ireland
1976	Commission for Racial Equality
1977	Advisory Council on Race Relations
1983	Black sections in Labour Party
1991	Census question on ethnicity
2003	Employment Equality (Religion or Belief) Regulations
2005	'Life in the United Kingdom' test introduced
2006	Racial and Religious Hatred Act

Introduction

I N 2006, THE LABOUR FORCE SURVEY found that for 6 per cent of the UK population aged 16 and over the first language spoken at home was not English. In the UK there are at least twenty different varieties of English, over forty dialects of overseas English and 56 different world languages, 12 of which are indigenous. Another survey found that there were at least twelve languages in Britain that could claim over 100,000 speakers. To some people, such linguistic diversity might seem surprising in the homeland of arguably the world's most successful modern language. These statistics, however, are indicative of the multitude of ways used by the citizens of modern Britain to communicate.

These languages, moreover, are closely linked with the ways in which people perceive themselves and their role in British society. For although the United Kingdom is a state, many people within this state think about themselves, their families and their local communities in quite different ways. One way of describing these individuals and the groups to which they belong is in terms of 'ethnicity'. Ethnicity is a highly complex and contentious concept. For the purposes of this chapter, however, it can be defined as the patterns of behaviour, cultural values and political affiliations shared by certain individuals who come together to form a group within a larger population.

According to the National Statistics agency, there were 3 million people in the British Isles from ethnic minorities in the 1991 census. The largest ethnic minority populations are found in Inner London and West Midlands Metropolitan County, and the smallest in the rural areas of Scotland, Yorkshire and Northumberland. Table 6.1 gives the figures for 2001 (and percentage proportions for 2001 and 1991), which show an increase in the proportion of the population from almost every ethnic minority (and the introduction of new categories of classification).

Additionally, the United Kingdom comprises four separate indigenous populations – one very large (English) and three small (Scottish, Welsh and Northern Irish). From one perspective, this arguably means there is a large number of people in the United Kingdom – around 20 per cent of the total

TABLE 6.1 Ethnic populations in 2001 and proportions in 2001 and 1991

Ethnic group	2001 population	2001 proportion of total UK population	1991 proportion of total UK population
White British	50,366,497	85.67%	94.5% (white)
White (other)	3,096,169	5.27%	Not a category
White Irish	691,232	1.2%	Not a category
Mixed race	677,117	1.2%	Not a category
Indian	1,053,411	1.8%	1.5%
Pakistani	747,285	1.3%	0.9%
Bangladeshi	283,063	0.5%	0.3%
Other Asian (non-Chinese)	247,644	0.4%	0.4%
Black Caribbean	565,876	1.0%	0.9%
Black African	485,277	0.8%	0.4%
Black (others)	97,585	0.2%	0.3%
Chinese	247,403	0.4%	0.3%
Other	230,615	0.4%	0.5%

Source: *Census*, 2001 and 1991

indigenous population – who do not have a straightforward relationship with the political state in which they live. In recent decades, this problematic relationship between the state and its ethnic and regional minorities has become the subject of one of the most important debates in modern British life, and in this chapter I want to examine some of the practices, attitudes and strategies which have emerged around this debate.

Ethnic and regional identity can appear in many forms. Historians, sociologists and anthropologists have discovered, however, that one of the most important ways in which ethnic groups identify themselves is through language. Not only is language the principal conveyor of symbols, ideas and beliefs which are of importance to the ethnic group, very often the language becomes a powerful possession in itself, something to be protected and preserved as the main badge of ethnic identity. Much of the time then, the alternative allegiances which constitute ethnic identity emerge specifically as tensions about language and the social status and cultural possibilities of different accents, dialects and vocabularies.

The recognition of ethnic status has significant legal, educational and social implications. But ethnic status, going back to our definition, also has important sociological and psychological implications for the kind of person the individual understands him/herself to be – that is, for an individual's identity. The point of departure for what follows is that a significant part of our individual identity is constituted through language – the language the world uses to communicate with us, and the language we use to communicate with the world. Putting all this together, then, these issues of ethnicity, identity and language are going to be our main areas of focus in this chapter. Specifically, I want to examine three inter-related issues – the usage and status of:

1   'standard' and 'non-standard' forms of the English language and implications for English and British identity
2   other indigenous British languages – Welsh, Scots and Gaelic – and the challenge to the domination of English
3   non-English languages brought to Britain by immigrants and other groups, such as Chinese and West Indian.

Varieties of English

In the nineteenth century, the notion of 'correct', 'good' or 'pure' English became something of an obsession for many literary critics, philosophers and educationalists. The result of this anxiety was the invention of an ideal form of the English language, covering aspects of grammar, vocabulary, pronunciation and so on, but also importantly linked to ways of acting, kinds of belief and systems of value. Such an ideal was needed to support Britain's self-image as a great industrial and imperial power, and to measure various kinds of linguistic deviance. The fact that this ideal or 'standard' English was an invention did not appear to worry those who used it to condemn the linguistic 'errors' made by the vast majority of the British population. It must have seemed strange to a person from Northumberland or Somerset, for example, regions with dialects evolved over 1,000 years and completely immersed in local history and local geography, to be told that the way they spoke was wrong – according to the arbitrary rules invented by certain intellectuals and scholars! In the twenty-first century, it has been most commonly argued that in most social situations an upper-class accent is a disadvantage and there are actually now speech coaches who will help 'posh' people lose their accents, whereas thirty years ago, everyone else was trying to acquire them. This has to be linked to the perception that class is nowadays more about celebrity than breeding, especially as many of the prestigious events on the social calendar, and the magazines that cover them, will now be overrun with the famous as much as the aristocratic, the only connection between the two groups being that both are comparatively rich.

The question of the correct way to speak and to write English continued to exercise a very great influence in British life throughout the twentieth century. Many people even today adhere to the model of standard English (or 'received pronunciation' as it is sometimes referred to) invented in the nineteenth century, believing it to be the real or true English language, a fixed linguistic structure against which deviations and mistakes can be measured. These people remain anxious about what they consider to be falling standards in spoken and written English, feeling that this is in some way related to Britain's wider economic, cultural and political status. Letters are written to the 'quality' newspapers (such as *The Times*, *The Independent*, *The Daily Telegraph* and *The Guardian*) and to the British Broadcasting Corporation (BBC), both radio and television, about bad practices in spoken and written English. In the early days of broadcasting, the 'BBC accent' was the hallmark of correct spoken English and newscasters are still seen as 'custodians' of the language. But in recent years this 'BBC accent', like its close relation 'the Queen's English', has in itself become a minority form; one of the few people likely to be heard speaking 'the Queen's English' is the Queen herself, in her Christmas Day speeches to the Commonwealth (and even she has been accused of loosening her speech in recent years). The clipped pronunciation and mannered voice of Prince Charles, as well as his constant use of the impersonal pronoun 'one' – as in 'one feels one's responsibilities' – is also somewhat of a throwback to an earlier stage in Britain's linguistic history. Although versions of the 'BBC accent' still exist – for example, in some sports commentary such as tennis, cricket, equestrian events or in some arts programmes – it is now more likely to be used for satiric or ironic purposes. To an extent, this debate has been won by the pluralists, and been replaced by a new concern over written English. Here, rules and standards are far more deeply ingrained, but the need to write 'correct English' is coming increasingly under pressure as new technologies such as the Internet and text messaging encourage compressed forms of expression such as 2moro (tomorrow), 4eva (forever), gna/gonna (going to), gr8 (great), thort (thought), tmoz (tomorrow), ttyl (talk to you later) and y (why).

A growing informality is apparent, fuelled by the diversity of 'Englishes' among different ethnic and regional communities, despite concerns in some quarters that, for example, it is possible for a student to gain a first-class degree without being able to write grammatically correct English to the standards upheld by their parents' generation. The counter argument is that visual culture is taking over from written culture and that a 'post-literate' society will be a more rounded one in terms of its creative thinking, less hung up on words, more capable of thinking in terms of ideas and images.

Adequate command of English still constitutes a major part of modern British education, even for those who do not speak the language regularly at home or outside the classroom. One way in which the fixation with the language manifests itself is in the debates surrounding the educational significance of William Shakespeare. Of course, to anyone familiar with it, Shakespearean language can hardly be thought of as a viable means of communication in the twenty-first century. Nevertheless, Shakespearean language is felt by many to represent the pinnacle of British cultural achievement, and it is widely argued that in his poetry and plays Shakespeare captured the essence of English (though not British) identity. To those taking this line, it therefore appears obvious that young British people, of whatever ethnic origin, should become familiar with Shakespeare's work so that they can appreciate the history and the society of which they are now a part. Drawing on these opinions, a 'Shakespeare industry' has become established, linked in many significant ways with other major industries such as publishing, leisure, tourism and heritage.

On the other hand, some people claim that Shakespeare's relevance is only historical, and that modern education should be dealing more with students' contemporary practices, values and beliefs. Both in terms of theme and language, it is argued, Shakespeare has limited significance for those from different ethnic backgrounds possessing important cultural and linguistic traditions of their own (it was, for example, widely questioned in 2000 whether Shakespeare's works should remain standard texts in British schools). The same could also be said of certain sections of the indigenous British population which have traditionally been excluded from the high cultural institutions where 'Shakespeare' has been enshrined for so long. For example, cultural critics have long claimed that a television soap opera such as *Coronation Street*, set in contemporary Manchester and detailing the experiences of a community of working-class people, was of far greater interest and significance to millions of people throughout Britain than anything by or about Shakespeare. This is because the themes, language and accents of *Coronation Street* are closer to what most British people experience in their daily lives. This is a contentious argument, as it might be seen to deny people from working-class or ethnic backgrounds access to a valuable cultural experience. The emphasis on regional accents was underscored by the decision of the French government, in an agreement with the BBC, to help French schoolchildren improve their English by broadcasting programmes such as *Open All Hours* (set in the north), *EastEnders* and *Only Fools and Horses* (both featuring Cockney accents and Estuary English) in teacher training colleges and secondary schools. The launch of the initiative, in a Paris school in September 2001, was scheduled to coincide with the European Day of Languages.

Regional variations in accent, vocabulary and pronunciation, as practised by the characters in *EastEnders* or *Coronation Street*, are of great importance in British life, as well as having an important bearing on the question of standard English. Some of the more easily distinguishable accents are those of Cornwall, the West Midlands, Tyneside, Northern Ireland and Clydeside, although to a sensitive ear, there are dozens of separate regional accents in Britain, and hundreds of minor linguistic peculiarities which set one region, one town, even one village, apart from another.

The city of Liverpool, for example, has a very strong and recognisable accent, known as 'Scouse', deriving from a mixture of Lancashire, Irish and Welsh influences, and those speaking with this accent are referred to as 'Scousers'. One version of 'Scouse' was brought to national and world attention by the success of The Beatles in the 1960s. The phrases, slang and inflections which characterised the speech of The Beatles however, were but one version of what is in fact a highly complex set of linguistic practices operating within the city of Liverpool.

One factor influencing all the varieties of English in contemporary Britain is the economic and cultural domination of the United States of America. Especially since the end of the Second World War, the issue of American influence on British life has been hotly debated. Some people fear that sharing a language with the most culturally successful nation on Earth will erode Britain's own linguistic identity and also accounts for Britons' woefully poor grasp on other European languages, while others argue that the global dominance of English ensures Britain's continuing cultural vitality. It does seem that through exposure to popular music, cinema, and computer technology, British people are becoming more and more familiar with the various speech patterns of the USA, even learning to differentiate between them (for example, Southern drawl, New York nasal, Californian rising into-nation). Distinctive American rhythms, intonations and slang are becoming common throughout Britain, not only in pubs and clubs, but to an increasing extent also in more formal contexts such as education and the media. Much British popular music since the 1960s, for example, is heavily influenced by American styles. Against this, part of the attraction of groups such as Stereophonics (Wales), The Proclaimers (Scotland) or Elbow (Manchester) is hearing the singers using their local accents. At the same time, it is clear that English, albeit American English, remains the dominant language of diplomacy and of popular culture, and it could be argued that this has given British people cultural and economic opportunities they might otherwise not have had.

All the issues raised in this section have important implications for the question of British identity. The ways in which the English language is used continue to be of great importance, for those who adhere to standard English as well as for those who accept and rejoice in the latest slang words and phrases. The number of official or authoritative bodies who accept that language is a constantly changing and vibrant part of culture is increasing. For example, dictionary compilers are more likely to include recent slang words than they used to be. The *New Compact Penguin English Dictionary* has entries for 'pants' (awful), 'manky' (dirty or rotten) and 'dis' (to show disrespect), but there are new words appearing in playgrounds all the time. A 2001 survey of 7- to 14-year-olds listed scores of buzzwords, ranging from the familiar such as 'wicked', 'radical' and 'dingbat', to the less common, such as 'savage' or 'vicious' (for excellent), 'trev' (a designer-clothes wearer), 'minging' (ugly or disgusting) and 'talk to the hand' (because I'm not listening). Unsurprisingly, television shows provide many new catchphrases, from the 'whazzup' of Budweiser commercials to the 'boyakasha' of the Ali G Show. 'Doh!' is among the young the most popular expression of stupidity these days, and it is therefore interesting to note that in 2001 Homer Simpson was voted Britain's most popular comedy character (pushing Basil Fawlty into second place). Other words, of course, fade out of fashion: only the over-30s would show their appreciation by calling anything 'brill', 'ace', 'fab' or 'naff', but 'cool' has shifted in and out of common vocabulary on a regular basis and the young continue to have their own 'slanguage'. For example, current favoured words in two parts of Britain are 'sick' (London) or 'tidy' (Wales) for 'good', and 'buff', 'peng' (London) or 'bangin'', 'mint', 'lush' (Wales) for 'good looking'. Rhyming slang remains common in young street culture, though its connections with Cockney are far off, and the emphasis is on using celebrities' names in a way that makes the commonplaces of everyday teenage life more interesting. Some examples are: 'Britney Spears' for beers, 'Wallace and Gromit' for vomit and 'Brad Pitt' for shit.

The possibility of a single, ideal English language was always remote, both because of its artificiality and because of the active role played in cultural life by accent and regional variation. But such an ideal is becoming less and less viable, given both the speed with which language circulates in the technological age, and the number of British people for whom the English language is deeply problematical. With regard to this latter group, I now want to discuss those non-English languages which are, nevertheless, indigenous to the British Isles.

Gaelic, Scots, Welsh

Before modern technology made travel and the spread of information so much quicker, it was possible for people from different parts of the British Isles never to hear the English language spoken. From the influx of European invaders and migrants who began to come to the islands around 2,000 years ago, a great number of distinctive local dialects, as well as a smaller number of discrete languages, emerged. But as English evolved into the successful international language it is today, these other, mainly Celtic, languages tended to be marginalised. For many people, this predominance of the English language is a problem in that it deprives individuals and communities of a distinctive local cultural inheritance. Instead it collapses all history and all possible experience into a homogeneous yet spurious Britishness. A character of James Joyce's describes a conversation at his school in Ireland with his teacher, who is an Englishman:

> The language in which we are speaking is his before it is mine. How different are the words *home*, *Christ*, *ale*, *master*, on his lips and on mine! I cannot speak or write these words without unrest of spirit. His language, so familiar and so foreign, will always be for me an acquired speech. I have not made or accepted its words. My voice holds them at bay. My soul frets in the shadow of his language.
>
> (James Joyce, *A Portrait of the Artist as a Young Man*)

For many minority language speakers, Joyce manages to capture in this passage the social and personal frustrations of being caught between a way of speaking which is specifically attuned to local experience and local history and an all too 'familiar', too dominant language such as English, in which they are expected to communicate.

Gaelic is the language of the Gaels, Celtic invaders from Europe who came to the British Isles in the second and third centuries before the beginning of the Christian Era. Gaelic rapidly became the principal language of Ireland, and later it was also widely spoken on the west coast of Scotland where many Irish Gaels emigrated in later years. (The census of 2001 showed that out of a Scottish population of 5.06 million, 1.2 per cent – about 58,650 people – spoke Gaelic in some form, continuing a steady decline in numbers since the first census recording in 1891 when there were 210,000 speakers.) Scots Gaelic was recognised as an official EU language in 2009.

Gaelic remained the first language of Ireland until the middle of the nineteenth century, when the Great Famine (1845–48) decimated the population. Death, mass emigration and the association of Gaelic with poverty and backwardness combined to marginalise the language, so that by the time the southern part of Ireland gained partial independence from Britain in 1922, Gaelic was only spoken in small pockets (called Gaeltachts) in the north and the west of the island.

This marginalisation did not go unopposed, however. During the 1890s a cultural movement known as the Celtic Revival became very influential throughout the British Isles, and this movement was closely linked with the idea of political independence for Ireland. An important part of its programme was the restoration of Gaelic as the first language of Ireland. This was felt to be necessary because, going back to the introduction to this chapter, language was seen as the crucial element of a distinctive identity, and therefore it was not possible for Irish people to achieve real freedom if they continued to speak English.

With regard to promoting Gaelic projects, the Northern Ireland Office has spent only a fraction of the amount spent on Scottish Gaelic and Welsh, but it has still been welcomed as official acknowledgement of the importance of Gaelic for the cultural health of the community. The city of Belfast has bilingual schools, a Gaelic newspaper until 2008 (called *Lá Nua*, meaning 'Day', which began publication in 1981) and a number of Gaelic radio and television programmes broadcast by the BBC and independent stations. While use of the language is now declining in the south, voluntary Irish classes flourish throughout Northern Ireland. All this activity is encouraging for Gaelic supporters, although whether the language can truly escape its sectarian heritage and help resolve the political divide in Northern Ireland remains a hotly debated question.

One of the most interesting British languages, precisely because of the debate as to whether it is a distinct language or merely a dialect of English, is Scots. Scots is descended from the Northumbrian dialect of Old English, and at one time forms of the language existed in all the non-Gaelic regions of Scotland, including the remote Shetland and Orkney Islands. By the sixteenth century one particular form of Scots supported a highly developed cultural and political tradition entirely separate from England. At that point, however, a number of factors combined to force Scots into decline, the most important of which was the union of the Scottish and the English Crowns in 1603. After the abolition of the Scottish parliament in 1707, Scots, like Irish Gaelic in the nineteenth century, began to be rejected as a sign of cultural backwardness, and the ruling classes attempted to purge their speech of any remnants of the old Scots tongue. Despite interest in what came to be known as 'Lallans' (Scots for 'Lowlands', as opposed to the mostly Gaelic-speaking Highlands) among some poets and novelists of the eighteenth century, the language survived only among the peasantry and, after the industrialisation of Scotland during the nineteenth century, among the urban working class.

Scots was under constant threat throughout the twentieth century because, unlike Scottish Gaelic, most people do not regard it as a separate language but as a deformed version of English, or as an artificial dialect invented by the romantic writers of the eighteenth and nineteenth centuries. Both of these misconceptions add to the stereotypical notion of Scots that tends to be reproduced in the popular imagination as the 'sign' of Scottishness – words such as 'wee' (small), 'braw' (fine, good), 'lassie' (girl) and so on, as well as a heavily inflected accent when speaking English. Mr Scott, from the original *Star Trek* series (played by an American actor James Doohan), possesses probably the most famous, and least convincing, Scots accent in popular culture. The comedian Gregor Fisher, who plays the part of working-class Glaswegian Rab C. Nesbitt in a BBC Scotland television series of the same name, is the nearest one will find outside Scotland to a genuine Scots speaker on television, though it would be very difficult for anyone who did not speak English as a first language to understand the characters in the programme.

Scots received little institutional support in the twentieth century. Until 2011, it was not recognised for census purposes, and a survey of 1,000 Scots in 2010 conducted by the Scottish government found that 64 per cent do not think Scots is a language though 85 per cent of those surveyed claimed they spoke it to a greater or lesser extent (the proportion fell to 58 per cent among frequent speakers and rose to 72 per cent among those who said they never speak Scots). As with the Gaelic language in the Republic of Ireland, it is only among a relatively small number of historians, critics and writers that Scots is valued; indeed, this intellectual support confers on Scots a sort of cult status, granting the language a vogue somewhat at odds with its shrinking working-class base. The familiar argument is that despite its impoverished condition, the language articulates a way of life, a way of thinking about the world, a way of being Scottish, that cannot be adequately expressed in English. This argument is rejected by many however, and not only by those 'Unionists' who maintain that Scotland's future depends on remaining an English-speaking region of the United Kingdom. The revival of Scots is also dismissed by many nationalists (seeking separate national sovereign status for Scotland) and devolutionists (seeking an autonomous Scottish parliament while remaining part of the United Kingdom) who feel that, given its history of strong cultural and political independence, Scotland does not need the support of an artificially resurrected language. This latter understanding of the relationship between language and national or ethnic identity is in marked contrast to the feelings underpinning the most successful non-English language of the British Isles: Welsh.

Like Scotland, since the nineteenth century Wales has had great difficulty in asserting its cultural independence from England. Before the Education Act of 1870, which prohibited teachers from using Welsh as a medium of education, about nine out of ten people spoke the language. As with all the minority languages mentioned so far however, Welsh became stigmatised as the language of the poor and the backward, and when the southern part of the country began to industrialise, it was only in rural areas such as the counties of Gwynedd and Dyfed in the north and west that Welsh managed to survive.

Since the 1960s, however, a new attitude towards the language has become evident. The rise of Welsh political nationalism has encouraged a pride in the Welsh language, and in recent years the ability to speak Welsh has become a highly prestigious attribute. This pride has manifested itself in many ways, but the basic impetus is towards the conversion of Wales into a fully bilingual country.

Many people began in the 1960s by abandoning anglicised names in favour of Welsh ones, while for those who had not yet mastered the language, it was possible to assert a Welsh identity simply by using the heavily inflected Welsh accent. Once over the border, all road signs are now given first in Welsh and then in English, as are most job descriptions, and the language has had great success at all levels of education. Welsh programmes represent well over 50 per cent of the country's radio and television output, and the success, for example, of the annual Eisteddfod festival adds to the sense of an autonomous nation supporting a distinctive national culture. In 2001, 21 per cent of the population in Wales said they could speak Welsh – a rise largely associated with the language now being taught in schools (20 per cent were able to read Welsh; 18 per cent able to write Welsh; 24 per cent able to understand spoken Welsh). This augurs well for the future of the language, and is in marked contrast to Scottish Gaelic, where the highest percentage of speakers are sixty-five and over. However, some Welsh nationalists argue that the success of the language has been achieved at the cost of a coherent political programme, and that central government support for various cultural initiatives does not represent a relinquishing of power, but merely a way of redistributing it.

We should remember that Welsh is reviving, not revived, and in the industrialised south, Swansea, Cardiff, Glamorgan and the Rhondda valley, where over half the population lives, Welsh is still to all intents and purposes a foreign language. Even so, the relative success of the language has been difficult for many English people to cope with. One recurring image is that of the English tourist feeling intimidated and offended by their

FIGURE 6.1 'Britain Visitor Centre' showcases the separate countries of the UK

exclusion from the Welsh conversations of local bilingual communities. Stories such as these reflect more, perhaps, on the insecurity of English people who hold an idea of Britishness specifically invented to incorporate the various identities of the British Isles under one, English-led banner (some controversy was sparked by the government repeatedly appointing several non-Welsh-speaking secretaries of state for Wales). For it hardly seems strange that Welsh people should wish to converse in their own language, nor that in the absence of political self-determination this should represent a valuable means of identification for them. In autumn 2001, it was suggested that an unofficial citizenship exam for English people planning to move to Wales would be a test of their ability to pronounce Llanfairpwllgwyngyllgogerychwyrndrobwllllantysiliogogogoch, the longest place name in the world after the Maori names of some towns in New Zealand. The town's county council clerk argued that newcomers needed to mix in with the community more, and that pronouncing the town's name correctly would be a good start, especially for people who had moved from England. Local people, however, refer to the town as Llanfair PG, rather than calling it by its full name, which in English means 'The church of St Mary in the hollow of white hazel near the rapid whirlpool by the church of St Tysilio of the red cave'.

It may be that, despite repeated measures to support them, given time and the global domination of American English noted in the last section, Gaelic, Scots and Welsh, as well as other non-English languages of the British Isles such as Cornish (from Cornwall) and Manx (from the Isle of Man), will one day cease to be living languages, preserved only in the artificial confines of the library and the university. Welsh appears to be in a reasonable state of health, but Gaelic and Scots may give cause for concern to their supporters and speakers. It might be wondered why, having being so neglected for so long, Britain's non-English languages have aroused so much interest in recent years. Certainly there has been concern about the fate of Gaelic, Scots and Welsh since the beginning of the twentieth century, but one could argue that it is only since Britain's non-indigenous ethnic minorities began to work for proper recognition of their distinctive cultural heritages that the islands' Celtic minorities have begun to see their languages in a new perspective. I will now turn to those non-indigenous languages.

New languages, new identities

Since the end of the Second World War (1945), immigration has become an issue of increasing public and political concern in Britain. Not only that, but the very terms in which the question of immigration is considered are also highly charged. If you reread the previous two sentences, you will see that the words I have used at the beginning of this discussion of immigration and ethnicity are 'issue', 'concern' and 'question'; other terms invariably found when this subject is raised are 'problem', 'solution', 'answer', 'debate', etc. For many people, such language is itself part of the 'problem' in that it only allows immigration and ethnicity to be discussed as anomalies in an otherwise efficient system, anomalies that 'we' – that is, the established indigenous population of Britain – need to resolve. Being constituted a 'problem' or an 'issue' or a 'cause for concern' even before their arrival in the country has serious implications for the way in which ethnic communities perceive their relations with the state and with Britishness generally. More recently, political commentators have observed that, aside from cultural benefits, only by welcoming migrants will European countries be able to increase their long-term rate of growth and also pay for the future pensions of those currently in work.

People have been migrating to and from Britain for centuries, and as long as this has been so, native and immigrant have been constantly reviewing their mutual relations. In 1596 the parliament of Queen Elizabeth I issued an edict limiting the number of black people entering England. This may be seen as the first of a large number of measures taken by British governments in an effort to define exactly what kinds of people have had the right to enter Britain and claim citizenship. The years since 1945 have seen numerous Immigration and Citizenship and Race Relations Acts, all in an effort to supply British identity with a legal and constitutional basis. Over this more recent period, two opposing attitudes appear to be at work. If, as some commentators suggest, increased population mobility is becoming a characteristic contemporary experience, then cultural and political systems which used to construe immigration and ethnicity as 'problems' may no longer be applicable. Such systems, indeed, it is argued, were never acceptable in the first place. On the other hand, with the break-up of the Soviet Union, the re-unification of East and West Germany, and the growth of Europeanism, the issue of borders, national and ethnic identity has become very important throughout Europe. Britain, as we have already seen, has its own internal borders and identities, a situation which has led to its unique political constitution. The exact nature of Britishness however, has become even more complex in the decades since 1945 with the influx of a new range of ethnic identities, and the subsequent emergence of new ways of being British.

There have been well-established Black, Chinese and Indian communities in Britain since the nineteenth century, especially in London and some of the bigger seaports such as Liverpool and Cardiff. The post-war period has seen the arrival of people from many geographical backgrounds – West Africa, the Caribbean, Hong Kong, India, Pakistan and so on, countries and regions known as the 'New Commonwealth' (as opposed to the 'Old

Commonwealth' of Canada, Australia and New Zealand). Traditionally, the most positive response in mainstream Britain to immigration from the New Commonwealth has been mild interest in the possibility of viewing exotic cultures at close hand. Asians, for example, have been 'contained' by mainstream British culture in terms of the 'colourful' or 'alternative' practices – food, clothes, music, religion and philosophy – brought from their homelands.

The multitude of identities brought by immigrants from that part of Asia are frequently collapsed into one exotic 'brown' identity which can then be more easily accommodated by modern 'multicultural' Britain. The Indian restaurant and the Pakistani newsagent or corner shop are established parts of British life, and certain other stereotypical traits and practices – Yoga, the Sikh and Muslim turban, the raga (the distinctive pattern of Indian music), arranged marriages, as well as of course the 'strange' way of speaking English – have become representative of what to most people seems a tolerable degree of difference within a larger British identity. It is, however, decreasingly appropriate to speak of a homogeneous British Asian experience. For example, those of Indian origin, according to government and independent statistics, are the most likely to vote, have considerable savings or achieve top exam results of all ethnic groups (including white), while Bangladeshis are the least likely.

FIGURE 6.2 People from numerous ethnic backgrounds populate the UK

The identity of Indian and other people in Britain is complicated by a history of colonial relations, and this in its turn is linked with the other major form of response to modern immigration. Since the nineteenth century, certain theories regarding the relations between race, nation and culture have led to the development of ideas which cast immigration and ethnicity in a very negative light. Influenced by these ideas, much of the modern British response to immigration has been characterised by xenophobia and racism. Racism in modern Britain can take two forms. An older, biological racism tends to be linked with violence and aggression, as for example, during the 1960s and 1970s when extreme right-wing elements went on 'Paki-bashing' sprees, and even developed political organisations based on repatriation of immigrants. This form of racism is increasingly rare, although it would be a mistake to underestimate the capacity of certain outmoded 'scientific' discourses of race to feed the cycle of racial hatred inherited from earlier times.

The newer, cultural form of racism is more subtle. It claims that it is unfair to ask people from a particular background to accept the kind of changes in lifestyle necessary for them to become proper British citizens. For example, one former politician caused a controversy in the 1990s with his 'cricket test': Lord Norman Tebbit argued that if people living permanently in Britain support other nations in sporting or other cultural events, then they have not sufficiently adapted themselves to British life, and cannot therefore legitimately be called British. Tebbit used the example of the way in which many black Britons support the West Indies cricket team, but the point was intended to apply to any instance of cultural 'treason'. Indeed, the issue of sporting affiliation has become even more heated since the publication of an article in a prestigious cricketing journal in 1995 which suggested that it would be a mistake to expect any 'ethnic' sportsperson selected to represent Britain, even if born here, to be as committed as a 'real' (that is, white) Briton.

According to political theorist Bhikhu Parekh, Asian migrants to the US will sooner call themselves American than those to Britain will describe themselves as British, though the latter will adopt a more local identity quite readily, identifying themselves as from a particular town or city. Following summer riots that were not inter-racial but which involved different ethnicities in looting and attacks on property in British cities, the historian David Starkey courted controversy in August 2011 by claiming during a *Newsnight* televised discussion that

> the problem is that the whites have become black. A particular
> sort of violent destructive, nihilistic gangster culture has become
> the fashion and black and white boys and girls operate in this
> language together. This language which is wholly false, which is

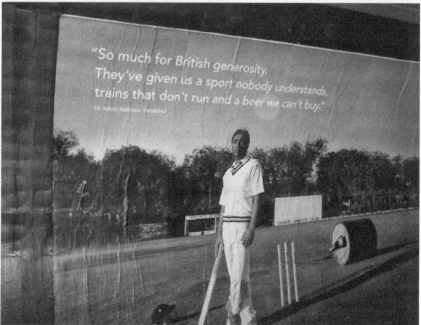

"So much for British generosity. They've given us a sport nobody understands, trains that don't run and a beer we can't buy."

Mr Ashish Malhotra, Faridabad

FIGURE 6.3 (a) and (b) Cricket developed into the national sport of England in the eighteenth century and was exported throughout the Empire, with the first internationals played in the mid-nineteenth century

this Jamaican patois that has been intruded in England and that is why so many of us have this sense literally of a foreign country.

Though at first sparked by the police shooting in Tottenham of a black man called Mark Duggan, this lawlessness seemed to mark a shift towards questions of relative perceptions of inner-city poverty and attitudes to theft, as opposed to the agendas of earlier 'race riots'. For example, following high-profile investigations into racially motivated attacks on Damilola Taylor and Stephen Lawrence, race relations in Britain reached what some considered a crisis in 2001, when several northern cities were hit by a spate of 'riots'. In Oldham in May, in Burnley in June and in Bradford in July, clashes between whites and blacks resulted in considerable damage and national fears about Britain's future as a multiethnic community. Reasons for the violent outbursts are open to discussion, but facts suggest some of the inequalities behind them: for example, in Oldham, the infant mortality rate among Muslims is three times higher than that of whites, while life expectancy is lower; adult health is worse and Muslims in the town are several times more likely to be unemployed. Government statistics report that about 50,000 people in the town experience some of the worst social conditions in the country, and the cotton mills which brought Pakistanis and Bangladeshis to Oldham in the 1950s to 1970s closed down twenty years ago. Perhaps not surprisingly, in a 2001 survey, 19 per cent of Britons cited race relations and immigration as a major concern, where only 3 per cent had said the same in 1996 (the average 2001 figure for other European countries was higher, however, at 21 per cent). In Oldham, a temporary eight-foot-high metal mesh fence was erected in the Hathershaw district, and while the home secretary said there would be no official Belfast-style ring-fencing, some white and Asian communities in the town have asked for more 'peace barriers'.

It does seem clear that Britain's ethnic minorities do not have a straightforward relationship with the state. People from the Commonwealth coming to live in Britain have as a rule identified with it as the 'mother country', and the vast majority have sought to become good citizens. Yet, the uncertainty of status, the forms of racism invariably experienced, as well as the very act of displacement from familiar places and practices, means that individuals will often wish to preserve, and indeed emphasise, their ethnic identity. Of course, not all ethnic minorities will understand their relationship with the host country and the English language in the same way. Each community brings its own assumptions and aspirations, its own cultural values and beliefs, to the affiliation with British identity. When one considers that there are many such ethnic communities in Britain, all experiencing different levels of assimilation and alienation; and when one further considers that different generations will not engage with the available identities in the same ways, then one may begin to appreciate that the question of what is and is not 'British' has become extremely complex in recent years. It now appears, in fact, that the practices, attitudes, beliefs and values that come together to form any identity are enmeshed in an intricate web of similarities and differences, and this web covers every area of modern British life – religion, politics, work, leisure, culture and education. Nowhere can this complicated situation be seen more clearly than through the subject upon which we have been focusing throughout this chapter – language.

Many British people do not use English as a first language, but speak instead the language of their home country, or of their parents' home country: indeed in 2010 it was reported that in inner London 55 per cent of primary school pupils do not have English as a first language, after a decade of loosened immigration entry controls under a Labour government keen to address falling population figures (the percentages for Birmingham, Bradford and Leicester are over 40 per cent). Chinese people living in Britain, as a more long-standing example, have not traditionally placed a high priority on integration into the host community. In a city such as Liverpool, which has one of the largest Chinese populations in the country (higher than the 0.4 per cent national figure in 2001), it is clear that Chinese people make less use of the English language than the city's other ethnic minorities. There are a number of reasons why this might be: the extreme difference between the Chinese and English languages; the hope of many Chinese people eventually to move back to their native country; the wish to preserve a valued cultural heritage; the unwillingness to 'lose face' by speaking English badly. Whatever the reasons, the older Chinese population of Liverpool have maintained a low profile in the social and economic life of the city and as a consequence a high proportion of the community still speak very little English. Chinese children on the other hand, whether immigrants or born in the city, learn to speak the language of their parents (usually Mandarin or Cantonese) at home, but have to learn English for school and for their other interests outside the community. This bilingualism can influence the ways in which the younger Chinese population understand their status in the contemporary life of Liverpool. Familiar both with the traditions of their parents and with the facts of modern British life, the younger people appear to possess greater confidence than their parents and grandparents, and are not afraid of raising the profile of their community. The Chinese New Year has become a major event in the social and cultural life of Liverpool, and street names in the area known as 'Chinatown' are given in English and Chinese. At the same time, these young Chinese people have problems which are different from the ones faced by their parents and different again from the ones faced by the city's other ethnic minorities. Bilingualism is just as likely to bring a sense of being marooned between identities as it is confidence. Third-generation Chinese, having different familial, religious and cultural values, will accept (or deny) their British identity differently to third-generation West Indians, Indians or Irish people. In fact, generalising about such relatively small populations can be dangerous, emphasising once more the political as well as social complexity of issues of ethnicity and language.

One of the most interesting examples of the complexity of modern British ethnicity is illustrated in the language brought by migrants from the Caribbean. People from the West Indies – mostly Jamaica, but also Trinidad, Guyana, Barbados, the Windward and Leeward Islands – were actively recruited for the British labour market in the years after the war when business was beginning to recover and unemployment was low. When these people came to Britain they brought with them their cultural traditions, the most obvious and important one being their language. But what was this language?

Standard English is the official language of Jamaica and many of the other West Indian islands. But most West Indians speak a version of 'Jamaican Creole', a language developed from the slave culture of the eighteenth and nineteenth centuries. Members of many West African tribes were brought over to the West Indies, and they spoke different languages, so to communicate amongst themselves they developed a form of language known as 'pidgin'. Pidgin drew on the language of the slave-masters – English – but reworked it using the linguistic forms of the numerous West African languages. And this language is basically the same one that has become known as Jamaican Creole (a 'creole' is a 'pidgin' dialect that has become a standard language for a particular community).

Many people would not consider Jamaican Creole to be a distinct language in itself, but merely an exotic form of standard English. This is certainly true at one level, yet according to linguists and anthropologists, it is possible for West Indian people to derive 90 per cent of their vocabulary from English and still speak a language that is not English. This is because language involves much more than words. Language involves complex physical and mental strategies, verbal styles and techniques, narrative genres and traditions, tones of voice, turn-taking protocols, speech rhythms and a hundred other things, some of them immensely subtle. As a gesture towards this subtlety, consider this short passage from a poem called 'I trod', written by the Black British writer Benjamin Zephaniah and published in 1985:

> I trod over de mountain
> I trod over de sea
> one ting I would like to see is
> up pressed people free
> I trod wid I eye peeled . . .
>
> (Benjamin Zephaniah, *The Dread Affair*, Arena 1985, p. 86.
> Reproduced courtesy of The Hutchinson Publishing Group.)

This example is interesting in a number of ways. The theme, first of all, is one that is very significant in Caribbean history and one that emerges in much Black British culture – the search for freedom. The poet uses the device of a physical journey over the landscape to represent the quest for a means to remove the spiritual and political scars of slavery. This theme is supported by the language of the poem, in which there is an attempt to reproduce the accents and pronunciations of Jamaican Creole – 'the' becomes 'de', 'thing' becomes 'ting', 'with' becomes 'wid'. Instead of being 'oppressed', these people are 'up pressed', a 'neologism' (a new word invented by the writer) that suggests both the pressure coming down on the people from above, and the people's determination to resist that pressure. This reworking of the language is also a way of linking past and present, as the refusal of standard English is part of the process whereby Black British people resist their 'enslavement' in contemporary Britain. In danger of becoming part of a permanent Black British underclass and thereby repeating the cycle of slavery and mastery, Zephaniah celebrates his West Indian identity by emphasising his distinctive speech patterns and rhythms in the face of Anglo-Saxon cultural domination.

The analysis should not stop here however. The phrase 'I eye' is not typical of Jamaican Creole (in which it would be 'me eye'), but derives from the discourse of Rastafarianism. This religion, which encompasses both a spiritual and a socio-political outlook and which is associated with certain cultural practices such as reggae music, marijuana and dreadlocks (a hair style), originated in Jamaica and has in recent years become one of the dominant images of West Indian identity. Rastafarians reject words such as 'me', 'my' and 'we' in favour of a single word ('I'), which celebrates the unique identity of the individual speaker and his/her unique relationship with Jah (the Rastafarian notion of God). At the same time, Rastafarianism is far from dominant among Britain's West Indian population which, typically of the wider British situation with regard to religion, encompasses a range of Christian, Islamic and atheistic positions. In these few lines, therefore, the poet can be seen as identifying with a very specific group. Analysis of the poem also shows the complex connections between contemporary British society, Caribbean history and a particular religious system.

Two points should be noted. The first is that even from the fairly sketchy reading provided here, it is possible to appreciate that Zephaniah's position is not *typical* of black Britishness, itself a contentious term, but shows instead the diversity of language and identity available to a British person of West Indian ethnicity. The second point is that Jamaican Creole, if not an *actual* separate language, certainly operates as a separate language for those members of the West Indian community who speak it to signal their lack of identity with dominant British culture. If Jamaican Creole is at one end of the spectrum, and Standard English is at the other, then a person born in Britain of West Indian parents has potential access to all the variations and nuances of language in between. How the individual from an ethnic community speaks will depend upon that highly complex cultural web mentioned earlier, incorporating different backgrounds, different generations, different levels of assimilation, different desires.

In recent years, other images and role models have helped to reveal the complexities involved in ethnic identity. The Notting Hill street carnival around Ladbroke Grove in London, which began as a local celebration of West Indian culture, is now the biggest event of its kind in Europe, such that in 2001 the authorities argued that it had outgrown its venue and would have to be moved. This cultural festival has in the past seen clashes between black Britons, organised racists and the Metropolitan police, but more recently it has been peaceful and hugely successful, attracting up to two million people from all over the country, and indeed the world, with floats participating in the procession around the three-mile route coming from as far afield as South Africa and Australia. Likewise, the television programme *Desmond's*, about a barber shop owned by a West Indian family, relies for much of its comic effect on the differences in perception between the older generation, born in the Caribbean and speaking variations of Jamaican Creole, and the children, born in London and speaking English with a typical London accent. Both the street carnival and the television programme confront the confusion arising from the wide range of identities available;

FIGURE 6.4 A Gujarati Hindu temple in Preston

both attempt to offer positive, enabling options rather than insisting on a final decision for or against Britishness.

The same can be said of the enormously popular television series *Goodness Gracious Me* which parodies cultural stereotypes of the British, Indians and particularly Indians in Britain. The show, a comedy featuring four British Asian actors, often reverses familiar scenarios, and so celebrated sketches feature a group of rude and loud Indians going for an 'English', and a party of Indian tourists coming to London for its spiritualism and simple, exotic way of life.

Conclusion

What we have seen then, is that regional accent, as well as dialects and languages such as Gaelic, Scots and Welsh, challenge the apparent homogeneity of the English language (and the British identity which it supports) from well-established positions within the state. Further, we have seen that although sharing some of the same concerns and strategies, ethnic groups from Asia, from the Caribbean and from other parts of the world pose a different kind of challenge to British identity. All the issues examined in this chapter have important implications for British identity, and they impact in significant ways throughout the cultural and political life of the country. By way of conclusion, I want to demonstrate this by looking briefly at three areas which are of great importance to British people of whatever background or allegiance – popular music, work and sport. These areas are examined in other parts of this book, but here I wish to focus upon them specifically in relation to the issues of ethnicity and language which have been our concern in this chapter.

Music is one of the principal ways in which ethnic identity is manifested. Ireland, for example, has a vibrant folk music culture, encompassing strong traditional elements as well as an *avant-garde* interested in experiment and innovation. For Irish people living in Britain, or for British people wishing to identify with what they consider to be an 'Irish' way of life, folk music offers a readily accessible means of ethnic identification. In the absence of a Gaelic language, certain distinctive sounds and rhythms come to be associated with Ireland and Irishness, and these effects are invariably reproduced whenever Irish identity is invoked. This close link between identity and cultural practice is always liable to stereotyping, however, as we have noted with much of the material mentioned so far; the same sounds and rhythms that produce a positive identification for some will suggest a whole range of negative, comic, racist images for others.

Folk music is also very popular and active in Scotland and Wales, where it fulfils slightly different functions, while nevertheless continuing to serve as a badge of cultural heritage. The English folk scene, on the other hand, although widespread and successful, tends to attract a more specialist audience, and the music does not play the part in national life that it does in the Celtic countries. One reason for this, perhaps, is that during the period of the rejuvenation of Celtic folk music – roughly since the 1960s – English folk has had to compete with another kind of music in which England has been consistently successful – 'rock n' roll'. This form of popular music developed in the United States of America in the 1950s, and, once again, the fact that the vast majority of songs were in the English language meant that young British people had an advantage when it came to producing rock n' roll music of their own. There is a widespread belief among both English and non-English speakers, in fact, that effective rock n' roll, unlike contemporary dance music, can only be produced through the medium of the English/American language. For example, most of the entries for the Eurovision Song Contest – an annual event attracting huge television audiences across Europe, but nevertheless evoking much derision and amusement amongst 'genuine' rock musicians – are now in English, a trend started by the Swedish group Abba in the 1970s. It is certainly true to say that since the 1960s, British rock musicians have been responsible for some of the most interesting and successful innovations in the genre, though the fragmentation of popular music into myriad styles and fusions has meant that 'rock' has developed a somewhat antiquated image, particularly for those attracted by world music, the new R&B (rhythm and blues) or the electronic and dance scenes.

Despite legal and voluntary moves towards 'equal opportunities' for all, some kinds of employment in modern Britain tend to attract certain kinds of people speaking in particular ways. At one level, this is explicable with reference to social class and gender. At another level however, the way one speaks and the ethnic background with which one identifies have always played a major part in the kinds of work one can expect to find (or not find) in Britain. Certain associations between ethnicity and employment – the Chinese laundry or (food) take-away, the Indian restaurant, the Irish 'navvy' (i.e. building labourer), etc. – have in some cases become so established in popular culture that it can be difficult for individuals from these ethnic communities either to imagine or to be accepted in different employment contexts. Much contemporary popular culture in fact, turns on the comic exploitation, or (more subtly) the dramatic refutation of these stereotypes. The very currency of these images however, or the desired 'surprise' effect when they are shown to be untrue, points to the fact that most British people still accept them as having some basis in reality.

A typical example of ethnic employment stereotyping is the association of West Indians with the rail system. Many of the Caribbean people who came to Britain in the 1950s and 1960s were invited specifically to work for

British Rail, and this remains an option for second- and third-generation West Indians. At the same time, black Britons are under-represented in many areas of employment, and especially in the professional sector or the higher corporate echelons. In some quarters, those who have made the break-through into higher paid, more prestigious jobs, tend to be haunted by the ambiguities of 'tokenism' and 'positive discrimination' – that is, the racist accusation that they have been selected especially to give the impression of equality of opportunity rather than on personal merit.

Whereas Welsh, Scottish and Irish accents appear to be acceptable as indicators of certain kinds of 'natural' ethnic qualities, it is very rare to hear a lawyer or a politician or a media broadcaster speaking Jamaican Creole. This is a result, as already indicated, of institutional pressure certainly, but also, it seems, of personal choice. Black British professionals, that is, tend as a rule to speak a version of Standard English, apparently because they (or their parents, if it is the language of the home and family) have decided that this is more suitable to their professional status.

With the London Olympics taking place in 2012, it is more than ever apparent that one area in which black Britons have made a major contri-bution to national life is sport. Indeed in some sports, such as athletics, boxing and soccer, people of Afro-Caribbean ethnicity far outstrip their level as a percentage of the population. The success of people of West Indian origin in representing Britain in sport has generally not been equalled by other minority ethnic communities – Indian and Chinese, for example – and the reasons for this are not clear. However, while some regard the success of black athletes as a positive thing – the full identification of people of Afro-Caribbean origin with Britain – others see it as a sign of the lack of opportunity for black Britons in other areas of society, as a way of diverting dangerous social and political tensions into harmless leisure activity and as a way of consolidating racist myths about the physical prowess of black people, as opposed to the supposed mental superiority of Caucasians.

While sport still does much to concentrate national and ethnic identity, the cultural ambiguities upon which ethnicity relies can help to expose the narrowness of traditional sporting affiliation. Again, Ireland is an interesting case in point. The soccer team representing the Republic of Ireland has had great success in recent years. Many of the players representing the country at international level were in fact born in Britain, but claim Irish citizenship through their immigrant parents or grandparents. A high percentage of these sportsmen, in fact, are of mixed race origin, possessing English, Scottish and Caribbean ties as well as Irish. This phenomenon has extended, in a highly popular and accessible way, the possible range of Irish identity, no longer restricted to the 3.5 million who live in the Republic itself, but incorporating the huge number of people throughout the world – more than 70 million according to some estimates – who identify to some degree with Irishness.

Finishing a chapter on British identity with an example from a non-British country nicely captures the complexity of the issues we have been discussing here. The ethnic, racial and linguistic factors operating in modern British society make for a highly sensitive, highly nuanced set of possibilities, in which identity is under constant pressure, not only from the society in which one lives, but also from the person one believes oneself to be.

Exercises

1   Choose a particular regional accent and try to identify some of the stereotypical characteristics that are associated with it. What are the principal differences between British English and American English – vocabulary, grammar, intonation? List some examples.

2   Why do some British people insist on speaking minor languages and dialects, even when they are bilingual? Try to identify some words or phrases from Scots, Welsh and Gaelic that have entered into the English language and are used regularly in Britain today.

3   What special 'problems' are faced by minority ethnic communities in Britain? What additional factors influence *young* British people from minority ethnic backgrounds?

4   Try to obtain a current listing of the British Top 40 music chart. How many of the singers/groups are British? How many are American, or some other nationality? How many are black?

5   Compose a sentence defining exactly what you understand by the phrase 'equal opportunity'.

6   What is Cockney rhyming slang and do you know any examples? Can you think of any other similar cases of communities constituted through language, speech or word-play?

Reading

Dabydeen, David *et al. The Oxford Companion to Black British History.* Oxford University Press, 2008. An original reference book covering the subject from Roman times to the twenty-first century.

Foster, Roy. *Paddy and Mr Punch: Connections in Irish and English History.* Allen Lane, 1993. Influential series of essays exploring the historical relations between Ireland and England in a scholarly yet readable way.

Gilroy, Paul. *There Ain't No Black in the Union Jack: The Cultural Politics of Race and Nation.* Hutchinson, 1987. Classic analysis of race relations in contemporary Britain.

Lammy, David. *Out of the Ashes: Britain after the Riots.* Guardian Books, 2011. Through an examination of his own upbringing and experience, a black British politician tries to make sense of the summer 2011 city riots that started from incidents in the London boroughs he grew up in.

Phillips, Mike. *London Crossings.* Continuum, 2001. Phillips, born in Guyana, but brought up in Britain as a child, offers a portrait of London and the role it played in (re)making black British identities.

Solomos, John. *Race and Racism in Britain.* 2nd edition, Macmillan, 1993. A wide ranging introduction to the poltitics of race in Britain.

Thorne, Tony. *Jolly Wicked, Actually: The 100 Words that Make us English.* Little, Brown, 2009. A different way of approaching the English people: through the idiosyncrasies of their vocabulary.

 # Cultural examples

Films

Route Irish (2010) dir. Ken Loach. Drama about private security contractors returning from the Iraq War to life in Liverpool.

Attack the Block (2011) dir. Joe Cornish. Aliens invade south London to meet the ruffneck teens of a drugs and violence council estate.

A Clockwork Orange (1971) dir. Stanley Kubrick. Pre-punk alienation of white British youth, manifested in violence and a specialised group language.

Goodbye Charlie Bright (2001) dir. Nick Love. Bittersweet film about five boys growing up on a south London council estate one summer.

Twin Town (1996) dir. Kevin Allen. Swansea-set tale of two brothers, starring Rhys Ifans. Sometimes called the Welsh *Trainspotting.*

Ratcatcher (1999) dir. Lynne Ramsey. Life on a Scottish housing estate in the 1970s.

East is East (1999) dir. Darren O'Donnell. Comedy about cultural differences as an Asian family, with a white mother, grow up in Lancashire with a stern traditionalist Muslim father. Follow up *West is West* (2010, dir. Andy DeEmmony) was far less well received.

The Crying Game (1992) dir. Neil Jordan. An exploration of national, political and sexual identity in Ireland and Britain.

Books

Amit Chaudhuri, *Afternoon Raag* (1993) A highly praised poetic and evocative novel recounting the life and thoughts of an Indian student at Oxford.

James Joyce, *A Portrait of the Artist as a Young Man* (1916) Classic exploration of the tensions between family, nation, religion and art.

Steven Kelman, *Pigeon English* (2011) The story of Harri, an eleven-year-old newly arrived in England from Ghana to live on the ninth floor of an inner-city housing block on an estate overrun by a local gang called the Dell Farm Crew.

Hugh MacDiarmid, *A Drunk Man Looks at the Thistle* (1926) A poetic plea for a modern
Scots language to support a modern Scottish identity.

Colin MacInnes, *Absolute Beginners* (1959) Race relations and riots in 1950s London,
as seen through the eyes of a jazz-loving teenager.

Caryl Phillips, *The Final Passage* (1985) Novel about the great emigration in the 1950s
from the Caribbean to England, and the life that a young woman, Leila, finds there.

TV programmes

Da Ali G Show. Controversial sketch show in which a Jewish man plays an offensive,
ignorant glitzy white streetsmart guy who adopts black hip hop culture.

Al Murray The Pub Landlord. Tongue-in-cheek live performances by a comedian
parodying the bombast of a stereotypical British bigot.

Rab C. Nesbitt. Comedy with a sharp edge about the adventures and opinions of a
working-class Glaswegian.

Goodness Gracious Me. Very successful satirical comedy programme written and
performed by four British Asians.

Music

The best way to chart annual developments in British music is by following the results of
the Mercury Awards, won in 2011 by P J Harvey with her examination of historical
conflict and present-day nationality: *Let England Shake.*

Tinie Tempah (popular Nigerian British Rapper from London).

Emeli Sandé (Scottish R&B and Soul recording artist and songwriter, from Aberdeen with
a Cumbrian mother and Zambian father).

Jem (Welsh singer songwriter whose work includes elements of rock, new wave-styled
electronica and trip-hop).

RunRig (Scottish folk-rock group including many songs in Gaelic).

Clannad (Irish group crossing folk and popular divide, singing many songs in Gaelic and
Breton, the Celtic language of Brittany in northern France).

Websites

www.peevish.co.uk/slang/index.htm
Ted Duckworth's exhaustive dictionary of British slang.

www.guardian.co.uk/news/datablog/2011/may/18/ethnic-population-england-wales
2011
ethnic population of England and Wales broken down by local authority.

www.askoxford.com
Guide to English usages, grammar and expressions.

www.netlingo.com
Guide to internet language words and conventions.

www.jewish.co.uk

Guide to Jewish culture and activities in the UK.

www.angelfire.com/ga/isbglasgow

Website for the Islamic Society of Britain. Good links page.

www.languagelearn.net

Association for Language Learning homepage.

www.hecall.qub.ac.uk/studying/ukirelan.html

Website devoted to the languages of the UK, including Welsh, Cornish, Manx and Scottish Gaelic and Irish.

www.ayecan.com

Scottish government website about the Scots language.

www.nuacht24.com

Online Irish Gaelic daily newspaper.

www.halfandhalf.org.uk/lcc.htm

Website devoted to the story of Liverpool's Chinese community.

Religion and heritage

Edmund Cusick

Timeline

1532	—	Formation of Church of England
1580	—	Formation of Congregationalists
1652	—	Formation of Quakers
1653	—	Formation of Methodists
1760	—	Board of Deputies of British Jews
1774	—	First Unitarian Chapel in London
1833	—	John Keble: Oxford Movement
1843	—	The Free Church splits from Church of Scotland
1850s	—	Broad Church formed
1880s	—	Christian Socialism
1942	—	British Council of Churches (all non-Roman Catholic)
1948	—	World Council of Churches
1972	—	United Reformed Church (Congregational and Presbyterian)
1978	—	The London Mosque, Regent's Park
1980	—	Modern English Church of England Service
1988	—	Lord Chancellor censured by Free Church for attending Roman Catholic funerals
1994	—	First Church of England woman priest
1995	—	Hindu Temple, Neasden
1995	—	Sheffield rave services condemned
2001	—	Archbishop Carey: 'Tacit atheism prevails'
2006	—	First black Anglican Archbishop John Sentamu
2010	—	Pope Benedict visits Britain

Introduction

THE TIMELINE FOR THIS CHAPTER provides a quick snapshot of key religious movements, milestones and changes in the UK over the last five hundred years. Most will be touched upon in this chapter, which will be looking at the importance of public and private religion in the lives of British people and considering the role that notions of 'heritage' have come to play in ideas of national identity in recent years.

A peculiarly British phenomenon is the presence of *established* churches such as the Church of England. These churches have an official constitutional status within the legal and political framework of Britain, and the Christian religion is to some degree woven into every level of British life: government, education, architecture, the arts, broadcasting and many other areas. In Northern Ireland, religion has had the extra political significance of marking the line between Catholic and Protestant para-military factions. At a personal level, Christianity may have been encountered in the form of prayers or hymns that were taught at school, or personal acquaintance with a local vicar or a chaplain at a hospital. Philip Larkin, in his poem 'Church Going', is not himself a believer, but accepts that there is a role for churches with their 'tense, musty, unignorable silence'. Most British people feel in some way reassured by the background presence of this religion, even if they do not wish to become actively involved with it. When in 2001 a voluntary question on religious affiliation was included for the first time on the census form, 72 per cent of respondents described themselves as Christians.

Yet, despite the official uniformity provided by an established church, and the shared heritage of, for example, religious music and the Lord's prayer ('Our father, Which art in Heaven'), the religious experiences available in contemporary Britain form a complex and remarkably varied picture. The fact that Britain is commonly assumed to be a Christian country (and a majority of people feel themselves to be 'Christian' in terms of their general principles) is undermined by a number of factors: the rapidly declining levels of people's involvement with the churches to which they nominally belong; the sharp decline in the value which young people attach to Christianity; the growth of a range of New Age religious practices; and the presence of large Hindu, Sikh and Muslim communities as a result of post-war immigration. All of these changes result in considerable differences between the religious identity of the segments of society and of different generations.

One way in which this 'ingrained' religious identity of British people is communicated is through the physical landscape. The historical evolution of British religion is visible to any visitor. In the countryside, every village will have one or more churches, and even quite small English towns usually have a range of different churches, representing Protestant and Catholic belief, most of which have been present in Britain for two centuries or more, though in larger towns and cities new churches such as those of the Church of Jesus Christ of Latter Day Saints (the Mormons), Jehovah's Witnesses or Christian Science and Friends' Meeting Houses (Quakers) may also be seen. The visitor will also notice a large range of church buildings that are no longer in use as places of worship. Some lie derelict, while others have been converted to new uses as apartments, restaurants, warehouses or even nightclubs. The traditional distinction between Anglicanism and Roman Catholicism was that the former emphasised the primacy of the individual conscience while the latter stressed the need for the observance of authority. This ideological rift is nowadays much blurred. Partly owing to the Ecumenical Movement, Anglicans and Roman Catholics have far more in common than separates them. Both churches are facing shrinking futures.

Alongside this decline in Christian practice over the last fifty years, particularly in the big cities, there has been a rise in other faiths. In addition, in many high streets, bookshops have extensive sections devoted to mythology, witchcraft, palmistry, spiritualism and related subjects. Off the high street, particularly in seaside, market or university towns, there are small shops selling incense, crystals, relaxing music, jewellery and books on magic and meditation. In gross terms, the people who attend the churches are few, elderly and overwhelmingly female. The people in the New Age shops are young, enquiring and unbound by any sense of religious duty, motivated rather by their generation's belief in personal freedom. These all indicate Britain's changing religious environment.

Another part of this change is the way in which religious buildings have become a part of what is called 'British heritage'. One obvious example is the 'marketing' of a number of great cathedrals, which are to be found across the UK, though this is particularly noticeable in medieval cities such as Chester, York, Winchester and Durham. These buildings are now both religious centres and centres of tourism. A new meaning to the term 'heritage' has arisen – heritage now reflects the intervention of the tourist industry to recreate images and artifacts from Britain's past. The 'heritage industry' has grown rapidly to become one of the fastest developing, and most visible, of Britain's areas of employment and enterprise. It is also one that promotes a particular version of Britain which celebrates continuity, tradition and conservative values.

Partly for this reason, Christianity in Britain is in many ways more of a cultural force than a spiritual one. Table 7.1 indicates that the number of practising Christians is in fact much more in balance with, than exceeding, that of other faiths.

In the 1990s there were, nominally, 27 million Anglicans in Britain. That is, almost two-thirds of the adult population claimed to belong to the Church of England. However at the same time the Anglican church had less than two million registered members. Membership signifies active involvement with the Church, for example in attending services and offering financial contributions. By 2008 the number calling themselves Anglican was 13.4 million. Between 1960 and 1985 the Church of England's registered membership halved, while the number who think of themselves as belonging

TABLE 7.1 Religions in the UK

	Thousands	*%*
Christian	42,079	71.6
Buddhist	152	0.3
Hindu	559	1.0
Jewish	267	0.5
Muslim	1,591	2.7
Sikh	336	0.3
Other religions	179	0.3
All religions	45,163	76.8
No religion	9,104	15.5
Not stated	4,289	7.3
Total no religion/not stated	13,393	23.2
Total	58,789	100.0

Source: 2001 Census

TABLE 7.2 Church members by country (% of adult population)

	1985	*1992*
England	11.6	10.1
Wales	17.0	15.0
Scotland	32.4	29.4
N. Ireland	81.6	82.7
Total	15.6	14.4

Source: *UK Christian Handbook* 1994/5
Christian Research Association

TABLE 7.3 Religion breakdown

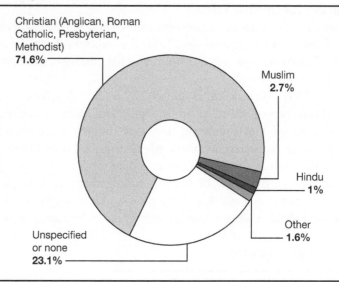

Christian (Anglican, Roman Catholic, Presbyterian, Methodist) 71.6%

Muslim 2.7%

Hindu 1%

Other 1.6%

Unspecified or none 23.1%

to the Church, in comparison, barely changed. This apparent contradiction between those who choose to think of themselves as Anglicans and those who are actively committed to Anglicanism is perhaps the single most important feature of British Christian life, and is discussed in more detail below.

There are 5 million Catholics in Britain. However, on any given Sunday more Catholics than Anglicans will attend a church service – it has been estimated that in Britain 23 per cent of Catholics registered as church members actually attend regularly, as against less than 10 per cent of non-Catholics. Nevertheless Catholic church attendance is also in decline. The northwest of England and the west of Scotland (particularly Liverpool and Glasgow) have had historically, and retain today, a distinctively Roman Catholic heritage. Liverpool is Britain's only Catholic city. But church attendances there are also down and there is a shortage of priests.

There have, however, been sporadic exceptions to the story of Catholic attrition in Britain. In the political arena, the advent of the Blairs made Catholicism fashionable for a time. (Cherie Blair is a Catholic and their children were sent to the smart Jesuit Catholic school Brompton Oratory. Tony Blair converted after leaving office.) Although the decline in numbers of vocations to the priesthood and the retirement of priests have led to closure or amalgamation of churches, some parishes have been revitalised by young priests coming from India or Africa. After the Pope's visit in 2010 there was an increase in vocations. So in the Westminster diocese the number of priests in training has currently risen to twelve.

The visit itself was interesting. It was the first papal state visit to Britain (Pope John Paul's 1982 visit was pastoral, so he didn't meet the Prime Minister, for example). There was extensive media coverage of the event in supposedly secular Britain. Despite apprehensions inside and outside of the Church, it was very successful. Grassroots clergy grumbled about the costs (£10 million) and felt that the Vatican's attempts to micro-manage the event which entailed pilgrim groups pre-registering and meeting as early as 3 am to be bused to London would end in tears. It didn't, largely thanks to good organisation and the involvement of Lord Patten as the diplomatic welcomer. Secular writers were afraid that the Church's paedophilia scandals and the fact of the Pope's German nationality would derail the visit. In the event people were seduced by the Pope's conciliatory tone and gentleness of manner. They were charmed by the personality of the 83-year-old man who met survivors of clerical sexual abuse, pointedly greeted female clergy from the Church of England in ecumenical services, and spoke of reconciliation and rapprochement between the churches. Much of the emphasis, during the Pope's visit, was on the inter-faith nature of the modern world. He united Christians against an enemy he identified as 'secularism'. Consequently there were several 'inter-faith' services. It was striking that no comment was expressed in the media about the absence from these ceremonies of people from outside the Christian and Jewish religions. During the entire visit, there was virtually no mention of Islam, Hinduism or of any other faiths widely practised in Britain. Ironically he beatified the nineteenth-century Cardinal John Henry Newman, who during his conversion from Anglicanism to Roman Catholicism declared: 'I shall drink – to the Pope, if you please – still, to Conscience first, and to the Pope afterwards'.

Earlier, in 2001 pessimistic sound bites on religion were attributed to two senior clergymen, the Anglican Archbishop of Canterbury, Dr George Carey and Cardinal Cormac Murphy-O'Connor, the Catholic Archbishop of Westminster. Dr Carey, addressing a congregation in the Isle of Man, declared Britain to be a country where 'tacit atheism prevails'. He said that British society concentrated only on the 'here and now' with thoughts of eternity rendered 'irrelevant'. Cardinal Murphy-O'Connor, speaking to a gathering of 100 priests in Leeds, said 'Christianity as a background to people's lives and moral decisions and to the Government and to the social life of Britain has almost been vanquished'.

Both statements generated considerable publicity. There were laments about the state of the nation, on the one hand, and complaints about the churches' defeatism on the other. However both clergymen went on to offer rays of hope. Dr Carey said that despite massive changes, religion had survived and there was growth in churches in Africa, the Far East and 'signs of real life' in Europe. Cardinal Murphy-O'Connor said that clergy should use this difficult period in the Church's history 'to change the culture of

Catholicism'. He believed the answer for the Church could lie in new movements, such as Youth 2000 and New Faith, and the building of small Bible-study and prayer groups. He said 'these small communities are the secret for the future of the Church'. In 2011 Archbishop Vincent Nichols endorsed Prime Minister David Cameron's statement to the Pope: 'You have made us sit up and think.' And in the wake of scandals involving journalists and the police and of rioting, a debate on moral values did enter political discourse.

From the 1960s till recent times religious issues in Northern Ireland have been overshadowed by 'the Troubles' – the continuing violence generated by the unresolved political issue of whether Northern Ireland should form part of the UK or of a united Ireland. The religious differences between Protestants and Catholics have thus been exacerbated, as Nationalists want Northern Ireland to be part of a Catholic country (with the South) while Unionists want the province to belong to a Protestant country – that is, the UK. It is often implied by British people that 'the Troubles' are based on religion, but it is probably more accurate to see the conflict as political, or even tribal, at root, a stand-off in which the communities have both looked to their differing churches for support. At no time has either Church condoned the use of violence in the dispute. And in fact meetings between religious leaders, including that between Pope Benedict and the Archbishop of Canterbury, Rowan Williams, have helped to reduce religious strife. As Table 7.2 shows, church membership in Northern Ireland, like attendance, far exceeds that in evidence on the mainland of the UK, and this is the case in both Catholic and Protestant communities. This is probably largely for political and cultural reasons, as church-going is an important way both of establishing solidarity within a community, and of defining its differences with other communities.

Wales has a separate religious tradition in which Methodism and the Congregational church have traditionally played an important part, both churches laying an emphasis on individual devotion and strict adherence to puritanical rules of abstention from worldly behaviour, such as drinking and fornication (sex outside of marriage). 'Chapel' (the word means a small, simple church) has come, in Wales, to represent the ordinary people who embraced non-conformism (a form of Protestantism comparatively extreme in comparison to the Church of England). Welsh chapels are plain and unadorned, and Welsh non-conformist Christianity has traditionally had no concept of the minister as priest (one with unique spiritual powers and authority to administer sacraments such as the Eucharist or Holy Communion) but has a strong sense of the prophetic tradition (preachers inspired directly by God). There has been no established church in Wales since 1920 – the Anglican church in Wales is known as 'the Church in Wales'. Nearly all Welsh denominations hold at least some of their services

FIGURE 7.1 The Church in Wales offers services in English and Welsh

in Welsh, particularly in Welsh-speaking areas. The past devotion of the Welsh (as well as changing population patterns) is evident in the appearance of chapels, many of which are now neglected, in the most remote areas, and the smallest of settlements.

The established church

The Church of England occupies both a political role and a spiritual one. The organisation is referred to as 'the Church of England' when considering its place in the constitution or life of the nation, and as 'the Anglican church' when its spiritual or theological identity is at issue. Because it is the body chosen by and connected to the British political system of government, the

Church of England is the established church (it differs, however, from the Church of Scotland). It is thus formally tied to both parliament and to the monarchy. So when Rowan Williams, the current Archbishop of Canterbury, makes pronouncements they are given national weight by his 'political' office.

Partly because of this link, the relation between religious principles and the personal morality of members of the royal family is closely observed and, as noted in the introductory chapter, is of continuous interest to the British people and the tabloid press. Though the monarch's religious role no longer includes 'the divine right of kings' (the idea that the monarch's rule is endorsed by God), people still expect the royals to set personal standards in social and religious institutions such as matrimony. Revelations in the mid-1990s about the adulterous liaisons of both Prince Charles and Diana, Princess of Wales mattered to many people because the prospective monarch will become the head of the Church, the institution which above all others is supposed to offer moral guidance to the country. Likewise, prominent politicians in the UK are still expected to endorse religious belief and to attend church occasionally, while the Church is expected not to get involved in party politics.

The fact that the Church of England has also been known as 'The Tory Party at Prayer' has less to do with any identification with the political policies of Conservative governments than with its role as a guardian of the past, and of established views. It is, as British people will say, conservative with a small 'c'. On rare occasions the spiritual and the perceived political function of the Church may come into conflict – the memorial service held after the Falklands war aroused anger from many Conservative politicians because of its emphasis on the Christian values of forgiveness and compassion for all in the war, including the relatives of Argentinean forces killed, an attitude not shared by those who felt that the national church should identify itself only with the victorious British forces. The Church of England is, in fact, also represented within the armed forces – every regiment has its chaplain and barracks have their own chapels. It is not unusual to see stained glass windows commemorating British Armed forces (through the flags or insignia of local regiments) or of Royal Air Force squadrons within English churches, and particularly in cathedrals. Another confrontational and difficult moment for the church arose when a tent camp was established outside St Paul's Cathedral in October 2011 by Occupy London, a group protesting against economic inequality. The church asked the protesters to leave and then backed off amid clerical resignations.

The presence of the established Church is evident in numerous ways in British life. British coins bear the head of the monarch plus the Latin initials 'F. D.', signifying that the monarch is Defender of the Faith, a title given to Henry VIII by Pope Leo X in 1521. In 1995, Prince Charles caused some controversy among traditionalists by suggesting that at his coronation he would like to be known as Defender of the Faiths (plural) in recognition that Britain was no longer an exclusively Christian country. He again caused controversy in 1996 when he suggested that money from the 'millennium fund' (a fund of money from the National Lottery which is intended to finance projects to enhance Britain's cultural life and national prestige) should in part be spent on mosques. Despite many moves towards multi-culturalism in Britain, sections of the tabloid press reacted with hostility to this suggestion, seeing mosques as a symbol of a foreign and minority religion despite the fact that British Muslims now outnumber adherents of most British Protestant denominations. Meanwhile, even government reforms to the House of Lords in 2001 did not include giving a formal place in the Lords for religions outside the Church of England.

The churches and society

Methodists, Presbyterians, Baptists and Quakers share much the same struggle as Anglicans and Roman Catholics to retain the interest of the population at large. The divisions within Christianity which separated the denominations alienated potential members, and, although they have been addressed by the reconciliatory ecumenical movement, none of the older churches is really thriving.

However, in day-to-day life Britain's churches are very involved in its culture. Church halls are used for whist drives, jumble sales, play groups, badminton, barn dances, sales of jam by the Women's Institute, and an array of other events for charity and local causes which may be entirely secular. Most of the Church's cathedrals hold concerts of classical music, both secular and religious, and may also hold exhibitions of paintings. Nearly all British cathedrals have a gift shop, for buying cards, tapes, ornaments and books, and many also have a 'coffee shop' or cafe where visitors are encouraged to come and eat. It is perhaps because of this greater flexibility in their use, as well as because of the aesthetic or historical appeal of beautiful buildings and stained glass, that, while church-going is in marked decline, attendance at cathedrals (both by tourists and by worshippers) is on the increase. In 2010, Canterbury Cathedral had 1.05 million visitors – more than London Zoo.

Religious tourism for recreation is also very popular, taking the place that pilgrimage for a spiritual purpose held for previous ages, and converging on the same sites: Iona, Bardsey, Walsingham, Glastonbury. Holy Island (Lindisfarne), for example, which is situated off the Northumbrian coast near Berwick, and which combines a peaceful atmosphere and dramatic setting with the sites of some of the earliest Christian settlements in

Britain, receives more than 300,000 visitors a year, most of them British. Such spiritual tourism is not always welcome, however – such is the demand for property for retreat houses and meditation centres that local people complain of not being able to afford houses on the island, which cost twice as much as they do on the mainland.

Throughout the period between the 1960s and the turn of the new century the Church was in a state of change. Conscious of its rapidly diminishing appeal to the population at large, it attempted to change traditions, in some cases hundreds of years old, in order to be more modern and hence attract more worshippers. The decision in 1992 to admit women as priests and bishops, in particular, proved controversial and divisive, resulting in many priests leaving the faith to take up holy orders in the Roman Catholic Church. Those Church of England priests who were most opposed to women priests may feel at home there but, ironically, many Catholics do not welcome what they see as their male chauvinism, and themselves see the advent of Catholic women priests as both desirable and inevitable.

A further illustration of the shift in the manner of religious expression occurred in 2001 when Tony Blair offered the Americans the redundant Greenwich Dome to cover the site of Ground Zero, the New York site of the Twin Towers destroyed in the terrorist attacks of 11 September. He was perhaps intending to capitalise on the melding of religious belief with heritage, to cement the Anglo-American 'special relationship' and to bolster the flagging tourist industry. His offer was not taken up. Meanwhile, for Anglicans the issue of ordination for homosexuals remains extremely divisive, and in the Catholic Church people are disillusioned both by the Vatican's mishandling of the scandal of paedophile priests and by the imposition of a new liturgy for the mass in 2011.

Some people disaffected from Anglicanism and Catholicism by the above changes are drawn to the unchanging continuity of the Orthodox Christian church. They like the certainty of fixed values. 'Was, is and will be' is an Orthodox expression which appeals to them, as also the motto of one British website: 'Telling the Truth since AD33'. Orthodox Christians in Britain now number 350,000.

Atheism in recent years has been given an increased prominence. When Brendan Behan described himself as 'a daylight atheist', someone who only believes in God when one of life's crises hits, he wasn't treating it seriously. However, a number of secularists, including Christopher Hitchens of the New Atheism movement and Professor Richard Dawkins, have given a serious profile to atheism in the culture. The latter's *The God Delusion* (2006) was widely read. It spoke to many people who could not bring themselves to have a religious faith and reassured them that kindred spirits shared their non-belief in a god. The last major period of faith and doubt possibly was in the nineteenth century when Darwinism (despite Darwin himself remaining a committed Christian) appeared to threaten a Christian account of the world. Atheists are given comfort in their rejection of institutional religion by statements from Professor Dawkins such as: 'why any circles worthy of the name of sophisticated remain within the Church is a mystery'.

Background religion

The English capacity for compromise can be seen to have emerged in what we could call 'half belief' or 'passive belief'. While membership of all Christian churches in Britain, and churchgoing, are in steep long-term decline, active Christianity in Britain is not in general being replaced by atheism, but rather by a less taxing, and harder to define 'passive Christianity' (a vague belief in a God, and a vaguer belief in Christ, but a strong adherence to the idea of being Christian). As suggested earlier, the contradiction at the heart of Christianity in Britain is that while most of the population believe themselves to be in some sense Christian, they have no commitment to, little knowledge of or belief in things that the Church regards as central to Christianity. Winston Churchill reputedly said: 'I'm not a pillar of the Church, I'm a buttress. I support it from outside.' There is in many quarters of the non-churchgoing-population an assumption that being English automatically qualifies one for membership of the Church of England and hence confers the right to be considered a Christian. This position is made easier to hold by the Church of England's status as the established Church. As the Church's rituals of baptism, marriage and funeral have traditionally been extended to anyone who lives within the parish of a particular church, it has been easy to assume that membership of the Church, too, is a right that everyone shares. Thus the English choose the Church of England, but choose to stay away from it – preferring a loose sense of association with it to actually attending its services. Despite this, overall more people still attend church on Sunday than football matches on Saturday. Moreover, events such as 9/11 or 7/7 spark an increase of up to 20 per cent in attendance. Surveys of religious attitudes in Britain regularly reveal a higher percentage of people who claim to be Christian than of people who claim to believe in God, implying a 'cultural Christianity' in which no orthodox spiritual faith in a divine Being is necessary, however strange such a concept may be to a traditional believer.

Most British people, it can be said, live in a state of 'popular religion', which, while loosely based on Christianity, would not be recognised as faith by most priests. In moments of crisis, it is the Christian God in some form to whom they will turn in private prayer. Such religion requires no active participation, but may be satisfied, for example, by listening to radio or TV broadcasts. A 'Sunday Service' is broadcast nationally every week while morning radio programmes have 'Prayer for the Day' slots – uplifting spiritual thoughts offered to the nation. The foremost news and current affairs radio programme, *Today*, early morning on Radio 4, has a popular multi-faith slot: *Thought for the Day*. Its contributors include Rabbi Lionel Blue (Jewish), Professor Mona Siddiqui (Muslim), Indarjit Singh (Sikh) and Akhandadhi Das (Hindu). Radio 4 also broadcasts *Something Understood*, a Sunday night reflection on spiritual matters. Likewise, *Songs of Praise*, a weekly televised Christian act of worship (described by the BBC as 'the longest running religious TV programme in the world') that focuses on hymn-singing, is still very popular, as is the Welsh S4C Sunday programme *Dechrau Canu, Dechrau Canmol* ('Start to Sing, Start to Praise').

The same enjoyment of passive religion is evidenced by the local and national newspapers which carry a weekly column on spiritual decisions written by a pastor. In Scotland, some local papers carry a daily sermon. Across the UK, religious broadcasting, which produces thoughtful programmes of high quality, is surprisingly popular. On an average Sunday in Britain six hours of religious programming will be broadcast by the BBC and independent television companies, and four hours by BBC radio. In general, it is the older generations who watch such programmes. In keeping with British reticence on the subject, religion only occasionally features in television drama. One exception was *Brookside*, a now defunct soap opera set in Liverpool, whose storylines have included a Catholic priest who leaves the church after an affair with one of his parishioners and another where the focus was a cult of extreme evangelical Christians. On BBC television, *The Vicar of Dibley* is a comedy drama series based around the life of a woman priest in the Church of England, and derives much of its humour from the clash of expectations between the traditional role of a clergyman and the new clergywoman. Likewise the comedy series *Rev* is deliberately located not in a rural parish but in inner-city London.

Other world religions in Britain

Britain has approximately 2,869,000 Muslims, the majority of whom were born in the UK. Others have arrived from the Indian sub-continent or from African countries. The larger Muslim communities are concentrated in the industrial cities of the Midlands, in London, Bradford and Strathclyde, and in the textile towns of Yorkshire and Lancashire where in the 1960s the clothing industry attracted workers from overseas. Additionally, immigrant communities who arrived in Britain from colonies and ex-colonies in Asia, West Africa and the Caribbean in the 1950s and 1960s tended to concentrate in particular areas – notably London, Birmingham, Glasgow and the big

TABLE 7.4 Attendance at religious ceremonies (thousands)

	1992	1998	2001
Christian denominations			
Anglicans	1,808	980	800
Roman Catholics	2,049	1,230	900
Presbyterian	1,242	1,010	850
Church of Scotland	700	600	550
Methodists	458	379	350
United Reformed Church	148	121	115
Baptists	170	277	250
Quakers	18	15	13
Other faiths			
Muslims	1,200	1,000	1,600
Hindus	400	350	559
Sikhs	500	400	336
Jews	410	285	267

Source: 2001 Census, *Religious Trends* No 2, 2000/2001, Christian Research Association, *Whitaker's Almanac*

industrial towns of northern England – and this has led to large communities of Muslims, Hindus and Sikhs in these areas. Glasgow, Newcastle and Leeds have sizable Muslim populations. Britain's Muslim population is predominately Sunni, with only around 25,000 Shias. For the first generation of Asian settlers, the practice of Islam and the heritage of Asian culture are inextricably intertwined. For their children, who have grown up in Britain, however, Islam is a cultural and religious force in its own right, so that many young Britons of Asian origin may think of themselves as British Muslims, rather than as Asians or as black Britons. Whereas in the 1980s only a fifth of the Muslims in Britain claimed to actively practise their religion, in the 1990s that figure rose to half.

For this generation the challenge is to continue to find ways to integrate the religious traditions of Islam into contemporary British life and to create a new British Islamic identity. It is a process which involves some difficulty, exacerbated by the fact that although Britain has laws of blasphemy that could be invoked when Christians were offended by Martin Scorsese's film *The Last Temptation of Christ*, Muslims who objected to Salman Rushdie's *The Satanic Verses* had no legal recourse. The Rushdie Affair, as it came to be known, in many ways started abroad. Objections to Rushdie's blasphemy against the Prophet in his book were first voiced in India, and later in Pakistan and, of course, Iran, from where the Ayatollah Khomeini issued his *fatwa*, which Rushdie heard on Valentine's Day 1989. In Britain, the famous organised book burnings only began the month

TABLE 7.5 Main ethnic groups by religion (2001)

Great Britain	Percentages								
	White British	White Irish	Mixed	Indian	Pakistani	Bangladeshi	Black Caribbean	Black African	Chinese
Christian	75.7	85.7	52.3	5.0	1.1	0.5	73.7	68.8	21.1
Buddhist	0.1	0.2	0.7	0.2	–	0.1	0.2	0.1	15.1
Hindu	–	–	0.9	44.8	0.1	0.6	0.3	0.2	0.1
Jewish	0.5	0.2	0.5	0.1	0.1	–	0.1	0.1	0.1
Muslim	0.1	0.1	9.7	12.6	91.9	92.4	0.8	20.0	0.3
Sikh	–	–	0.4	29.2	0.1	–	–	0.1	–
Any other religion	0.2	0.3	0.6	1.7	0.1	–	0.6	0.2	0.5
No religion	15.7	6.2	23.3	1.8	0.6	0.5	11.3	2.4	53.0
Not stated	7.7	7.4	11.6	4.7	6.2	5.8	13.0	8.2	9.8
Total (=100%) (thousands)	50,366	691	674	1,052	747	283	566	485	243

Source: Census 2001, Office for National Statistics; Census 2001, General Register Office for Scotland

before. The affair raised awareness of Islam in Britain and several groups emerged into the public eye. For example, the Bradford Council of Mosques attacked Rushdie, while trying to create a political Muslim collective, and the Women Against Fundamentalism group defended him while trying to dislodge stereotypical views of Muslim women. Meanwhile British law did not recognise that any blasphemy had occurred.

In 1996, there was a widespread boycott by Muslims of religious education classes in schools (which, by law, may teach about other religions but must be predominantly Christian). Despite there being state-funded schools offering an education which is distinctively Anglican, Catholic or Jewish, no state money had by then been awarded to assist in creating a Muslim school. (This situation was not redressed until the year 2000.) The anomaly arose possibly because Islam was still seen as intolerant, or even as a threat, by many conservative Britons, whose folk-memory of Islam was in terms of the medieval Crusades (a word used with a positive emphasis in Britain generally, but which must have adverse connotations for Muslims). Young British Muslims, however, represent an important strand in British identity, feeling themselves to be in the forefront of the development of Islam in Europe. Positive cultural public images have been supplied by Sami Yusuf, the pop singer, and Jeff Mirza, the stand-up comedian.

The bombings on the London Underground in July 2005 ('7/7') prompted some unpleasant anti-Muslim feeling when it was discovered that the perpetrators were from northern England. However, they also concentrated the minds of the majority-peaceful Muslim community to whom this form of extremism is every bit as threatening as to the British mainstream population.

The government remains apprehensive about relations between Christian and Muslim groups and continues to seek mediation and compromise. For example in 2006 it proposed that 25 per cent of places at new faith schools should be made available to children not of the dominant faith. However, it then swiftly backtracked on this proposal in response to a negative reaction, mainly from the Catholic Church.

The history of the presence of other faiths and peoples, and their role in public life in Britain, is not widely known. For example, Asian performers are recorded in London in the seventeenth century and Indian sailors, called Lascars, were living in London at the end of the eighteenth century. England had several Indian professors in the 1800s and a British India Society was established in 1839 (under the influence of the first widely known Indian nationalist Rajah Rammohun Roy) followed by a London Indian Society in 1872. Already, by the middle of the nineteenth century there were significant Indian communities in London, Southampton and Liverpool, though they were smaller than other black communities in Britain. As an indication of this level of cultural presence, it is worth noting that Queen Victoria – who never visited India – asked a Muslim servant, Abdul Karim, to teach her Hindustani. The founding President of the London Indian Society, Dadabhai Naoroji, also one of the early presidents of the Indian National Congress, was the first Indian elected to the British Parliament, in 1892, when he stood as a Liberal candidate in East Finchley, while another Parsi, Mancherjee Merwanjee Bhownaggree, a merchant from Bombay, was elected Conservative MP for Bethnal Green Northeast in 1895.

There is therefore a long cultural heritage of Asian people and faiths in the UK. This was well demonstrated in 1995, by the opening of the largest Hindu temple outside India, in Neasden in London. This event attracted much media interest since it was the only such structure to be built outside India for a thousand years. It used largely volunteer labour and was paid for entirely by donations from the Hindu community. Now, the majority of Hindus live in Greater London although Birmingham, in the Midlands, has also become a centre of the community. Many British Hindu families came from India and Sri Lanka but considerable numbers also arrived from Uganda and Kenya, when they were expelled by the authorities there in the early 1970s. There are now Hindu temples across the UK in major cities and towns.

The Sikh community is also well represented in Britain and is concentrated in particular areas – for example, in Southall and Gravesend in Greater London. Most early post-war migrants, in the 1950s, came from the

FIGURE 7.2 Local Lions welcome Indians to the Llangollen International Eisteddfod

Jat caste, and were predominantly men. At first they would hold a *diwan* or religious meetings at home, often in all-male households, but soon set up *gurdwaras* (Sikh temples) for Sunday services. Their families followed from the Punjab in the 1960s, and stronger domestic and religious ties were established.

Britain has the second largest Jewish population in Europe. Most Jews live in London, but there are several hundred Jewish congregations in the UK, many Jewish schools and synagogues serving both the Orthodox faith and the minority Reform group. The Chief Rabbi Jonathan Sacks is a well-known and respected public figure who has debated with the atheist Professor Richard Dawkins in the media. Fears have been voiced that nowadays half of Jewish men are marrying non-Jewish women, and that this will lead to a decline in faith and religious observance.

Finally, the Rastafarian religion has had a sizable cultural influence in Britain. Rastafarians' philosophy of life was originally based on their adaptation of the Christianity they experienced in the colonial West Indies. They see themselves as Israelites displaced from their homeland, and Babylon is the collective name for all countries of exile outside Africa. Rastafarians have been influential in many cultural ways in Britain. Their 'dreadlocks' hair style is shared by some New Age travellers or crusties and they were probably influential in promoting a climate of tolerance towards soft drugs, a major aspect of their religion, in the 1980s. They staked out their territory in urban areas of cities like Liverpool with graffiti such as: 'Toxteth Not Croxteth' meaning that marijuana was welcome in Toxteth, but not the heroin which was available in another district of the city.

Though the religious group is small, millions appreciate the characteristic Rastafarian music, reggae, and particularly that of Bob Marley and the Wailers. Marley's music has been enormously influential, even with many British white punk bands such as The Clash, Stiff Little Fingers and The Ruts, plus more mainstream groups like Culture Club and UB40, through to mainstream hits by celebrities like Peter Andre. Among other black British groups displaying Rasta influence have been Aswad, Misty in Roots and Steel Pulse, while the critically acclaimed and widely published Rastafarian poets Benjamin Zephaniah and Levi Tafari have raised the profile of Rastafarianism, promoted the interests of ethnic minority groups generally and contributed to the transformation of British cultural identities.

Religious festivals

One of the most obvious examples of religion in contemporary British life is in the progression of the year through festivals and significant dates. Oxford University's terms are named Michaelmas (feast of St Michael the archangel), Hilary (St Hilary) and Trinity (a Sunday in June). The Anglican Church has traditionally divided the year according to a liturgical calendar – basing the year around a number of key religious feasts and thus creating holidays such as Whitsun, named after the feast of the Pentecost which is celebrated on the seventh Sunday after Easter, when the Holy Spirit appeared to the apostles. British life is punctuated by such national holidays, some of which still have a religious meaning, but many of which are now largely secular festivals. An example of the latter is Mother's Day which is based on Lady's Day (25 March), a celebration of the annunciation to Mary that she was pregnant with Christ, who was to be born nine months later on 25 December. Some public festivals have roots in the pagan religions that held sway in Britain before the arrival of Christianity, lost religions whose customs are being recreated and celebrated by a new generation of 'pagans', who celebrate seasonal events such as the winter and summer solstices (mid-points), by meeting out of doors at ancient sites of worship, most famously at Stonehenge.

The name Easter is derived from the name of the Saxon goddess of spring, Eostre (related to a Mediterranean pagan goddess mentioned in the Bible, Astarte). In some areas, Easter rituals, as well as celebrating the resurrection of Christ, include ceremonies which were once probably part of pagan fertility rites, though now performed in a spirit of secular fun, for example, the rolling of eggs down hills or the eating of pancakes on Shrove Tuesday, at the beginning of Lent, the period of fasting before Easter (observed by few Christians in Britain, in contrast with the month of Ramadan, observed by the majority of Muslims). Well dressing is common in Derbyshire where in 1349 there may have been a ceremony of thanks at Tissington for surviving the Black Death. For most non-religious British people Easter is an occasion for the exchange of chocolate, though this chocolate is usually in the shape of an egg or a rabbit (the Easter Bunny), both symbols of fertility. Many British people who never normally go to church will attend a service on Easter morning. The day after Easter Day, Easter Monday, is also a public holiday.

The first of May or May Day is a public holiday introduced by a Labour government. It is a socialist revival of a much more ancient pagan festival of Beltane which is still celebrated by Morris dancers, who dance traditional dances, clad in straw hats and with bells on their ankles, around a maypole. In places such as Oxford (where there is a tradition of greeting the dawn on May Day morning), Morris dancers are likely to be joined by neo-pagans: young people dressed in the fashions of youth counter-culture – ex-army coats trousers and boots, dreadlocks, strings of coloured beads or leather thongs worn as bracelets or necklaces, and pierced noses and ears. That such people will share the same celebration as well-heeled middle-class students and conservative middle-aged people points to the deeper rhythms of British life which unite people who otherwise feel themselves to be profoundly different, politically and culturally.

Hallowe'en, on 31 October, is a British festival that now shows many traces of American influence. For example children are now beginning to play 'trick or treat'– that is, to call at houses on Hallowe'en dressed in macabre fancy-dress costumes and ask for sweets. This new and growing fashion, pagan in origin, can be contrasted with the Christian tradition of groups of carol-singers going from door to door at Christmas, singing in exchange for coins or refreshments. Carol singing is in marked decline. Some people feel uneasy about Hallowe'en. It was originally a pagan festival of remembrance for the end of the old year (according to the pagan calendar) and of communion with the dead. It is celebrated principally by children, who enjoy the frightening atmosphere created by make-up, masks and costumes on the theme of ghosts, witches, spectres and skeletons. While in the 1960s and 1970s schools would enthusiastically participate in Hallowe'en, from the 1980s onwards many schools, particularly in Scotland, which had a particularly strong Hallowe'en tradition, banned the celebration, because of pressure from Christian parents who believed the festival was connected with black magic and witchcraft, or because it encouraged children to go out unsupervised, at night.

Guy Fawkes Night (the fifth of November), also known as 'Bonfire Night' or 'Fireworks Night', is another example of how a festival which is now seen as entirely secular can grow from religious origins. While, again, its origins lie in pre-Christian pagan customs (a fire festival to welcome the winter) this custom of gathering to light outdoor bonfires, and, to burn effigies symbolically representing the old year, was adapted by the Christian state in the seventeenth century to commemorate the defeat of a Catholic plot (the gunpowder plot) to blow up the Houses of Parliament. Like Christmas, Bonfire Night is remarkable in being one of the few customs which actively unite British people. All across the UK, everyone is acutely aware of, if not participating in, festivities typically consisting of a display of fireworks around a bonfire, on which a human effigy of Guy Fawkes is burned.

The role of the traditional churches as part of the British state is most obvious on Armistice Day (the Sunday nearest to 11 November). This day is also known as 'Poppy Day', as many British people, particularly of the older generations, will wear a red paper poppy to show that they remember those who have died fighting for their country. (In the First World War many British soldiers were killed in battle in the wheat fields of Flanders, which had poppies growing in them.) All over the country, ceremonies which combine military drill and Christian ritual are held to remember the war dead, especially those killed in the 1939–45 war. This is principally a time of mourning and of celebration for the generations who have lived through the Second World War, and those who died. However, even many young people, who feel uncomfortable about the solemnity and emphasis on the past of Poppy Day, also feel that some of their sense of identity as British subjects is defined by this day. Even if the themes of patriotism and military service are not those with which they personally identify, the commemoration ceremonies held in schools, churches and town centres provide an annual reminder of another history of British identity – one that now needs to be negotiated alongside strengthening links with the EU.

For those without significant religious festivals, Christmas (25 December) is without question the single most important event in the British social, religious and cultural calendar (though it should be noted that in Scotland, where it was not until the 1950s that Christmas Day became a public holiday, the alternative celebration of 'Hogmanay' or New Year has historically been of much greater importance and, in the Highlands of Scotland particularly, remains so). Christmas Day is the one time when people feel the need to re-enact the importance of the family and most young people who otherwise live elsewhere will still spend that day with their parents. For most British families the Christmas period is the only time, apart from weddings and funerals, when the 'extended family' – including different generations and the children of different branches of the family, are gathered together. It is the time when, as John Betjeman put it in his poem 'Christmas': 'girls in slacks remember Dad / And oafish louts remember Mum'. For many people, this proves to be something of a strain, as British people are not used to sharing their lives so closely with so many other relatives for several days, and this is reflected in statistics for violent domestic crime.

While the Christmas festival, celebrating the birth of Jesus, is of course a religious one, it could be argued that for most British people, any religious meaning is very slight, and the celebration consists chiefly of drinking and eating, especially Christmas dinner of turkey, roast potatoes, Christmas pudding (a very rich fruitcake), mince pies (sweet fruit pies of mixed dried fruit and brandy), the giving of presents and the watching of special Christmas programmes on television. Passive religion, however, is more popular at Christmas than at any other time, with many people listening to carol services on the radio, such as that broadcast by the BBC from King's College in Cambridge. For many British people, the Christmas story has sentimental appeal, if only because it reminds them of when they first heard it as children, and it is this, rather than religious faith, which makes the church seem more attractive at Christmas. Generally speaking, public performances of the nativity story of Jesus' birth, which is primarily reserved for children's school plays, take a second place to pantomimes and productions of Dickens's *A Christmas Carol* across the country. In 2006 for the first time the Royal Mail's Christmas postage stamps omitted any religious reference.

Some Christmas traditions are of fairly recent manufacture. Prince Albert, Queen Victoria's consort, introduced the Christmas tree to Britain from his native Germany. Father Christmas or Santa Claus's red uniform and white beard is said to have been inspired by a Coca-Cola advertising campaign in the 1920s. Despite the widespread commercialism however, most British people do derive some religious meaning from Christmas and, for this one time in the year, will participate in Christian ceremony. They will also listen to the monarch's only annual talk to the nation, which has an ostensibly religious purpose. It is broadcast on both radio and television and the queen or king asks for God's blessing on the British people. For most of the nation this is a dated occasion devoid of any religious meaning, and indeed, of any meaning at all. While in the 1970s up to 27 million people, more than half the population, watched this broadcast, in 1994 this number had fallen to around 15 million, and in 2005 to 8 million. For many it is simply 'a tradition' – part of the Christmas ritual.

The New Age

'New Age' is a broad term devised to describe the renewal of interest in a range of approaches to the spiritual dimension which promote individuals' ability to discover and develop their own spirituality. Whereas Christianity is seen by many as emphasising adherence to a strict moral code (for example through the ten commandments, the Bible, confession or sermons), New Age religions concentrate on developing the spiritual awareness which they believe is present in each person. Their practices have a huge variety in their origin – some being revivals of the pagan magical and religious systems that Christianity replaced in Britain, some being extensions of Eastern meditative and religious practices, and some, such as yoga and t'ai chi, being concerned with physical exercises. It may be that the presence of an increasingly diverse multi-ethnic community in Britain has boosted the popularity of some practices. For example, interest has grown in vegetarianism and veganism (large Hindu and other communities have added a considerable market for vegetarian food, which has in turn stimulated British caterers and retailers, and thus aided their popularity) and while thirty years ago vegetarian options on a pub menu were rare, they are now standard. The practices of Chinese medicine, meditation and yoga are also rapidly increasing in Britain.

The belief in reincarnation, to which many young people who have been influenced by paganism adhere, is one which, while alien to older generations brought up under Christianity, is fundamental to Hinduism, for example. The young are also more sympathetic to the Tibetan idea of *bardo*, a transitional state between life and death where for a time the living and dead are in communication. In an 'orderly' way the oldest die first and the younger await their turn. Similarly, it is not unusual for young British people involved in the New Age to talk about 'karma' (a religious idea of divine cause and effect passed on through different acts and incarnations, derived from Hinduism). Other New Age practices have a distinctly European origin, stemming from a revival of interest in Celtic myth and culture, or from new publicity given to old systems of occult knowledge through for example the Kabbalah or palmistry. Hundreds of thousands of people are involved directly in activities such as meditation or astrology (the belief system where people's personalities and destinies are determined by the star signs under which they are born). But more significant is the effect of these beliefs on the overall sense of how British people see themselves and their world. A quarter of British people, for example, claimed in a recent survey to regularly read their horoscope as published in a magazine. Many more will read their horoscope as a form of light-hearted entertainment, but will still hope for good news. TV programmes that explore 'inexplicable' phenomena are also extremely popular, as was Mystic Meg, a TV seer formerly on the BBC's weekly National Lottery show who predicted the type of person destined to win the jackpot each week. Also, business people have adopted many alternative spiritual practices, as a cure for stress and as a source of inspiration or energy. Feng shui is also used to create a comfortable working environment for offices. Finally, a small but growing number of people among the professional classes are choosing Buddhism.

The term 'New Age' is used to link all of the above activities, and this grouping has some justification, not least because those who have an interest in one of these practices often also have an interest in others. The term itself is derived from astrology, which holds that every 2000 years the solar system enters a new age. The Piscean age (from the sign of the fish) which started approximately at the birth of Christ was the Christian age (Pisces is seen by astrologers as the sign of self sacrifice and mass movements), while the New astrological era will be that of Aquarius. (Aquarius is the sign of individualism, and hence of any religion which allows individuals freedom.)

Some of the increasingly popular practices that have been placed by the media in the New Age category are distinctively religious. For example Wicca (witchcraft, or worship of British forms of the Mother Goddess, often associated with the practice of magic) and Buddhism are religious preoccupations. Interest in oriental medicine, health food and yoga, however, does not require or imply faith. Many facets of the New Age, such as the interest in astrology or in Eastern meditation, are religious in the sense that they involve establishing a link between individuals and a spiritual realm. However, in other ways these activities seem more like hobbies than parts of organised religions because they involve individual study or meditation rather than a formal organisation with its own hierarchy and moral code.

FIGURE 7.3 The question is both religious and experiential in this work by artist John Bernard, originally from West Africa

New Age groups are thus the antithesis of the highly controlled, brainwashed 'cults' which fascinate newspaper editors in Great Britain (such as followers of the Unification Church, known as 'Moonies').

New Age practices, in the widest sense, are one of the most important, and most rapidly developing areas of religious change across Britain, and must be considered seriously. Aspects of the New Age have permeated very different sections of British society: from business people turning to meditation as a release from the stress of pressurised, urban, executive life, to the Donga tribe – young pagans who have abandoned normal British society and who live, largely, out of doors, and who came to national prominence for their role in actively protesting against the government's appropriation of sites of rare natural value to build new motorways.

In many ways, currents of New Age religion have enabled changes which have occurred in British life since the 1990s to find a religious expression. The rising tide of concern for the environment, for animal welfare and rights (a subject the British think themselves very concerned with, though they have fewer domestic animals *per capita* than for example the Dutch), for conservation, and for green or ecological politics, has helped to create a climate in which religions such as paganism, which celebrate the

Earth and its wildlife, fulfil a need for many people. A powerful element within the identity of young British people is a sense of identification with the countryside, and a resentment of the loss of countryside to modern building, and in particular, of the road-building programme, which successive governments have pursued. This may have encouraged the mainstream churches to rediscover their ecological roots and to offer slogans such as 'Live Simply so that Others May Simply Live'.

Famously, while statistically very few young people seek active involvement in any of the national political parties, and there is generally much cynicism about politics in British life, concern for the landscape is an area for which there is genuine enthusiasm. Many environmental protesters endure poverty and physical hardship to fight new road building. Such activity earns considerable sympathy from many Britons of all generations. TV coverage of campaigners against the Newbury road bypass and a new runway at Manchester airport turned one young male protester called 'Swampy' into a national hero. Far more young people are involved in such 'single issue' protests than in party politics, as referred to elsewhere in this book. Whereas for previous generations the sense of belonging to a nation may have been expressed through such institutions as the church, the armed forces or in some cases, a university or a public school, many of the young generation find their ideals and their sense of belonging in nature and in the land itself.

While Christianity is identified politically with authority, the Establishment and the older generation, many New Age beliefs, and paganism in particular, are identified with the young and the disaffected. The most visible adherents are 'New Age travellers', who, in the hot summers of the 1980s, fought annual battles against the police to reach Stonehenge, Britain's most important ancient site, because they believed that they had both the right and the duty to celebrate the summer solstice and, in particular, to name their children there. The latter idea offers an example of how quickly an idea essential to identity – the ritual of naming – can become part of British sub-culture, and how the New Age generates its own 'instant' mythology through which people define themselves.

The British appetite for passive religion, and the commercial forces of tourism show their influence on pagan sites as well as Christian ones. Stonehenge is one of Britain's most popular attractions, receiving 750,000 visitors a year, many of whom are drawn by a vague, but powerful, sense of communion with some other world, or mystic power, which lives on in the imagination of the visitors, if not in the stones themselves. The young New Age pagans who worship at the stones are in a sense a natural extension of British instincts rather than a violation of them, despite their anti-establishment posture.

Religious differences: age and sex

The decline of Christianity in Britain is not due to individuals losing their religion, but rather to a process of generational change. A generation which was very religious, at least in terms of church attendance and social attitudes, and which has been the mainstay of church life in England over the last thirty years is literally dying out, and being replaced by a generation which cares far less for church observance, and for Christianity in general. Christianity is associated for young people with the unfashionable and unnecessary code of restrictive, negative morality of the value systems of their parents or grandparents. Many associate a figure such as the Pope with an authoritarian patriarchal Jehovah and tend to see Christianity, and Catholicism in particular, as a series of prohibitions – 'don't take drugs', 'don't have sex', 'don't get drunk' and 'don't swear'. One thinks of Blake's 'Garden of Love': 'Priests in black gowns were walking their rounds / And binding with briars my joys and desires'. As such it has very little appeal and has also been seen as male centred, dictating women's lives: under Catholicism, women cannot be priests, or use contraception, or have an abortion. Attempts by some within the Church to integrate elements of 1990s youth culture into worship, including some ideas borrowed from New Age spirituality and others from the 'rave' music scene, have caused problems and controversy. They have been backed by many bishops as an attempt to bridge the enormous cultural gap between the Church and young people, yet resisted by many ordinary worshippers who cannot reconcile flashing lights, amplified electronic music and cinema screens as part of recognisable Christian worship. A visitor to a church service in Britain will be struck by the advanced age of the worshippers: many congregations are largely made up of women in their sixties or seventies, or still older. The chief exceptions to this are evangelical congregations, both within the Church of England and outside it in churches such as the House churches, Baptists or Pentecostals, which place a strong emphasis on a dramatically emotional conversion-experience, and conservative moral values and family structures (for example, no sex except in marriage).

One example of the gulf between the Church and society was the Church's hostility towards the National Lottery. The Church was once again seen as basically prohibitive. While some serious commentators on national life agreed with its reservations about the damaging effects particularly on poor people of the compulsion to gamble, and those of extreme wealth on the winners, the week in 1996 when the Church raised its strongest objections was also one in which nine out of ten British people bought a lottery ticket for a £40 million jackpot. The church may still try to exercise its role as moral guardian of the nation, but few people take this seriously enough to be guided by it in their own lives. This is even more the case with the young. For them, Christianity is profoundly unfashionable. It is significant that, almost in imitation of the sub-cultural pagan practice of wearing occult jewellery whose meaning is known only to another 'initiate' of the sub-culture, Christians have, in Britain, increasingly embraced the symbol of the fish (an ancient secret sign used when Christianity was itself a minor religion, a cult) rather than the cross, as a badge to identify themselves only to other believers.

Church weddings, despite the aesthetic attraction of historic church buildings and music, are in decline. The comment of one future bride, 'We're not religious at all, we don't believe in God but we want to get married in a church' sums up the confused motives behind many such weddings – the fact that the wedding is a Christian ritual, involving religious vows, is somehow invisible to those used to passive religion. The hit film *Four Weddings and a Funeral* offered an illustration of the lack of religious interest in the church at English and Scottish weddings, which is, paradoxically, matched by the cultural importance to the upper classes of having a church wedding. Christening – the Christian rite of baptism – is now becoming rare. David Beckham said after the birth of his son: 'I definitely want Brooklyn to be christened, but I don't know into what religion yet.'

It should be noted that, while the Church is dominated by men, surveys reveal that in groups of every age women are more likely to acknowledge the importance of religious experience than are men. In both New Age groups and in Christian churches, it is women who predominate. It may be that British women are more open to spiritual practice and belief than men (a survey conducted for Channel 4 found that roughly half of British women believed in astrology, while only a quarter of men shared that belief). It may be that men are simply more reluctant to show religious feeling outwardly. No men's magazines have astrology columns, but almost every woman's magazine has its own named astrologer. Two-thirds of the private clients of leading astrologers are reported to be women.

The heritage industry

A major cultural change in British life from the 1970s through to the present has been that Britons spend more leisure time and money on visiting historical sites and exhibits. It has been argued that the growth in the heritage industry has in some ways filled a gap left in people's lives by the loss of a religious dimension. Reverence for the past could be seen as replacing the religious reverence of previous generations. Britons who, a generation before, might have gone to church, now spend their Sunday visiting a stately home or exhibition of local 'heritage' – a modern pilgrimage. The Jorvik Centre in York (the town's modern name is derived from Jorvik, its Viking name) was the first purpose-built centre for heritage tourism. The life-size plastic Vikings of Jorvik have been followed by other exhibition centres showing everything from Oxford scholars to highland Scottish crofters. Such exhibitions use mannequins dressed up in historic costume, in restored or imitation historic houses, shops, castles or factories. They may even be staffed by actors dressed in historic costume. Paradoxically, the increasing secularisation of British life has led to less leisure time on Sunday for many, as since the 1990s shops have begun to routinely open on Sundays, giving the traditionally quiet Sabbath day more a feel of 'business as usual'.

The attraction of a 'museum culture' does not just extend to the remote past, but applies even to the twentieth century, and to areas of life that have only recently been part of normal life, rather than historical curiosities. In South Wales, for example, (where coal mining was until the 1980s the dominant industry, but has now almost disappeared) it is possible to be guided around a redundant coal mine by men who used to work as miners there, but who are now only dressed as miners to show tourists around. While much of this repackaging, particularly in metropolitan areas, might seem to be arranged or created for foreign tourists, in fact most of the visitors to many such attractions are British, being reintroduced to their own past through the professional presentation of a host of corners of its geography and commerce. As justifications for the former 'greatness' of Great Britain fall away, it could be said that its people turn to the past to find symbols of their identity, and indeed, their importance. Of these, the stately home is one of the most enduring as well as the most successfully marketed to the public.

In some ways the Church has benefited from this – the great cathedrals which combine Christian heritage and monuments from the past, have never been so popular. In other ways, too, the British could be accused of living in their past. Many films lovingly recreate Edwardian England, particularly those of Merchant–Ivory, who have specialised in finely detailed costume dramas and adaptations of literary classics such as *A Room with a View* and *Howards End*. Other films such as *The Remains of the Day* and *Pride and Prejudice* are profitably sold around the world as an image of an ideal Britain, and eagerly consumed by Britons themselves as a kind of national myth. The common elements of the aristocracy, venerable buildings and English eccentrics occur over and over in such films, offering a picture of a quaint gentle England. *Downton Abbey* is a striking recent example.

Fantasies of the Britain of previous generations, particularly of rural Britain, predominate in television drama series such as *Emmerdale* or *Downton Abbey* and in advertising – notably for various brands of bread, biscuits and cakes. Historical settings are also used in some of the numerous 'situation comedies' which British people watch. *'Allo 'Allo* and *Foyle's War* for example, are set during the Second World War, a time which many in the older generations look back to with nostalgia and pride. The celebrations in 1995 to commemorate the fiftieth Anniversary of VE (Victory in Europe) Day were the occasion of a collective nostalgia for the comradeship and certainties of wartime. It should be stressed, however, that children and young people in general know very little about 'the [1939–45] war' – the defining moment in twentieth-century British history, and the flooding of print and broadcast media with images of the war in the half-centenary year 1995 made very little impression on them. For example a popular television series *Goodnight Sweetheart*, with a hero who, by means of time travel, has a double life – one part lived in the wartime 1940s, and one lived in contemporary Britain – appealed only to the old, with their hunger for nostalgia. In 2006 a regular sketch on *The Catherine Tate Show* mocked the cheerful poverty of the 1940s and 1950s and the lack of sophistication of the ordinary people.

Another feature of the British fascination with the past is the re-creation of the world – particularly in rural areas far from London – as a series of places defined by some cultural product. Thus one is able to go on an excursion not just to another place, but, at least imaginatively, to another time. For example the Lake District is advertised as Wordsworth's home, the Yorkshire Moors as 'Brontë Country' and even towns used for very recent productions – parts of Yorkshire for the television series *Heartbeat* (now

FIGURE 7.4 Several steam railways have been revived by enthusiasts as tourist attractions

known as 'Heartbeat Country') – or Harry Potter films have become marketed in this way, and there is a steady demand from the public for such
attractions.

The Harry Potter film of 2001 and its sequels form an interesting
glimpse into the way Britain has come to be imagined, and then marketed.
Locations for the film include the remote Scottish Highlands at Glen Nevis,
buildings such as Oxford's historic Bodleian Library and Alnwick castle, a
preserved steam railway at Goathland and Gloucester cathedral. All of these
sites, illustrating the recent industry that has grown up around British
countryside, history and nostalgia for the recent past, are already part of
'heritage' Britain. Not on the heritage trail, but more representative of life for
the great majority of UK citizens, is the ordinary house where Harry Potter's
story begins, filmed in a suburban cul-de sac in Bracknell. The contrast
between these two Britains is reflected in road signs. Alongside Britain's real
geography, through which one is guided by blue motorway signs and green
trunk road signs there is an alternative network of reddish-brown road signs
– indicating the presence of 'heritage' Britain. This may be formed of real
places – castles, stately homes, preserved factories – or of invented attractions.
For example, in north Wales it is possible to journey through the tunnels of
an abandoned mine now converted into 'King Arthur's Labyrinth' – a site
with no connections to Arthurian legend, but one where an underground
heritage display has been erected. There was an equally disjunctive *Dr Who*
exhibition at Llangollen. For a country declining economically, there is an
added commercial incentive to turn to the past – not just for nostalgia but for
a product that, for example, is unavailable in the US, yet which is also linked
to many of the people who come as tourists from that country. The latter will
also show at least as much interest in the contents of Table 7.6, the current
line of succession to the British throne, as will the locals.

Conclusion

The question of the role that religion plays in establishing British identity is
a complex one, and one that reveals great differences between people of
different ages in Britain. For a large number of British people over fifty,
religion is a quiet and distant but important presence in their lives. It is a
touchstone of shared British identity at great national or public occasions
and a continuing link with the past. It is also a source of comfort available
at times of private or personal tragedy and celebration, such as weddings
and funerals, when religion becomes temporarily of far greater importance
for all generations.

In England, even many of those who do not believe in Christianity feel
a sense of attachment to the Church of England. While they may never

TABLE 7.6 Current line of succession to HM Queen Elizabeth II (b 1926)

1 HRH The Prince of Wales (Prince Charles; b 1948), eldest son of Queen Elizabeth II
2 HRH The Duke of Cambridge (Prince William; b 1982), elder son of The Prince of Wales
3 HRH Prince Harry of Wales (b 1984), younger son of The Prince of Wales
4 HRH The Duke of York (Prince Andrew; b 1960), second son of Queen Elizabeth II
5 HRH Princess Beatrice of York (b 1988), elder daughter of The Duke of York
6 HRH Princess Eugenie of York (b 1990), younger daughter of The Duke of York
7 HRH The Earl of Wessex (Prince Edward; b 1964), youngest son of Queen Elizabeth II
8 James, Viscount Severn (b 2007), son of The Earl of Wessex
9 Lady Louise Windsor (b 2003), daughter of The Earl of Wessex
10 HRH The Princess Royal (The Princess Anne; b 1950), daughter of Queen Elizabeth II
11 Peter Phillips (b 1977), son of The Princess Royal
12 Savannah Phillips (b 2010), elder daughter of Peter Phillips
13 Isla Phillips (b 2012), younger daughter of Peter Phillips
14 Zara Phillips (b 1981), daughter of The Princess Royal
15 David Armstrong-Jones, Viscount Linley (b 1961), son of Princess Margaret, the Queen's late younger sister
16 The Honourable Charles Armstrong-Jones (b 1999), son of Viscount Linley
17 The Honourable Margarita Armstrong-Jones (b 2002), daughter of Viscount Linley
18 The Lady Sarah Chatto (b 1964), daughter of Princess Margaret
19 Samuel Chatto (b 1996), elder son of Lady Sarah Chatto
20 Arthur Chatto (b 1999), younger son of Lady Sarah Chatto

attend church services, they like to know that they are there, and would feel robbed if they were taken from them. For a number of people, the Church of England encapsulates in its rituals, liturgies, hymns and music a distinct cultural expression of Englishness. For that minority of the population who adhere actively and strongly to Christianity, this element of religion as expression of national identity is also there but is probably less important. In Wales and Scotland, membership of the respective communions of the Anglican church serves more to divide them off from their fellow Welsh and Scottish people. Religion becomes an expression of difference or trans-nationalism, that is, of possible allegiance to Englishness.

For young British people whose parents were born elsewhere in the world, religion – such as Hinduism or Islam – is one important strand of their identity: a key element in the culture that marks their own contribution to Britishness as distinctive and creates a link with another heritage elsewhere. Their religion can be a source of estrangement from the rest of the British population, when they are faced with a hostile tabloid media which talks only of Muslim or Hindu 'extremism'. However, a large majority of them refuse to be alienated, and have come to see all religions as, in the words of Indajit Singh, editor of *The Sikh Messenger*, 'overlapping circles of belief with much in common'.

For most people under about thirty, Christianity is associated with a past to which they feel they have little connection. Some will describe themselves as atheists, and many as agnostics, but for those who are interested in spiritual things, the New Age is more likely to attract them. While not part of a formal or organised system, such practices offer people freedom and individuality plus the possibility of exploring spiritual paths for themselves.

Exercises

1   Do you recognise the following phrases: 'To hide one's light under a bushel', 'to go the extra mile', 'to turn the other cheek'? What do they mean? How do you feel Christian ideas might be at odds with people's lives in Britain today?

2   Many British commentators try to link a decline in religious practice to a perceived deterioration in morals. Do you think this is a fair connection to make, and what signs or changes in Britain do you think lead people to argue that there has been a worsening of moral standards?

3   What are hot cross buns, Shrove Tuesday pancakes and Yule logs? When would they be eaten? Remembering that dates such as Valentine's Day (14 February) have a religious background, how would you map out the British calendar in terms of (a) Christian festivals and (b) significant dates for all faiths?

4   Where would you locate the following ten World Heritage sites (established by UNESCO) on the map in Chapter 1: the City of Bath; Blenheim Palace; Canterbury Cathedral; Stonehenge; Westminster Palace; the islands of St Kilda; the Giant's Causeway; Hadrian's wall; Ironbridge; and the castles and town walls of Caernarfon, Conwy, Beaumaris and Harlech? Do you know, or can you find out, the natural or cultural significance of each site?

Reading

Davie, Grace. *Europe: The Exceptional Case: Parameters of Faith in the Modern World.* Darton Longman Todd, 2002. Argues that secularisation is not inevitable.

Dawkins, Richard. *The God Delusion*. Bantam Press, 2006. A polemical treatise against Christianity from an atheistic, Darwinian perspective.

Fowler, Peter. *The Past in Contemporary Society: Then, Now*. Routledge, 1992. Examines the extent to which our heritage is still with us in the present.

Haldane, John. *An Intelligent Person's Guide to Religion*. Duckworth, 2003. An accessible and even-handed account of some of life's dilemmas from a professor of philosophy.

Parsons, Gerald. *The Growth of Religious Diversity: Britain from 1945*. 2 vols. Open University/Routledge, 1993. Careful and thorough analysis of Britain and religion since the Second World War.

Ramadan, Tariq. *What I Believe*. OUP 2009. The Professor Of Contemporary Islamic Studies at Oxford asserts the rights, entitlements and responsibilities of Muslims in the West.

Visram, Rozina. *Ayahs, Lascars, and Princes: The Story of Indians in Britain, 1700-1947*. Pluto, 1986. Reveals the largely unknown heritage and history of Hindus, Muslims, Sikhs and Parsis from India in the UK.

 # Cultural examples

Films

My Son the Fanatic (1997) dir. Udayan Prasad. Comic treatment of the efforts of a Pakistani taxi driver to clean up the morals of his northern English town.

Four Lions (2010) dir. Chris Morris. A satirical analysis of the relations between 'home-grown' terrorists and their religious roots – an Islamic *Dad's Army*. In four months it grossed £3 million in the UK.

Priest (1993) dir. Antonia Bird. A social drama exploring the conflicts between Catholicism and homosexuality in an impoverished Liverpool parish.

No Surrender (1985) dir. Peter Smith. Rival Catholic and Protestant Irish factions collide in a Liverpool club.

Bhaji on the Beach (1993) dir. Gurinder Chadha. A trip to Blackpool for a group of Punjabi women becomes a source of mutual understanding and solidarity.

Leon the Pig Farmer. (1992) dir. Vadim Jean and Gary Sinyor. Young Jewish Londoner moves to rural Yorkshire.

Excalibur (1981) dir. John Boorman. New Age philosophy and Celtic magic projected onto the myth of Arthur's England.

Truly, Madly, Deeply (1991) dir. Anthony Minghella. One woman's private trauma of grief after bereavement.

The Wicker Man (1973) dir. Robin Hardy. A cult movie with a horrifying ending in which a mainland policeman discovers pagan fertility rituals, including human sacrifice, still dominate the society of a small northern island. Inferior remake: 2006.

The Lord of the Rings (2001) dir. Peter Jackson. J.R.R. Tolkien's fantasy masterpiece portrays the struggle between good and evil in a quest for the one magic ring.

Books

Asian Women Writers' Collective, *Flaming Spirit* (1994) Edited by Rukshana Ahmad and Rahila Gupta. Religion, identity and nostalgia for home are common themes in this collection of stories from Asian women across Britain.

David Lodge, *How Far Can You Go?* (1980) Analysis of modern Catholic faith and responsibility in Britain.

Jenny Newman, *Going In* (1995) A British account of entering a French convent and the relationships between the religious and secular worlds.

Salman Rushdie, *The Satanic Verses* (1988) The novel whose portrayal of Islam sparked a major controversy over blasphemy and free speech.

Hanif Kureishi, *The Black Album* (1995) Novel of Anglo-Pakistani youth growing up in London against the backdrop of the Rushdie Affair.

David Hare, *Racing Demon* (1990) David Hare's intelligent and questioning play about two Church of England priests engaging in theological debate and sociological comment in contemporary south London.

John Betjeman, *The Best of Betjeman* (1978) Poems including nostalgic views of his youth, but also 'In Westminster Abbey', a devastating critique of English religious attitudes.

Peter Stanford, *The Extra Mile* (2010) A fascinating personal account of pilgrimages undertaken to Iona, Walsingham, Holywell, etc.

TV programmes

Restoration. BBC 2 programme where viewers voted on which heritage building to restore.

Songs of Praise. Perennial Sunday evening favourite in which a congregation and community are visited by the BBC for a weekly service.

Father Ted. Comedy series about three Irish priests and their sometimes less than spiritual lifestyle.

The Vicar of Dibley. Sitcom about a woman vicar written by the author of *Four Weddings and a Funeral.*

Rev. A comedy series about a vicar who has moved from rural Suffolk to the problems of inner-city multi-ethnic London.

Websites

www.churchofengland.org
   Church structure: what it means to be Anglican.
www.bbc.co.uk/religion/religions/islam
   Extensive information about the Islamic faith and culture in the UK.
www.buddhanet.net
   Simple introduction to Buddhism, beliefs, practices and meditation.
www.mysticplanet.com/8diction.htm
   New Age dictionary of terms from 'accupressure' to 'yoga'.
www.orthodoxengland.org.uk/hp.php
   A resource covering the history and practice of Orthodox Christianity.

Conclusion: Britain towards the future

Peter Childs

IN THE YEARS SINCE THIS BOOK was first written, there has been a general shift from a literate to a visual culture, with numerous concerns expressed over literacy levels alongside a realisation that the young are outstripping the older generation in their technological understanding. In many respects the UK still looks to the US for cultural directions (e.g. the rise among the middle classes of the HBO boxset as an adjunct to Americanisation), but British culture has generally remained outward looking, partly because of increased ethnic diversity. In terms of language there is the evolution into dominant forms of expression of texting and social networking (email perhaps increasingly focused on use in the workplace and on those used to letter writing) alongside the huge shifts in accents and linguistic informality. There has also been an interesting rise of professional language and the shift towards customer-service etiquette. There continues more virulently than ever a fraught relationship between the Tory party and the EU now that the Conservatives are in government again. East European and other migration has transformed understandings of migration and ethnicity as new accents permeate social spaces. While technology has wrought huge changes, there have been shifts in consumer behaviour since the 'credit crunch', then recession (e.g. the return of car boot sales, dine-in for a tenner deals, coupons and so on). There is arguably a general feeling in British culture that we should reappraise the status and role of economics in our society. This view has partly come to prevail because of the failure of banks which operated outside easily understood ethical norms and seemed heedless of human consequences when they lent freely and then withdrew credit. This is allied also to a general perception that money is corrupting traditional aspects to British life. For example, when the much-loved chocolate-makers Cadburys were taken over by the multi-national corporation Kraft, a sense of values and history were lost along with livelihoods; similarly, when football clubs like Chelsea, Liverpool and Manchesters United and City are owned by overseas businessmen commercial logic will be applied to a cultural institution that is bound up with family, 'religion' and heritage. The previously endorsed 'common sense' view that the free market is the most efficient way of organising life in the West has been challenged since the bail-out of the bankers and the nationalisation of banks in 2008. This was preceded by over a million protesters marching on the streets of London against the Iraq war in February 2003 and since followed by mass opposition to the cuts imposed by the Conservative–Liberal Democrat coalition government in 2010 and 2011 (the UK has seen student occupations, strikes and riots). At the moment, the economic aspect to British identity seems wrapped up in larger forces and the fate of Western economies. As a protest against capitalist economics, demonstrators pitched tents outside St Paul's Cathedral in central London for months in the second half of 2011, reminiscent of the days when students would occupy campus buildings during their protests. Under the banner of the worldwide 'Occupy Movement', the St Paul's campers left the Anglican Church in a difficult position, caught between condoning lawlessness on their doorstep and evicting from Church land people protesting against inequality. This dilemma was felt more keenly when the tents prevented the new lord mayor from being anointed on the steps of the cathedral for the first time in 800 years.

The future in Britain now looks more unstable than it has for many years. After several decades in which standards of living have risen and prosperity and growth have appeared natural, people are starting to question whether the future will be 'better'. A survey in December 2011 for *The Observer* newspaper found that only 32 per cent of people thought that today's youth would have a better living standards than their parents. There is here a notable change in expectations: for example, in 2003 43 per cent of people expected their children to have a higher quality of life when the children reached their current age, but the figure had dropped to 23 per cent in 2011. This can be contrasted with the New Labour theme tune of 'Things Can Only Get Better' at the seminal election in 1997. Subsequent to that victory 40 per cent of British people, who polls often reveal to be comparatively pessimistic, thought that 'Britain is getting worse as a place to live'. In 2011 the percentage had risen to 61 per cent. The current Conservative government works with the slogan of 'Keep the Country Safe', which echoes the ubiquitous 'Keep Calm and Carry On' revived wartime official red label that adorns tea-towels and coffee mugs. The future is not perceived to be bright by most people in Britain, but it is also true to say that it does not look much better elsewhere in Europe.

Europe

Britain is part of the continent of Europe, part of the European Union and its extensive single market for trading, but not part of the Eurozone, 17 European Union countries that operate a single currency. At the start of 2012, only the first of these is not in doubt. As the 27 countries of the European Union met in December 2011 to address the financial crisis that had engulfed the operation of the single currency, Prime Minister David Cameron insisted on a discussion of amendments the British government wished to see to the proposals that had been put forward. When this was curtailed, Cameron opted to exercise Britain's veto and withdraw from the summit. The future of the European Union, as well as the position of the euro, was thus to be discussed without Britain at the table. The possible consequences of this situation put Britain's place in the European Union in question, and further retreat from European unity would have more consequences for Britain's political and economic place in the world, for example in relation to the Commonwealth and the United States. Following Cameron's veto, the German newspaper *Der Spiegel* chose as its headline: 'Bye Bye Britain'.

European unity has developed into one of the most contentious issues of present day British politics. Since the Union's origins in the 1950s, Britain has been somewhat slow and reluctant to participate fully. It was not until 1 January 1973, following two years of negotiations, that Britain joined the European Community (EC). The decision, taken by the then-governing Conservative party, which has long been more divided by the issue of European membership than any other topic, was not without controversy. A national referendum was called on the matter in June 1975, and the British populace endorsed EC membership by a two-to-one majority despite considerable opposition from certain quarters. Until recently, and the fraught issue of the single currency, perhaps the element of EC membership that has caused most dissension between Britain and the EC is the Common Agricultural Policy (CAP). For years this was the central element of the EC budget, commanding over 60 per cent of expenditure, such that if the CAP was unfair the redistributional effects of the whole EC budget would also be unfair. Britain argued that, because of the CAP, the value of its contributions far outweighed the value of benefits received, and consequently the EC established two British refunds in the 1980s.

The Maastricht Treaty in 1992 changed the European Community to the European Union, but other main elements of the treaty included further arrangements for economic and monetary union, including adoption of a single currency (then called the ecu rather than the euro), provisions for an independent European bank, and the development of a common defence and foreign policy. A continued hostility to European integration on the right of British politics led to the 2001 election being fought by the Conservative party on the platform slogans of 'Keep the Pound' and 'Save the UK from a Federal European Superstate', and to those on the right, the euro and the Masstricht Treaty have transformed the EU from a union of democratic countries into a supra-national empire where decisions affecting citizens are not open to democratic control. The Conservatives lost the 2001 election and the following one in 2005, suggesting that the majority view in the UK on Europe is closer to scepticism than hostility, underlined by the British reluctance to take full advantage of their voting rights: the European Parliament elections of 1999 (23.3 per cent) and to a lesser extent 2004 (38.9 per cent) had a low turnout of the British electorate. In 2009 (34 per cent), for the first time the government polled less well than a party with no representation in the British parliament as the UK Independence Party (UKIP) won more votes than the governing Labour Party. Britain seems to remain deeply reluctant to participate fully in European initiatives, and one ex-prime minister has argued that the greatest missed opportunity for Britain occurred when it failed to join the Common Market in 1957, such that rules and precedents had been established by the time of British involvement in 1973.

Some commentators in the media have long argued that a high level of economic and political integration will radically change government and life in Britain. The current process of deregulation which began with the creation of a customs union will have radical consequences for national sovereignty

FIGURE 8.1 The flag of St George has replaced the Union Jack to signify Englishness within Britishness

FIGURE 8.2 The cross of St George on an English crusader

if taken to its conclusion. Subsequent further integration, such as adoption of the euro, has long been resisted on the basis that it means the sacrifice of certain national economic tools, including control of the interest rate, and an unacceptable degree of vulnerability to economic conditions in other countries. Those who take a negative view of European union argue that the chancellor should be able to control the British economy from Westminster and that legislation which governs the British populace, concerning the maximum length of the working week for example, should only originate from the British Parliament. Certain members of the now ruling Conservative Party, so-called Eurosceptics, have for many years split their party into two camps over the subject of Europe. A 2001 report from the European commission warned that two-thirds of those questioned said they believed giving up the pound would mean an end to national independence while 60 per cent said they thought the EU could not be trusted with British interests. The academic asked to review the figures in Brussels concluded that views about the euro were based upon 'prejudice and the innate conservatism of British public opinion'.

Britain's relationship with (the rest of) Europe can be considered in a number of ways, but in general it might be argued that the British have responded positively when the Europeans from the Continent have come to their shores, such as students on the EU's SOCRATES scheme, but have been hostile to legislation which may appear to be imposed at a distance from Brussels. For many people, the European presence in Britain in recent years has been most visible in the national sport of football, where managers like Roberto Mancini (Italian, at Manchester City) and Arsène Wenger (French, at Arsenal) have accompanied stars such as Fernando Torres (Spanish, at Chelsea), Patrice Evra (French, at Manchester United) and Robin van Persie (Dutch, at Arsenal) in a massive influx of European talent since the mid-1990s. The appointment in 2001 of Sven-Göran Eriksson, a Swede, to the position of England manager caused a national debate, as it was felt in many quarters that the team ought to be led by a fellow countryman, who would understand the local significance of football to the English, and the succeeding manager in 2006 was indeed English: Steve McClaren. When results were poor, the call went out again for 'the best man' to take the job, which led to the appointment of Fabio Cappello, only for underperformance in the World Cup in 2010 to lead to renewed calls for an Englishman to manage the side.

Alternatively, Britain has generally been hostile to the ways in which the nation's diet has come under repeated scrutiny by European officials (known to the British as bureaucrats) as they attempt to regulate and standardise agricultural production and markets across the European Union nations. Rumours concerning legislation over food and drink coming from Europe have become widespread in contemporary folklore, with stories of decrees from Brussels over the size of apples or the straightness of cucumbers fuelling British anti-European feeling. The image of 'the food mountain', built to stabilise markets and prices, has itself become a powerful symbolic landscape form for Europe in the popular press in Britain. The huge furore around beef and bovine spongiform encephalopathy (a fatal brain disease believed to be passed from infected cattle to humans), which led to a worldwide ban on British beef in the mid-1990s, also brought out the cultural politics of food production and consumption very starkly – especially so, perhaps, given the association of Britishness with beef (the epitome of this is William Hogarth's eighteenth-century painting 'The Gate of Calais', commonly known as 'O the Roast Beef of Old England', which hangs in the National Gallery in Trafalgar Square). The 'beef crisis' provoked in some Britons a 'patriotic' response of ignoring health warnings and continuing to eat British beef, simultaneously mocking people who were more cautious about their consumption habits. So, in a 2001 United Nations survey of domestic concerns, while for other Europeans 'Beef/BSE' came third in a poll of 'What would you say were the two or three most important problems facing your country today?', for the British it did not figure in the top twelve (the top three were, as often, law and order, health and unemployment).

It is widely understood, however, that food from the Continent has had a pervasive positive impact on British culture. Supermarkets now carry products that would have been hard to find twenty years ago: rocket, wild mushrooms, Parmigiano-Reggiano, crème fraîche, filo pastry, dry-cured bacon, pancetta, and a dozen kinds of rice, of pasta and of olive oil. However, of all people in the West, the British still spend the least part of their monthly income on food, though the middle classes eat out more and more, expecting in gastropubs to be served foods from around the world that they would not have heard of ten years earlier: pad thai, pho, pata negra, sushi, bulgogi and boutargue. The revolution in British restaurant food has been attributed to the influence of chefs such as the Roux brothers, who opened their restaurant, Le Gavroche, in the early 1970s, and served carefully chosen and prepared 'authentic' French food, as opposed to the imitation fare previously available in London. These were followed by chefs such as Raymond Blanc and Anton Mosimann, and then Nico Ladenis and Marco Pierre White. Arguably, it is this influence that has led to the enormous success of cookery programmes and TV chefs in recent years. These are sometimes not professional cooks but those who have simply learnt how to eat well for themselves, such as Nigella Lawson and Sophie Grigson. Many are celebrated because of their personalities as much as their cooking (James Martin or Jamie Oliver), while still more are valued simply for educating British people about the basics (Delia Smith). It is cookery books, though, that have changed most, as traditional, 'good English cooking' guides by the likes of Fanny Craddock and Jane Grigson were superseded in the 1970s by translations from French originals, and hundreds of recipe books by chefs like Blanc and Mosimann, which were subsequently emulated by homegrown authors and publications such as the ubiquitous River Café Cook Book, which itself then gave way to the cult of the River Cottage cookbooks by Hugh Fearnley-Whittingstall as more and more people looked to cook with healthy, organic and homegrown produce.

In an *Observer* poll in 2001, Britons were asked which was their favourite European country. The replies placed Spain (26 per cent) overwhelmingly in front, followed by France (13 per cent), Italy (12 per cent), Ireland (11 per cent) and Portugal (8 per cent). These figures complemented separate findings on Britons' choice of foreign holiday destinations, recorded as: Spain (27 per cent), France (20 per cent), Ireland (6 per cent), Italy (4 per cent) and Portugal (4 per cent). These were the top European destinations except for Greece (6 per cent); of non-European countries, only the USA (7 per cent) ranked in the top ten.

Over the last three decades, while remaining sceptical of economic and legislative integration, British people have become increasingly appreciative of European culture. Among the young, Europe is generally perceived positively and associated with many of the good things in life discussed above, from food to holidays. However, many remain concerned about the level of EU migrancy to Britain, which the government says has placed a strain on schools and public services after the addition of the eight 2004 accession countries. Following an influx of over 600,000 migrant workers from Eastern Europe in a two-year period, amounting to 1 per cent of the UK population, the Home Secretary put a cap of less than 20,000 on the number of low-skilled workers from Bulgaria and Romania who would be allowed to work in Britain when the EU expanded again in 2007. This reflects a long ambivalent relationship to change in Britain: analysts, pro-gressives and many politicians recognise that the influx of workers helps the economy and provides a needed labour force in certain industries, while others, particularly the old and conservative, fear that the recognisable society in which they grew up is changing too fast for their sense of belonging.

Multiethnic

While it is straightforward to offer figures and percentages of various kinds for the overall UK population, as in previous chapters, such statistics are usually more applicable to some ethnic groups than to others, and this can be for economic as well as cultural reasons (for example, research in 2007 by the Joseph Rowntree Foundation uncovered that chances of living in poverty are twice as great for other ethnic groups – the rate of poverty stood at 40 per cent – as for white Britons). So, when discussing language, it is important to realise that one in six primary school children does not speak English as a first language. These figures are also contextualised by the fact that half the ethnic-minority population is under 24, compared with one-third of the white population, and over half a million schoolchildren speak English as a foreign language. The youth culture of ethnic groups also varies, such that, for example, young people from ethnic minority backgrounds are a third less likely to use drugs than whites but it is also true that habits of drug-taking will vary across ethnicities. Similarly, more 16- to 19-year-olds from ethnic minority groups are in full-time education than whites. In terms of gender, women from ethnic minorities hold more educational qualifi-cations than white women, and black African women are twice as likely to be qualified above A level standard. Again, the proportion of Asian women who have separated or divorced is less than half that recorded among whites. Also, while Britain has the highest proportion of single mothers in the

European Union, rates vary from one in ten white women with children is a single mother to one in five Caribbean mothers. Last of these indicators, taken from the *Observer*'s 'Britain Uncovered' survey in March 2001, is the statistic that three-quarters of Pakistani and Bangladeshi women are in partnerships by the age of 25, 50 per cent more than white women.

The rise of multiethnic Britain has signalled great cultural changes for the entire population. Food in Britain has been revolutionised by exposure to cuisine from around the world and while eating out in Britain was once a dull affair for the connoisseur it is now transformed into a high-quality gastronomic experience in the many hotels, boutique restaurants and gastropubs that have embraced fine cuisine. Every market town has long had at least an Indian restaurant and a Chinese takeaway, but Thai restaurants are becoming nearly as common, shortly followed by Greek, Mexican, Iranian, Turkish, Norwegian and other eateries. This has not been solely because of migrants coming to Britain but also because travel abroad has given the British population a taste for foods outside the mainstream, ranging from halva to green curry. Celebrity TV chefs, such as Ken Hom (Chinese) and Anjum Anand (Indian), have introduced 'exotic' foods to the domestic diet and it has been said that this is a positive part of the rapid mongrelisation of British culture, such that the foreign secretary said in early 2001 that chicken tikka masala is now the national dish.

FIGURE 8.3 London's diverse ethnic population

In the arts, 'Ethnic' and crossover music particularly has become main-stream in recent years, with artists such as Dizzee Rascal, K.I.A., Nitin Sawhney and Tinie Tempah nominated for the prestigious Mercury Music prize and new r'n'b singers like Estelle dominating the charts. There are also the annual MOBO (Music of Black Origin) awards solely for black artists and an equivalent ceremony to celebrate the achievements of British Asians in the arts. Since the 1980s Asian musicians in Britain have been experimenting with rap, dub technology, jungle breakbeats, traditional Indian music and rock. In the mid to late 1990s Anglo-Asian artists with sitars, guitars and decks, such as Cornershop, Asian Dub Foundation, Fun-da-mental and Talvin Singh, broke into the pop charts. Across the board, Afro-Caribbeans have exerted a decisive stylistic influence on British youth and mainstream cultures as evidenced by the dance appropriation of aspects of rudeboy, Rasta, hip-hop and sound system culture. Hip-hop culture under-lines the creative assemblage that defines Afro-Caribbean youth styles in Britain, whether in music (mixing and sampling), dress (arranging assorted fake and real designer labels) or language.

A festival that epitomises the best multicultural aspects of modern Britain is the Edinburgh Mela. This is Scotland's biggest annual intercultural arts festival and its aim is to celebrate Scotland's mix of influences in music and the arts. The festival's roots are in South Asian cultures, and the Mela was originally created by a group of people from Bangladesh, India and Pakistan, yet the festival intends to reflect the diversity of what it means to be Scottish, while also bringing artists from around the world, from the late Nusrat Fateh Ali Khan to Papa Wemba, Bappi Lahiri and Musical Youth. It has become the most significant multicultural festival in Scotland, attracting people from all parts of the UK, and it showcases global stars such as the bhangra singer Malkit Singh (whose music features in the film *Bend it Like Beckham*) as well as fresh homegrown fusion music from bands Jinx, a ska/punk band from Yorkshire.

A debate that has often focused on issues of ethnicity has concerned asylum-seekers. Repeated UK governments have come under attacks for immigration control shortcomings but also for schemes such as distributing migrants from the ports where they arrive to cities around the country. Several councils declared that they could take no more refugee families and stopped providing homes for those who arrived, while others accused the Home Office of paying self-interested private landlords to house thousands of asylum-seekers in slums rather than use accommodation provided by the local authorities. More than 100 incidents were reported in Hull alone in the year following the introduction of refugees to the city in the summer of 2000. Around this time, the United Nations estimated that there are 37 million refugees across the world, only 0.5 per cent of whom are in Britain.

FIGURE 8.4 Long queues form every day outside the London Passport and Visa Office

As a contrast to those voices who see the demise of 'Britishness' in future years, there are those that consider culture, and identity itself, as pluralistic and multi-layered, while recognising the pressures that are currently questioning the limits of Britain. Perhaps most prominently in these quarters, the 'unsettling' of Britain was detailed by the Parekh Report on 'The Future of Multi-Ethnic Britain' in 2000. The report commissioned by the Runnymede Trust saw seven reasons why the idea of Britain is at a turning-point in the new century: globalisation, the country's decline as a world power, its role in Europe, devolution, the end of empire, the spread of social pluralism and post-war migration. The report's conclusion was that Britain ought to be recognised as the 'Community of communities' it has now come to be (and, for that matter, always was). Changes in the understanding of British culture and in the transmission of appropriate national stories, signs and symbols can follow through from this appreciation of present and past pluralism.

It is also clear that some British people consider a multicultural society to be a threat not just to their ideas of national identity but their very well-being. The suicide plane attacks on New York and Washington on 11 September 2001 brought cries of support and outrage from the British press and politicians, but it was also apparent that for some British people these extreme terrorist actions were hard to dissociate from their perceptions of Muslims in the UK, and the week following the American disaster were marked not just by calls for a greater understanding of religious and cultural differences but also by verbal attacks and acts of violence aimed at Muslim individuals and their families. This was put in another context by the 7/7 attacks on London transport in 2005. On 7 July that year four terrorists detonated bombs hidden in rucksacks on trains and buses in the capital. Two factors shed a particular light on understandings of the attacks that day: first, that the London Metropolitan police shot an innocent young Brazilian man at a tube station because they thought he had a bomb in his rucksack, and second, that the four bombers were all British Muslims. This resulted in an extensive inquiry into police procedures and racial attitudes but also into the perceptions among young British Muslims of their country. It is also notable that a Channel 4 survey of 500 British Muslims found that 24 per cent believed the four blamed suicide bombers did not perform the attacks.

Literature has provided a number of prominent contemporary examples of multiethnic Britain, from Salman Rushdie's *The Satanic Verses* through the works of Hanif Kureishi to Andrea Levy's *Small Island*. To take one celebrated book, Zadie Smith's debut novel *White Teeth* presents a series of metaphors for the heterogeneity of modern Britain. Her title of course plays with the idea that everyone is the same under the skin, but the novel charts the variety of molars, canines, incisors, root canals, false teeth, dental work and damage that constitute the history behind different smiles. The commonsensical idea of the uniformity of teeth, which can also be divided into a host of shades from pearly to black, is as much a fiction in the novel as the traditional template of Britishness. The prime examplars of traditional Englishness in *White Teeth* are a family called the Chalfens. The Chalfens are taken to be 'more English then the English' because of their liberal middle-class values, and also their tendency towards empiricism. However, they are in fact third-generation Poles, originally Chalfenovskys: not more

English than the English, but as English as anyone else. Smith rings this theme of hybridity and cross-fertilisation through numerous extended metaphors, drawn from horticulture, eugenics and the weather.

The most prominent person in the novel who considers herself to be 'a stranger in a strange land' is Irie Jones, whose mother is 'from Lambeth (via Jamaica)' and whose father is a white war veteran from Brighton. In the novel's metaphor, Irie sees no reflection of herself in the 'mirror of Englishness'. She turns to her grandmother and Jamaica for a sense of her 'roots' but concludes that the idea of belonging is itself a 'lie'. The other central family of the book, the Iqbals, have come to England from Bangladesh. Their second-generation children spend their teenage years apart, the one in London, the other in Chittagong. Each finds his identity is located elsewhere: Millat, living in London, wishes to be an American gangsta rapper before he becomes in the words of his father a 'fully paid-up green bow-tie wearing fundamentalist terrorist', while Magid, in Bangladesh, becomes 'a pukka Englishman, white suited, silly wig lawyer'. Their mother, Alsana, expresses the overall view of the novel: 'You go back and back and back and it's still easier to find the right Hoover bag than to find one pure person, one pure faith, on the globe. Do you think anybody is English? Really English? It's a fairy-tale.'

White Teeth's view of race relations, though far from perfect, seems more closely to resemble hopes for Britain's future than observations about its past. The book works politically far more at the level of representation than any kind of confrontation. The novel disseminates a multicultural view of London, where currently over 40 per cent of children are born to at least one black parent. And *White Teeth*, as the novelist Caryl Phillips concluded in his review of the novel, ably dramatises the fact that: 'The "mongrel" nation that is Britain is still struggling to find a way to stare into the mirror and accept the ebb and flow of history that has produced this fortuitously diverse condition.'

New technology

Finally, nothing seems to look to the future more than technology. In the last ten years, a number of new machines have materialised in a sizable number in most British homes. There are new gadgets in almost every room, like breadmakers and juicers in the kitchen, but most changes have affected communications and entertainment. These include digital cameras and camcorders, the Wii, Playstation and Nintendo Gameboy, home cinema speakers and projectors, hard-disk recorders and DVD players, smartphones and netbooks, MP3/4 players, and high-definition televisions. The trend is away from hard and towards soft media, meaning that CDs and DVDs will soon be a thing of the past, and every home will be able to access every song and film ever made, possibly for free if enough advertising accompanies it (e.g. Spotify). However, the greatest cultural change has been happening online, in social space, especially with Facebook, LinkedIn and Twitter.

Nevertheless, predictions that the Internet would kill TV appear to be premature. Just as the cinema survived the advent of home video, television is booming despite the growth of digital media and the attraction of social networks. British people watched an average of 3 hours and 45 minutes of television a day in 2009, 3 per cent more than in 2004 (according to Ofcom). Telly continues to take centre stage in people's evenings, boosted by the popularity of shows such as *The X Factor, Britain's Got Talent* and *Doctor Who*. This has been boosted by digital video recorders (DVRs), now in 37 per cent of homes, along with high-definition television, now in more than 5 million UK homes in 2010. All of which has been put forward as another nail in the coffin of film, which has now seemingly lost its battle with digital video, and has tried to advocate 3D as the new must-have auditorium experience (with television, as always, adapting to include the new cinema technology for the home). The increase in TV viewing has also been driven by the growth in the UK's ageing population: older people tend to watch more TV, with 65-year-olds watching over five hours a day on average. Digital television has nearly reached the 100 per cent threshold and old analogue signals have been turned off in nearly all regions. More people have access to a greater number of channels now, and for most people this amounts to many dozens whereas they only had five a few years ago. This has resulted in a larger number of viewing hours per individual. The addition of broadband as a viewing platform has also meant huge numbers of people, especially the young, do not need a television to 'watch television'. Young people also use Facebook and Twitter while watching the television, rather than switching it off. Manufacturers are of course now putting functionality on TV that allows people to use Facebook or watch RSS and Twitter feeds while watching a programme. On-demand television on catch-up facilities such as the BBC iPlayer and ITV Player have not eclipsed live TV but have added to viewing hours and access to the most popular programmes such as celebrity showcases like *Strictly Come Dancing* and *I'm a Celebrity Get Me Out of Here*. Simon Cowell's two ITV 1 talent shows *X Factor* and *Britain's Got Talent* accounted for four of the five most watched programmes of 2009, with the final of *Britain's Got Talent* becoming the show with the highest audience at 16.5 million viewers. Perhaps most interestingly, Ofcom research indicated the audience growth in video-sharing sites such as YouTube had slowed over the past two years, but radio popularity continues to grow, with a high of 90.6 per cent of the population tuning in at least once a week (though the amount of time spent listening to the radio had fallen by 5 per cent in the previous five years).

FIGURE 8.5 A range of book tie-ins, serials, and documentaries on DVD and tape are sold through the BBC shop

In 2001, 90 per cent teenagers under the age of 16 already had a mobile phone, and by now a mobile phone has become considered essential for almost the entire population, whereas in 1988 the figure for ownership stood at 3 per cent. For those who do not use social networking, text messaging and email have become the most common forms of communication as people value the flexibility of these forms of contact and many people increasingly consider telephone conversations unnecessary or inconvenient, perhaps turning to Skype or other services for long-distance or face-to-face business conversations. Even the Lord's Prayer has now been translated into a text message as part of a scheme to send church services to worshippers on their mobile phones. 'Our Father who art in heaven' has become 'dad@hvn', and the rest of the Prayer now reads: 'urspshl.we want wot u want&urth2b like hvn.giv us food&4giv r sins lyk we 4giv uvaz.don't test us!bcos we kno ur boss, ur tuf&ur cool 4 eva!ok?' The Muslim community has also already witnessed the benefits of text-messaging believers with their five daily 'calls to prayer'.

Overall, the speed of technological change has been embraced by the British, who have in recent years welcomed new developments such as broadband internet access, BlackBerrys, wireless and Bluetooth connectivity, handheld scanners, GPS (global positioning systems) and digital assistants, even though according to surveys most people do not use anything like half the features available to them on their gadgets.

Conclusion

The technological revolution has enormously changed people's lives in the home, challenging the idea of the family 'unit' by turning its members into consumers of myriad domestic leisure activities. Alongside this, post-war migration has greatly altered the ethnic population, and the rise of the European Union has meant that British people have thought more deeply about their national identities, some wishing to call themselves primarily 'Welsh/Irish/English/Scottish', and others 'European', 'Asian', 'African' or any one of a hundred other labels that often make 'British' a hyphenated nationality. The Britain the essays in this book have described is composed of various contrasting elements: asylum-seekers and moneyed gentry; settled suburban commuters and country farmers; women priests and male nurses; nostalgic OAPs, well-off babyboomers, and young NEETs (not in employment, education or training) who can only dream of ever owning a home – each experiencing a different version and expressing a contrasting view of the country when talking about their relation to Britain. Any of these experiences of being British is a product of individual identity and circumstance, formed by a range of factors such as gender, region, religion, work and schooling, and each of these alternative views would supply a picture of Britain which can only take a place in a mosaic of opinions. As much as if not more than ever, in the twenty-first century it is wrong to think that there is a single British character, rather than a plurality of cultural identities.

Exercises

1 What do you think are the arguments for and against multiethnic communities?

2 Despite new age legislation in 2006 to prevent discrimination, many people believe that some employers will continue not to give jobs to those over the age of fifty because they think older people are less likely to keep up with technological developments. To what extent do you feel the proliferation of new technologies adds to a generation gap in society? Are the young's attitudes towards the old different from what they were in the past?

3 A recent report stated that the five things Europeans think of when considering the UK are The Beatles, London, the royal family, the BBC and Shakespeare. To what extent are these things 'British', as opposed to English? What five things that are not English would you list as the most famous aspects to Britain?

4 In this conclusion, some of the influences of Europe on Britain have been mentioned. What would you consider the main British influences on European countries to be?

 Reading

Bragg, Billy. *The Progressive Patriot*. Bantam, 2006.

Davey, Kevin. *English Imaginaries*. Lawrence & Wishart, 1998.

Easthope, Antony. *Englishness and National Culture*. Routledge, 1999.

Gilroy, Paul. *There Ain't No Black in the Union Jack*. Routledge, 1992.

Hyder, Rehan. *Brimful of Asia: Negotiating Ethnicity on the UK Music Scene*. Ashgate, 2004.

Nairn, Tom. *After Britain*. Granta, 2000.

Phillips, Mike and Phillips, Trevor. *Windrush: The Irresistible Rise of Multi-racial Britain*. HarperCollins, 1999.

The Runnymede Trust. *The Future of Multiethnic Britain: The Parekh Report*. Profile, 2000.

Wright, Patrick. *On Living in an Old Country*. New edition. Verso, 2009.

Cultural examples

Films

Four Lions (2009) dir. Chris Morris. Satirical take on fundamentalism and terrorism inspired in part by the 7/7 bombings and centred on a foolish gang of British Muslims.

Bhaji on the Beach. (1994) dir. Gurinder Chadha. Film, mixing British realist and Indian musical styles, about a group of British Asian women from Birmingham on a daytrip to Blackpool.

Trainspotting (1995) dir. Danny Boyle. Shocking and funny tale of heroin addicts in Edinburgh based on the novel by Irvine Welsh.

Mike Bassett: England Manager (2001) dir. Steve Barron. Spoof comedy in which Ricky Tomlinson, from TV's *The Royle Family,* stars as a pre-Eriksson national football manager who quotes Rudyard Kipling while aiming to take England to the World Cup in Brazil.

TV Programmes

See www.bfi.org.uk/features/mostwatched for the British Film Institute's overview of Britain's favourite television over the decades.

Books

Nadeem Aslam, *Maps for Lost Lovers* (2004) Powerful novel by a British Pakistani writer about Britain transformed into another country through the eyes and culture of a pair of murdered lovers.

Nagra Dilgit, *Look We Have Coming to Dover!* (2007) Comical and insightful collection of poems by a Brtish poet whose verses relate especially to the experience of British-born Indians.

James Kelman, *Not Not While the Giro* (2007) Booker Prize winner Kelman shows the lives of young Scottish men who are only waiting for the next dole money or menial job to get them through the stark reality of their lives.

Zadie Smith, *White Teeth* (2000) Hugely popular comic novel of multiethnic life in London since 1947.

Victor Headley, *Yardie* (1992) Jamaican gangster pulp fiction set in 1990s Hackney, London. The novel looks at the post-war Afro-Caribbean immigrant experience in conjunction with the transnational drugs economy.

Jeff Noon, *Vurt* (1993) Novel set in a grim, comic Manchester of the future. In a world peopled by vurt, robo and dog beings, gangs escape cops through the use of cyber-technology.

Julian Barnes, *Letters from London, 1990–95* (1995) An assembly of English novelist Barnes's writing for *The New Yorker,* on a range of topics from the fortunes of Margaret Thatcher to the troubles of the royal family.

Websites

www.wired.com
   News and analysis of the technologies driving the information age.
www.cybertown.com A site on which you can live an online life with virtual cash in
   Cybertown.
www.ukip.org
   British UK Independence Party site.
www.speakout.co.uk
   Campaign to demand a referendum on Europe.
www.geocities.com/yes_euro/
   One 17-year-old's view of why Britain should unite further with Europe.

Glossary

Instead of a set of exercises and questions to end the book, we have noted down the following outlines of keywords. We would like you to use these as starting points for thinking about each of the terms, but also as an elementary glossary to which you may want, perhaps with the aid of a dictionary and other books, to add your own terms and short definitions.

Accent is the inflection given to, and modulation of, speech. It mainly indicates social class and should be distinguished from both *dialect*, which is a combination of accent intonation and local vocabulary (and indicates region), and *slang*, which is the use of ungrammatical English among people in the same generational/gender groupings.

Acronyms adopted widely in the 1980s to describe new social and cultural phenomena included: YUPPIES, young urban professionals; DINKIE, dual income no kiddies; NIMBY, people who were in favour of (say) gypsy sites but 'not in my back yard'. Mrs Thatcher was nicknamed TINA: There Is No Alternative. The word wrinkly, applied to an old person, was not an acronym.

ASBO (Anti-Social Behaviour Order). Introduced in 1998 to control youths who have been terrorising their neighbours predominantly on housing estates. Those being given ASBOs occasionally see them as something to be proud of: badges of honour.

Bingo wings. These are the unsightly flabby areas of flesh below older women's arms. They are visible as they raise their card and shout 'House' in the game of Bingo.

Bling (from hip hop) is a style of flashy, cheap jewellery worn by chavs. It includes gold sovereign rings for men and fake gold trinkets for women.

Chavs (from the Romani word 'chavi', meaning child) are young, working-class people who wear casual sports clothes and are seen as vulgar by many.

Consumerism is the idea that consumption, not production is the basis of capitalist society. Hence 'market forces' and 'value for money' can be brought into all aspects of public life. There are three stages of consumerism: goods; services (TV entertainment/pizza delivery); and experience (aerobics programmes/travel).

Do-gooders is a term of abuse for well-meaning, left-leaning liberals. They are seen as sincere but dangerous interferers, rather than as problem-solvers.

Drug culture is an alternative way of life that has produced a range of terminology for drugs. Heroin is 'smack'; cocaine is 'crack'; marijuana/cannabis is 'grass', 'hash' (short for hashish), 'shit', 'slate'. Addicts are 'smack-heads', etc.

Emos are a subset of Goths, but they are much more serious. They wear their hair across their faces and may practise self-harm as a form of exhibitionism.

(The) Establishment is a neutral term for the people who are traditionally believed to run Britain – the landed aristocracy, hereditary peers, long-established business interests ('The Beerage'). Alan Clark used it to distinguish those members of the Conservative Party who represent an old guard, as distinguished from those who currently hold political power.

Estuary English is a form of speech distinguished from 'received pronunciation' or 'proper English'. For example 'regimental' is pronounced 'regimen'au'. 'It'll' becomes 'i'uw'. Identified in 1984 by David Rosewarne, estuary English supplies speakers from different social backgrounds with a means of camouflaging their origins, whether cockney or public school. It is commonly used by, for example, traders in London's money markets.

Gender is a division into masculine/feminine which is socially constructed – as opposed to the male/female distinction of sex, which is biologically determined.

Generation X is from Douglas Coupland's novel *Generation X: Tales for an Accelerated Culture*. It identifies and defines a group of consumers born from 1964–9. They appear alienated from the values of their affluent parents (Baby Boomers) by their own uncertain prospects, but the difference may be to do with style. They are also known as Busters or Slackers. They welcome the internet, quirky advertising, grunge fashion and the idea of defining themselves.

Goths are young people of both sexes who dress in long black clothes and wear white makeup, to differentiate themselves from their peers. They are quiet and unlikely to be troublesome.

(The) **Grocer's Apostrophe** is a snobbish term for apostrophes wrongly placed by uneducated people in the following, for example: 'Cabbage's for Sale'.

Grunge was a term used by mid-1980s rock journalists to describe a confrontational form of hard-rock music. Despite its overtones of squalor and dirt it has come to describe a particular fashion look – one that is deliberately not smart.

Hegemony, from the Greek word for leadership, refers to a cluster of ideas, practices and connections which enables a small group of people to retain dominance. Formulation of the concept is associated with Antonio Gramsci.

Heritage has overtones of 'inheritance' and is about the transmission of traditional values. It is intended to be a dynamic outgrowth of static 'museum' culture and to indicate concern for the physical and historical environment. Since the 1980s Britain has had a heritage secretary. Some see it as just another contender in the struggle between ideologically opposed versions to 'officially' fix British cultural identity. It is thus an aspect of theme-park Britain.

Hoodies are teenagers who cover their faces with their hoods. When they were banned from Bluewater shopping centre, Tory leader David Cameron famously said that instead of despising them, people should show them more love. His approach was travestied by a government minister as 'hug a hoodie'.

Hybridity is mixing different styles of fashion, music, or anything else in order to come up with a better synthesis. Within this fusion the originals (with their conflicting messages) can sometimes still be detected. So BBC TV's 1990s Jane Austen series might place a more feminist overlay on the original texts.

Jobsworths are people who, when asked to be flexible, protest, 'it's more than my job's worth' (to deviate in any manner from prescribed rules). They are presumed to be narrowly bureaucratic, unthinking, time-serving employees, who hide within the public service. The use of this disparaging description may indicate that the speaker is part of a new, non-unionised, entrepreneurial Britain.

Laddism is a male culture that may be seen as a reaction to the idea of the caring, sensitive 'new man' produced by the feminist movement. So laddism is characterised by a climate of rough behaviour, excessive drinking ('lager louts') and all-male attendance at soccer matches. Magazines such as *Loaded* and *FHM* cater to it. It is imitated now by women, known as ladettes.

Moral panics are periodic bouts of hysteria, where the media (particularly the tabloid press) whip up national feeling about issues which have existed all along but have lacked the 'oxygen of publicity'. Examples would be: chaining of pregnant prisoners; teenage use of the drug Ecstasy; 'social-security scrounging'.

Muffin top is the roll of fat which spills over the waistband of hipster jeans.

NEETs is a term given by Whitehall to a group of young people (7.7 per cent of their age group) living on social welfare, who are 'not in education, employment or training'.

New Age is a broad term devised to describe the renewal of interest from the mid 1980s onwards in a range of approaches to the spiritual dimension which emphasise the individual's ability to discover and develop their own spirituality. The term comes from astrology: every 2,000 years the solar system enters a new age, the next one being the age of Aquarius (the sign of individualism). Influences are yoga and t'ai chi. It is associated with alternative culture: the occult, Tarot, astrology and hippy lifestyles. Most visible elements are New Age travellers and the Donga Tribe.

Outing is the practice of publicly declaring someone to be homosexual. It has been used particularly to identify the sexual orientation of, for instance, an Anglican bishop who opposes the ordination of homosexual clergy. Its use is controversial within the gay community.

Pagan was originally either a polytheist or someone who doesn't believe in a God at all, but now denotes a New Age movement aiming to recreate links with nature. Its adherents may be interested in: Wicca (see below), the occult, the book of shadows, spells, magic, witchcraft, athames and myriad rituals. Some pagans believe in the mind-expanding potential of drug use.

Political correctness is a term used to suggest that people are too sensitive about giving offence to oppressed or special-interest groups, which include women, gays and ethnic minorities. Language has been purged of many words: housewife; actress; stewardess; chairman. The word 'partner' has become substituted for husband/wife or (gay/lesbian/straight) lover.

Protestant work ethic is the idea that people must take responsibility for their own destinies and therefore not rely on others to support them but must work for themselves to 'justify their existence'. Robinson Crusoe exemplifies a robust self-sufficient practitioner.

Rhyming slang, though originally Cockney, is now incorporated into the language at large. To have a butcher's (hook) is to take a look. The nursery rhyme 'Pop goes the weasel' refers to pawning a suit (a 'whistle and flute'). Slang is often used to avoid obscenity: according to *Chambers Dictionary* a 'berk' (a common English word for a fool) is 'short for cockney rhyming slang Berkeley Hunt, for cunt', while 'Aris' (used in films such as *Lock, Stock and Two Smoking Barrels*) means 'arse' because it is an abbreviation of 'Aristotle', which rhymes with bottle, and 'bottle and glass' rhymes with 'arse' (see www.peevish.co.uk/slang/links.htm#british).

Sound bites are short expressions used by politicians and media commentators to compress ideas into an easily memorable form. The idea is that in a fast-paced modern work, where people have limited concentration spans, ideas have to be got over to them in succinct shorthand. Critics fear that their use leads to the over-simplification of complex arguments. Examples are rip-off Britain, spin doctors, Eurosceptics, dumbing down, cronyism.

Spin doctors are public relations people who manage the flow of information and news so as to cast their corporate or political employers in the best light. They time the release of bad news to coincide with major distracting events, arrange publicity stunts and feed positive information about their clients to the media.

Stakeholder society is the term used to describe Tony Blair's vision of 'active citizenship' in modern Britain.

Subculture refers to both alternative culture and to individual groups operating separately from mainstream society. Often it refers to rival gangs of mods and rockers, skinheads and bovver boys or punks, but it also refers to groupings of (mainly young) people with gentler outlooks: new romantics, goths and crusties, for example.

Tabloids are sometimes also known as 'red tops'. They include newspapers such as the *Mirror*, *Daily Star* and *Sun*. The last named, owned by Rupert Murdoch, is known for its daily nude on page three. Though despised by highbrows, their political influence is as great as that of the broadsheets, because of their greater circulation.

Theme park is an American concept, popularised by Disney based on recreations of fantasy worlds. It replaces the previous generation's seaside piers and amusement arcades. Popular British examples are Alton Towers, Madame Tussaud's and Camelot. The expression 'Theme-Park' Britain has been applied to attempts to package a slick, plastic, idealised and sanitised version of Britain's past. It is to be sold to foreign and domestic tourists and sustains various hegemonic interests. Traditional versions of Britain have been seen as engaged in this process. Castle banquets at Ruthin (Wales) and Bunratty (Ireland) are part of it, as are stately homes, and such industrial-archaeology sites as Styal Woollen Mill or Llechwedd Slate Mines.

The third way is the term used to describe Tony Blair's policies, which purported to carve a political niche between traditional left and right positions. It derives from the theories of the sociologist Anthony Giddens and in particular his book *The Third Way: the Renewal of Social Democracy* (1998).

Upstairs/downstairs represents the idea of Britain as 'two nations': masters and servants. Particularly in Edwardian Britain, servants lived in the basements of houses and owners on the upper floors. This division was reflected in respective power relations. The concept was revived by a popular TV series of that name and was in evidence again in 2002 in a new television serial of Galsworthy's *The Forsyte Saga*. Robert Altman's movie *Gosford Park* (2002) observes this social split from a new angle, as did Kazuo Ishiguro's novel *The Remains of the Day* (1989).

WAGs are the wives and girlfriends of footballers. They have become notorious for their rowdy behaviour and partying. There is a lot of moral panic about the example they set. They have been invidiously contrasted with the wives of England's 1966 World Cup winners.

Wicca is a revived witchcraft followed by some New Agers. Its practices include herbalism, divination and psychic healing. Partly because of its worship of a 'Great Goddess' it has attracted many feminists looking for alternatives to Christianity and Judaism. The popular image of Wicca was exploited by the cult film *The Wicker Man* (1973).

Index